"John Stott's *Christian Mission in the Modern World* is a small classic and remains surprisingly relevant for today. And no one is more qualified than Chris Wright to bring the discussion up-to-date—to expand, reframe and even sometimes disagree with Stott's work on certain issues within the evangelical and biblical commitment shared by both. This will prove to be an excellent basic introduction to mission and evangelism, along with providing a biblical understanding of salvation, dialogue and conversion for Christian mission. But it will also be a helpful guide to how evangelical thinking on mission has developed in the past four decades by two of its premier exponents."

Michael W. Goheen, author of *Introducing Christian Mission Today* and *A Light to the Nations*

All John Stott's and Chris Wright's royalties from this book have been irrevocably assigned to Langham Literature (formerly the Evangelical Literature Trust). Langham Literature is a program of the Langham Partnership International (LPI), founded by John Stott. Chris Wright is the International Ministries Director.

Langham Literature distributes evangelical books to pastors, theological students and seminary libraries in the Majority World, and fosters the writing and publishing of Christian literature in many regional languages. For further information on Langham Literature and LPI, visit langham.org.

CHRISTIAN MISSION

in the

MODERN WORLD

UPDATED AND EXPANDED

JOHN STOTT *and*
CHRISTOPHER J. H. WRIGHT

An imprint of InterVarsity Press
Downers Grove, Illinois

InterVarsity Press
P.O. Box 1400, Downers Grove, IL 60515-1426
ivpress.com
email@ivpress.com

InterVarsity Press® is the book-publishing division of InterVarsity Christian Fellowship/USA®, a movement of students and faculty active on campus at hundreds of universities, colleges and schools of nursing in the United States of America, and a member movement of the International Fellowship of Evangelical Students. For information about local and regional activities, visit intervarsity.org.

The Scripture quotations quoted herein are from the Revised Standard Version of the Bible, copyright 1946, 1952, 1971 by the Division of Christian Education of the National Council of the Churches of Christ in the U.S.A. Used by permission. All rights reserved.

While any stories in this book are true, some names and identifying information may have been changed to protect the privacy of individuals.

Some of the material in the chapter "Reflections on Salvation" is adapted from Christopher J. H. Wright, Salvation Belongs to Our God: Celebrating the Bible's Central Story *(Downers Grove, IL: InterVarsity Press, 2008).*

Author photo: Elizabeth Denbeigh
Cover design: David Fassett
Interior design: Beth McGill
Images: Emblems: ©S-E-R-G-O/iStockPhoto
          Dubai from above: ©Naufal MQ/Getty Images

ISBN 978-0-8308-4439-5 (print)
ISBN 978-0-8308-9893-0 (digital)

Printed in the United States of America ∞

Library of Congress Cataloging-in-Publication Data
Stott, John R. W., author.
  Christian mission in the modern world / John Stott and Christopher J. H. Wright.—Updated and expanded edition.
    pages cm
  Includes bibliographical references.
  ISBN 978-0-8308-4439-5 (pbk. : alk. paper)
  1. Mission of the church. 2. Evangelistic work. 3. Christianity and other religions. 4. Salvation—Christianity. 5. Conversion—Christianity. I. Wright, Christopher J. H., 1947- author. II. Title.
  BV601.8.S8 2015
  266—dc23

                                                                        2015033929

P 20 19 18 17 16 15 14 13 12 11 10 9 8 7 6 5 4 3 2 1

Y 32 31 30 29 28 27 26 25 24 23 22 21 20 19 18 17 16 15

To

the Lausanne Movement,

which shares its origins with this book

CONTENTS

PREFACE TO THE FIRST EDITION

Apart from my personal commitment to evangelism, both to evangelism through the local church and—since a mission in Cambridge University in 1952—to university evangelism, there are four particular experiences that have contributed to the writing of this book.

First, in 1968 I attended as an "adviser" the Fourth Assembly of the World Council of Churches at Uppsala. Finding myself allocated to section 2 ("Renewal in Mission"), I was immediately plunged into the thick of contemporary debate about the meaning of mission.

Then, although I was not able to attend the Salvation Today conference at Bangkok in January 1973, I naturally followed it with deep interest and concern. When invited the following year to deliver the annual Baker lecture in Melbourne (in memory of Bishop Donald Baker, New Testament scholar and former principal of Ridley College, Melbourne), I chose as my theme "Salvation Yesterday and Today." The substance of this lecture is reproduced with permission, and enlarged, in chapter four.

Third, the planning committee of the International Congress on World Evangelization at Lausanne in July 1974 asked me to give an opening address on the nature of biblical evangelism, and to seek to provide a biblical definition of the five words *mission, evangelism, dialogue, salvation* and *conversion*.

So when, fourth, Canon Jim Hickinbotham, principal of Wycliffe Hall, Oxford, invited me to deliver the 1975 Chavasse Lectures (in memory both of Bishop F. J. Chavasse of Liverpool, who had been principal of Wycliffe Hall, and of his son Bishop Christopher Chavasse, who had been master of St. Peter's College and chairman of the governing body of Wycliffe Hall), it seemed appropriate to take the same five words and elaborate what I had attempted to sketch at Lausanne. I am very grateful to the principal, staff and students of Wycliffe Hall for the kindly welcome and attentive hearing that they gave me, and for the stimulus of the question time that followed each lecture.

Although I have no wish to disguise myself or to conceal that I am a Christian of "evangelical" conviction, this book is not an exercise in party propaganda. I have no axe to grind, except to go on seeking to discover what the Spirit is saying through the Word to the churches. Nothing encouraged me more at Wycliffe than to hear the principal's concluding comment that he thought I had been "scrupulously fair" toward those with whom I have ventured to disagree. This has certainly been my aim. Besides, if I am critical of others, I desire also to be critical of myself and of my fellow evangelicals. Life is a pilgrimage of learning, a voyage of discovery, in which our mistaken views are corrected, our distorted notions adjusted, our shallow opinions deepened and some of our vast ignorances diminished.

Perhaps the greatest need in current ecumenical debate is to find an agreed biblical hermeneutic, for without this a broader consensus on the meaning and obligation of "mission" is unlikely ever to be reached.

John Stott
April 1975

PREFACE TO THE REVISED AND EXPANDED EDITION

I well remember buying *Christian Mission in the Modern World* in 1975, as a theological student in the midst of my doctoral studies on the Old Testament and ordination training at Ridley Hall, Cambridge. It came in the wake of the excitement generated by the reports of the first Lausanne Congress on World Evangelization in 1974 and its epoch-making Lausanne Covenant. Many of us as younger British evangelicals were taking courage from the resurgence of evangelical theology, in the face of the liberalism still dominating university theology departments. At the same time we were animated by the recovery of the historic evangelical social conscience, committed to an understanding of mission that included engagement with the social, economic, political and cultural realities of our day. And John Stott was our hero and mentor in both those realms. Had he not stood up to robustly defend a biblical, evangelical understanding of mission and evangelism in World Council of Churches gatherings? Was he not already urging us to be salt and light in society, to penetrate our culture rather than withdraw from it? This book, in its five pithy chapters, seemed to capture those concerns and fuel our zeal.

I had read many of the books he wrote in the 1960s, had relished the Bible readings he gave as a visiting speaker at the Cambridge

Inter-Collegiate Christian Union and the lectures with which he enriched gatherings of the Theological Students' Fellowship, and had heard him preach at All Souls Church, Langham Place. But I did not meet John Stott personally until 1978, at the National Evangelical Conference on Social Ethics, which he chaired and at which I had been invited (as a fresh young Anglican curate with a doctorate in Old Testament ethics) to give one of the morning Bible expositions. Our initial contact there led to ongoing friendship, culminating in our years of working together after he invited me to take on the leadership of the ministries he had founded within the Langham Partnership in 2001—years that included the pleasure of sometimes sharing with him his writing-retreat cottage in Wales, The Hookses, where I now sit to write this preface.

So it was with a great sense of personal debt as well as enormous privilege and not a little unworthiness that I accepted the invitation of the John Stott Literary Executors and InterVarsity Press to work on a revised edition of *Christian Mission in the Modern World*, to be released in the fortieth year since its original publication, with a request to relieve the book of some of its more dated material and to add some reflections of my own on each of the chapters. Just a word about each of those aspects of the task.

In revising John Stott's own chapters, I scrupulously avoided modifying his meaning at any point. I have removed references to debates of the 1960s and early 1970s that are long since lost in time and significance, along with some (but not all) of the names and writings of the sparring partners with whom Stott engaged, and the detailed history of some particular controversies. Even with that trimming, it is important for the reader to be aware that whenever Stott uses words such as recent, current or contemporary—he was writing in the context of the 1960s and 1970s. Knowing that Stott himself approved of the more gender-inclusive language that became more common in the 1990s and onward, I revised the predominant use of man and men that was still understood and accepted generically in the 1970s.

In preparing my own reflections, I was aware, first of all, that this book was created out of a series of five lectures that he had given in various venues, and in any lecture it is impossible to say all there is to say on any given topic. Readers need to be aware, therefore, that if they want a full understanding of the mind of John Stott on, say, "salvation," they need to graduate quickly from reading chapter four of this book to exploring the breadth and depth of *The Cross of Christ.*

Beyond that, I have tried to do three things, within limits of space and even greater limits of my own expertise. First, where John Stott himself continued to think and write on the topic of each chapter, I point that out with quotations and references wherever possible. Second, since each topic has continued to generate ongoing theological and missiological debate, I have tried to give some sense of where those debates have moved in the decades after 1975. One feature of the book that struck me again and again was how farsighted Stott was. At point after point, he mentions issues (sometimes only in passing) that have become significant or controversial matters in later years. By adding endnotes with whatever bibliographical information I could muster at a number of points, I hope this revised edition of the book may be a helpful primer for students in some areas of mission studies. And third, I have taken the liberty of sharing my own reflections, sometimes developing Stott's own line of thinking, sometimes diverging from it, and sometimes quoting at length from what I have written elsewhere. Where I do find myself expressing a point differently (or daring to disagree!), I like to think that were I to have the opportunity to discuss the matter with the author, we would come to a happy convergence of thought. That was often our experience when we did have such opportunities.

It is my pleasure and privilege to enable this fine little classic of John Stott to have a fresh lease of life, praying as I'm sure he did that it will strengthen faith, feed minds and energize biblical mission.

Chris Wright
March 2015

one

MISSION

John Stott

All Christians everywhere, whatever their cultural background or theological persuasion, must think at some time or other about the relation between the church and the world. What is a Christian's responsibility toward non-Christian relatives, friends and neighbors, and indeed to the whole non-Christian community?

In reply to these questions most Christians would make some use of the term *mission*. One can hardly discuss church-world relations and omit the concept of "mission." But there would be a wide divergence in our understanding of what our "mission" is, of what part "evangelism" plays in mission, and of what part "dialogue" plays in evangelism. I fear further that we would diverge from one another not only in our understanding of the *nature* of mission, evangelism and dialogue, but also in our understanding of the *goal* of all three. Possibly the terms *conversion* and *salvation* would figure somewhere in our definition of goals, but again there might be little consensus regarding the meaning of these words. My task, then, is to take this cluster of five words—*mission, evangelism, dialogue, salvation* and *conversion*—and to attempt to define them biblically, starting in this chapter with *mission*, and then devoting a chapter to each of the remaining four.

In recent years, relations between ecumenical and evangelical Christians (if I may use these terms as a convenient shorthand, for I recognize that they are by no means mutually exclusive) have hardened into something like a confrontation. I have no wish to worsen this situation. However, I do believe that some current ecumenical thinking is mistaken. But then, candidly, I believe some of our traditional evangelical formulations are mistaken also. Many ecumenical Christians do not seem to have begun to learn to live under the authority of Scripture. We evangelicals think we have—and there is no doubt we sincerely want to—but at some times we are very selective in our submission, and at others the traditions of the evangelical elders seem to owe more to culture than to Scripture. My chief concern, therefore, is to bring both ecumenical and evangelical thinking to the same independent and objective test, namely, that of the biblical revelation.

The first word we have to consider is *mission*. Before attempting a biblical definition it may be helpful to take a look at the contemporary polarization.

TWO EXTREME VIEWS

The older or traditional view has been to equate mission and evangelism, missionaries and evangelists, missions and evangelistic programs. In its extreme form this older view of mission as consisting exclusively of evangelism also concentrated on verbal proclamation. The missionary was often caricatured as standing under a palm tree, wearing a pith helmet and declaiming the gospel to a group of ill-clad "natives" sitting respectfully around him on the ground. Thus the traditional image of the missionary was of the preacher, and a rather paternalistic kind of preacher at that. Such an emphasis on the priority of evangelistic preaching sometimes left little room for any other kind of work to be counted as "real mission," including even schools and hospitals. Most adherents of the traditional view of mission, however, would regard education and medical work as perfectly proper, and indeed as very useful adjuncts to evangelistic work, often out of Christian compassion for the ignorant and the sick, though sometimes as being unashamedly "platforms" or "springboards" for evangelism—hospitals and schools providing in their patients and pupils a conveniently captive audience for the gospel. In either case the mission itself was understood in terms of evangelism.

This traditional view is far from being dead and buried. Sometimes it goes along with a very negative view of the world of culture and society. The world is like a building on fire, it may be said, and a Christian's only duty is to mount a rescue operation before it is too late. Jesus Christ is coming at any moment; there is no point in tampering with the structures of society, for society is doomed and about to be destroyed. Besides, any attempt to improve society is bound to be unproductive since unrenewed people cannot build a new world. A person's only hope lies in being born again. Only then might society conceivably be reborn. But it is too late now even for that.

Such world-denying pessimism is a strange phenomenon in those who say they believe in God. But then their image of God is only partially shaped by the biblical revelation. He is not the Creator who in the beginning gave humanity a "cultural mandate" to subdue and rule the earth, who has instituted governing authorities as his "ministers" to order society and maintain justice, and who, as the Lausanne Covenant puts it, because he is "both the Creator and the Judge of all people," is concerned for "justice and reconciliation throughout human society."[1]

At the opposite extreme to this unbiblical concept of mission as consisting of evangelism alone there is the viewpoint that has been advocated in the ecumenical movement since the 1960s. This is the view that God is at work in the historical process, that the purpose of God's mission, of the *missio Dei*, is the establishment of *shalom* (Hebrew for "peace") in the sense of social harmony, and that this

shalom (which is identical with the kingdom of God) is exemplified
in such areas as the battle against racism, the humanization of industrial relations, the overcoming of class divisions, community
development, and the quest for an ethic of honesty and integrity in
business and other professions.

Moreover, in working toward this goal God uses people both
inside and outside the church. The church's particular role in the
mission of God is to point out where God is at work in world history,
to discover what God is doing, to catch up with it and to get involved in it ourselves. For God's primary relationship is to the world,
it was argued, so that the true sequence is to be found no longer in
the formula "God-church-world" but in the formula "God-world-
church." This being so, it is the world that should set the agenda for
the church. Churches must take the world seriously and seek to
serve according to its contemporary sociological needs.

What are we to say about such identification of the mission of
God with social renewal? A fourfold critique may be made.

First, the God who is Lord of history is also the Judge of history.
It is naive to hail all revolutionary movements as signs of divine
renewal. After the revolution the new status quo sometimes en-
shrines more injustice and oppression than the one it has displaced.

Second, the biblical categories of *shalom*, the new humanity and
the kingdom of God are not to be identified with social renewal. It
is true that in the Old Testament *shalom* (peace) often indicates
political and material well-being. But can it be maintained, as serious biblical exegesis, that the New Testament authors present
Jesus Christ as winning this kind of peace and as bestowing it on
society as a whole? To assume that all Old Testament prophecies
are fulfilled in literal and material terms is to make the very mistake
that Jesus' contemporaries made when they tried to take him by
force and make him a king (John 6:15). The New Testament understanding of Old Testament prophecy is that its fulfillment *tran-*

scends the categories in which the promises were given. So according to the apostles the peace that Jesus preaches and gives is something deeper and richer, namely, reconciliation and fellowship with God and with each other (for example, Ephesians 2:13-22). Moreover, he does not bestow it on all people but on those who belong to him, to his redeemed community. So *shalom* is the blessing the Messiah brings to his people. The new creation and the new humanity are to be seen in those who are in Christ (2 Corinthians 5:17); and the kingdom has to be received like a little child (Mark 10:15). Certainly it is our Christian duty to commend by argument and example the righteous standards of the kingdom to those who have not themselves received or entered it. In this way we see the righteousness of the kingdom, as it were, "spilling over" into segments of the world and thus to some extent blurring the frontiers between the two. Nevertheless the kingdom remains distinct from godless society, and actual entry into it depends on spiritual rebirth.

Third, the word *mission* cannot properly be used to cover everything God is doing in the world. In providence and common grace he is indeed active in all people and all societies, whether they acknowledge him or not. But this is not his "mission." "Mission" concerns his redeemed people, and what he sends *them* into the world to do.

Fourth, such preoccupation with social change sometimes leaves little or no room for evangelistic concern. Of course we must give earnest attention to the hunger, poverty and injustices of the world. But we cannot then fail to have comparable concern or compassion for people's spiritual hunger, or fail to care about the millions who are perishing without Christ. The Lord Jesus Christ sent his church to preach the good news and make disciples, and we must not become so absorbed with legitimate social goals and activity that we fail to obey that command.

A BIBLICAL SYNTHESIS?

From the traditional view of mission as exclusively evangelistic and the current ecumenical view of it as the establishment of *shalom*, we ask whether there is a better way, a more balanced and more biblical way of defining the mission of the church, and of expressing the relationship between the evangelistic and social responsibilities of the people of God.

The need for such a balanced relationship was recognized within the ecumenical movement itself. At the Uppsala Assembly of the World Council of Churches in 1968, its recently retired secretary general, Dr. W. A. Visser 't Hooft, made the following fine statement in an opening address:

> I believe that, with regard to the great tension between the vertical interpretation of the Gospel as essentially concerned with God's saving action in the life of individuals, and the horizontal interpretation of it as mainly concerned with human relationships in the world, we must get out of that rather primitive oscillating movement of going from one ex-treme to the other, which is not worthy of a movement which by its nature seeks to embrace the truth of the Gospel in its fulness. A Christianity which has lost its vertical dimension has lost its salt and is not only insipid in itself, but useless for the world. But a Christianity which would use the vertical preoccupation as a means to escape from its responsibility for and in the common life of man is a denial of the incarnation, of God's love for the world manifested in Christ.[2]

Sadly, the issue was not clarified at that conference and remained a divisive issue among ecumenicals and evangelicals alike. The old polarization continues.

All of us should be able to agree that mission arises primarily out of the nature not of the church but of God himself. The living God of the

Bible is the sending God. Some have even applied the word *centrifugal*, normally used of the church reaching out in mission, to God himself. It is a dramatic figure of speech. Yet it is only another way of saying that God is love, always reaching out after others in self-giving service.

So God sent forth Abraham, commanding him to go from his country and kindred into the great unknown, and promising to bless him and to bless the world through him if he obeyed (Genesis 12:1-3). Next he sent Joseph into Egypt, overruling even his brothers' cruelty, in order to preserve a godly remnant on earth during the famine (Genesis 45:4-8). Then he sent Moses to his oppressed people in Egypt, with good news of liberation, saying to him, "Come, I will send you to Pharaoh that you may bring forth my people . . . out of Egypt" (Exodus 3:10). After the exodus and the settlement he sent a continuous succession of prophets with words of warning and of promise to his people. As he said through Jeremiah, "From the day that your fathers came out of the land of Egypt to this day, I have persistently sent all my servants the prophets to them, day after day; yet they did not listen to me" (Jeremiah 7:25, 26; compare 2 Chronicles 36:15-16). After the Babylonian captivity he graciously sent them back to the land, and sent more messengers with them and to them to help them rebuild the temple, the city and the national life. Then at last "when the time had fully come, God sent forth his Son"; and after that the Father and the Son sent forth the Spirit on the day of Pentecost (Galatians 4:4-6; compare John 14:26; 15:26; 16:7; Acts 2:33).

All this is the essential biblical background to any understanding of mission. The primal mission is God's, for it is God who sent his prophets, his Son, his Spirit. Of these missions the mission of the Son is central, for it was the culmination of the ministry of the prophets, and it embraced within itself as its climax the sending of the Spirit. And now the Son sends as he himself was sent. Already during his public ministry Jesus sent out first the apostles and then the seventy as a kind of extension of his own preaching, teaching and healing ministry. Then after his death and resurrection he widened the scope of the mission to include all who call him Lord and call themselves his disciples. For others were present with the Twelve when the Great Commission was given (see, for example, Luke 24:33). We cannot restrict its application to the apostles alone.

THE GREAT COMMISSION

This brings us to a consideration of the terms of the Great Commission. What was it that the Lord Jesus commissioned his people to do? There can be no doubt that most versions of it (for he seems to have repeated it in several forms on several occasions) place the emphasis on evangelism. "Go into all the world and preach the gospel to the whole creation" is the familiar command of the "longer ending" of Mark's Gospel, which seems to have been added by some later hand after Mark's original conclusion was lost (Mark 16:15). "Go . . . and make disciples of all nations, baptizing them . . . and teaching them" is the Matthean form (Matthew 28:19, 20), while Luke records at the end of his Gospel Christ's word "that repentance and forgiveness of sins should be preached in his name to all nations" and at the beginning of the Acts that his people would receive power to become his witnesses to the end of the earth (Luke 24:47; Acts 1:8). The cumulative emphasis seems clear. It is placed on preaching, witnessing and making disciples, and many deduce from this that the mission of the church, according to the specification of the risen Lord, is exclusively a preaching, converting and teaching mission. Indeed, I confess that I myself argued this at the World Congress on Evangelism in Berlin in 1966, when attempting to expound the three major versions of the Great Commission.

Today, however, I would express myself differently. It is not just that the Commission includes a duty to teach baptized disciples everything Jesus had previously commanded (Matthew 28:20), and that social responsibility is among the things that Jesus commanded. I now see more clearly that not only the consequences of the Commission but the actual Commission itself must be understood to include social as well as evangelistic responsibility, unless we are to be guilty of distorting the words of Jesus.

The crucial form in which the Great Commission has been handed down to us (though it is the most neglected because it is the most costly) is the Johannine. Jesus had anticipated it in his prayer in the upper room when he said to the Father, "As thou didst send me into the world, so I have sent them into the world" (John 17:18). Now, probably in the same upper room but after his death and resurrection, he turned his prayer-statement into a commission and said, "As the Father has sent me, even so I send you" (John 20:21). In both these sentences Jesus did more than draw a vague parallel between his mission and ours. Deliberately and precisely he made his mission the *model* of ours, saying "*as* the Father sent me, *so* I send you." Therefore our understanding of the church's mission must be deduced from our understanding of the Son's. Why and how did the Father send the Son?

Of course the major purpose of the Son's coming into the world was unique. Perhaps it is partly for this reason that Christians have been hesitant to think of their mission as in any sense comparable to his. For the Father sent the Son to be the Savior of the world, and to that end to atone for our sins and to bring us eternal life (1 John 4:9, 10, 14). Indeed, he himself said he had come "to seek and to save the lost" (Luke 19:10). We cannot copy him in these things. We are not saviors. Nevertheless, all this is still an inadequate statement of why he came.

It is better to begin with something more general and say that he came to serve. His contemporaries were familiar with Daniel's apocalyptic vision of the Son of Man receiving dominion and being served by all peoples (Daniel 7:14). But Jesus knew he had to serve before he would be served, and to endure suffering before he would receive dominion. So he fused two apparently incompatible Old Testament images, Daniel's Son of Man and Isaiah's Suffering Servant, and said, "The Son of man . . . came not to be served but to serve, and to give his life as a ransom for many" (Mark 10:45). The ransoming sin-offering was a sacrifice that he alone could offer, but this was to be the climax of a life of service, and we too may serve. "I am among you," he said on another occasion, "as one who serves" (Luke 22:27). So he gave himself in selfless service for others, and his service took a wide variety of forms according to people's needs. Certainly he preached, proclaiming the good news of the kingdom of God and teaching about the coming and the nature of the kingdom, how to enter it and how it would spread. But he served in deed as well as in word, and it would be impossible in the ministry of Jesus to separate his works from his words. He fed hungry mouths and washed dirty feet; he healed the sick, comforted the sad and even restored the dead to life.

Now he sends us, he says, as the Father had sent him. Therefore our mission, like his, is to be one of service. He emptied himself of status and took the form of a servant, and his humble mind is to be in us (Philippians 2:5-8). He supplies us with the perfect model of service, and sends his church into the world to be a servant church. Is it not essential for us to recover this biblical emphasis? In many of our Christian attitudes and enterprises we have tended (especially those of us who live in Europe and North America) to be bosses rather than servants. Yet it seems that it is in our servant role that we can find the right synthesis of evangelism and social action. For both should be for us, as they undoubtedly were for Christ, authentic expressions of the love that serves.

Then there is another aspect of the mission of the Son that is to be paralleled in the mission of the church, namely, that in order to serve he was sent *into the world*. He did not touch down like a visitor from outer space, or arrive like an alien bringing his own alien culture with him. He took to himself our humanity, our flesh and blood, our culture. He actually became one of us and experienced our frailty, our suffering and our temptations. He even bore our sin and died our death. And now he sends us "into the world," to identify with others as he identified with us (though without losing our Christian identity), to become vulnerable as he did. It is surely one of the most characteristic failures of us Christians, not least of us who are called evangelical Christians, that we seldom seem to take seriously this principle of the incarnation. It comes more natural to us to shout the gospel at people from a distance than to involve ourselves deeply in their lives, to think ourselves into their culture and their problems, and to feel with them in their pains. Yet this implication of our Lord's example is inescapable. As the Lausanne Covenant put it, "We affirm that Christ sends his redeemed people into the world as the Father sent him, and that this calls for a similar deep and costly penetration of the world."[3]

THE RELATION BETWEEN EVANGELISM AND SOCIAL ACTION

What, then, should be the relation between evangelism and social action within our total Christian responsibility? If we grant that we have no liberty either to concentrate on evangelism to the exclusion of social concern or to make social activism a substitute for evangelism, we still need to define the relation between the two. Three main ways of doing this have been attempted.

First, some regard social action as *a means to evangelism.* In this case evangelism and the winning of converts are the primary ends in view, but social action is a useful preliminary, an effective means to these ends. In its most blatant form this makes social work (whether food, medicine or education) the sugar on the pill, the bait on the hook, while in its best form it gives to the gospel a credibility it would otherwise lack. In either case the smell of hypocrisy hangs around our philanthropy. A frankly ulterior motive impels us to engage in it. And the result of making our social program the means to another end is that we breed so-called rice Christians. This is inevitable if we ourselves have been "rice evangelists." They caught the deception from us. No wonder Gandhi said in 1931, "I hold that proselytizing under the cloak of humanitarian work is, to say the least, unhealthy . . . why should I change my religion because a doctor who professes Christianity as his religion has cured me of some disease?"

A second way of relating evangelism and social action is better. It regards social action not as a means to evangelism but as *a manifestation of evangelism*, or at least of the gospel that is being proclaimed. In this case philanthropy is not attached to evangelism rather artificially from the outside, but grows out of it as its natural expression. One might almost say that social action becomes the "sacrament" of evangelism, for it makes the message significantly visible. Actions of love and compassion themselves "preach" the gospel message they flow from. We should not hesitate to agree with this, so far as it goes, for there is a strong precedent for it in the ministry of Jesus. His words and deeds belonged to each other, the words interpreting the deeds and the deeds embodying the words. He did not only announce the good news of the kingdom; he performed visible "signs of the kingdom." If people would not believe his words, he said, then let them believe him "for the sake of the works themselves" (John 14:11).

Nevertheless, this second view still leaves me uneasy. For it makes service a subdivision of evangelism, an aspect of the proclamation. I do not deny that good works of love did have an evidential value when performed by Jesus and do have an evidential value when performed by us (compare Matthew 5:16). But I cannot bring myself to accept that this is their only or even major justification. If it is, then still, and rather self-consciously at that, they are only a means to an end. If good works are visible preaching, then they are expecting a return; but if good works are visible loving, then they are "expecting nothing in return" (Luke 6:35).

This brings me to the third way of stating the relation between evangelism and social action, which I believe to be the truly Christian one, namely, that social action is *a partner of evangelism*. As partners the two belong to each other and yet are independent of each other. Each stands on its own feet in its own right alongside the other. Neither is a means to the other, or even a manifestation of the other. For each is an end in itself. Both are expressions of unfeigned love. Evangelism and compassionate service belong together in the mission of God.

The apostle John has helped me to grasp this by these words from his first letter: "If any one has the world's goods and sees his brother in need, yet closes his heart against him, how does God's love abide in him? Little children, let us not love in word or speech but in deed and in truth" (1 John 3:17-18). Here love in action springs from a twofold situation, first "seeing" a brother in need and secondly "having" the wherewithal to meet the need. If I do not relate what I "have" to what I "see," I cannot claim to be indwelt by the love of God. Further, this principle applies whatever the nature of the seen need. I may see spiritual need (sin, guilt, lostness) and have the gospel knowledge to meet it. Or the need I see may be disease or ignorance or bad housing, and I may have the medical, educational or social expertise to relieve it. To see need and to possess the remedy compels love to act, and whether the action will be evangelistic or social, or indeed political, depends on what we "see" and what we "have."

This does not mean that words and works, evangelism and social action, are such inseparable partners that all of us must engage in both all the time. Situations vary, and so do Christian callings. As for situations, there will be times when a person's eternal destiny is the most urgent consideration, for we must not forget that people without Christ are perishing. But there will certainly be other times when a person's material need is so pressing that he would not be able to hear the gospel if we shared it with him. The man who fell among robbers needed above all else at that moment oil and bandages for his wounds, not evangelistic tracts in his pockets! As the saying goes, "a hungry man has no ears." If our enemy is hungry, our biblical mandate is not to evangelize him but to feed him (Romans 12:20). Then too there is a diversity of Christian callings, and every Christian should be faithful to her own calling. The doctor must not neglect the practice of medicine for evangelism, and neither should the evangelist be distracted from the ministry of the word by the ministry of tables, as the apostles quickly discovered (Acts 6).

THE GREAT COMMANDMENT

Let me return now to the Great Commission. I have tried to argue that its Johannine form, according to which the church's mission is to be modeled on the Son's, implies that we are sent into the world to serve, and that the humble service we are to render will include for us as it did for Christ both words and works, a concern for the hunger and the sickness of both body and soul, in other words, both evangelistic and social activity. But supposing someone remains convinced that the Great Commission relates exclusively to evangelism, what then?

I venture to say that sometimes, perhaps because it was the last instruction Jesus gave us before returning to the Father, we give the Great Commission too prominent a place in our Christian thinking. Please do not misunderstand me. I firmly believe that the whole church is under obligation to obey its Lord's commission to take the gospel to all nations. But I am also concerned that we should not regard this as the only instruction that Jesus left us. He also quoted Leviticus 19:18, "you shall love your neighbor as yourself," called it "the second and great commandment" (second in importance only to the supreme command to love God with all our being), and elaborated it in the Sermon on the Mount. There he insisted that in God's vocabulary our neighbor includes our enemy, and that to love means to "do good," that is, to give ourselves actively and constructively to serve our neighbor's welfare.

Here then are two instructions of Jesus—a great commandment, "love your neighbor," and a great commission, "go and make disciples." What is the relation between the two? Some of us behave as if we thought them identical, so that if we share the gospel with somebody, we consider we have completed our responsibility to love him or her. But no. The Great Commission neither explains, nor exhausts, nor supersedes the Great Commandment. What it does is to add to the requirement of neighbor-love and neighbor-service a new and urgent Christian dimension. If we truly love our neighbor, we shall without doubt share with him or her the good news of Jesus. How can we possibly claim to love our neighbor if we know the gospel but keep it from them? Equally, however, if we truly love our neighbor we shall not stop with evangelism. Our neighbor is neither a bodiless soul that we should love only their soul, nor a soulless body that we should care for its welfare alone, nor even a body-soul isolated from society. God created the human person, who is my neighbor, as a body-soul-in-community. Therefore, if we love our neighbor as God made him or her, we must inevitably be concerned for their total welfare, the good of their soul, their body and their community. Moreover, it is this vision of the human person as a social being, as well as a psychosomatic being, that obliges us to add a *political* dimension to our social concern. Humanitarian activity cares for the casualties of a sick society. We should be concerned with preventive medicine or community health as well, which means the quest for better social structures in which peace, dignity, freedom and justice are secured for all. And there is no reason why, in pursuing this quest, we should not join hands with all people of good will, even if they are not Christians.

To sum up, we are sent into the world, like Jesus, to serve. For this is the natural expression of our love for our neighbors. We love.

We go. We serve. And in this we have (or should have) no ulterior motive. True, the gospel lacks visibility if we merely preach it, and lacks credibility if we who preach it are interested only in souls and have no concern about the welfare of people's bodies, situations and communities. Yet the reason for our acceptance of social responsibility is not primarily in order to give the gospel either a visibility or a credibility it would otherwise lack, but rather simple, uncomplicated compassion. Love has no need to justify itself. It merely expresses itself in service wherever it sees need.

Mission, then, is not a word for everything the church does. "The church is mission" sounds fine, but it's an overstatement. For the church is a worshiping as well as a serving community, and although worship and service belong together they are not to be confused. Neither, as we have seen, does "mission" cover everything God does in the world. For God the Creator is constantly active in his world in providence, in common grace and in judgment, quite apart from the purposes for which he has sent his Son, his Spirit and his church into the world. "Mission" describes rather everything the church is sent into the world to do. "Mission" embraces the church's double vocation of service to be "the salt of the earth" and "the light of the world." For Christ *sends* his people into the earth to be its salt, and *sends* his people into the world to be its light (Matthew 5:13-16).

PRACTICAL IMPLICATIONS

In conclusion, it may be helpful to consider what the realistic out-workings of this understanding of mission are likely to be. Evangelical Christians are now repenting of the former pietism that tended to keep us insulated from the secular world, and are accepting that we have a social as well as an evangelistic responsibility. But what will this mean in practice? I would like to explore two areas: Christian vocation and the local church.

I begin with vocation, by which I mean a Christian's life's work.

We've often given the impression that if a young Christian is really keen for Christ he or she will undoubtedly become a foreign missionary, that if they are not quite as keen as that they will stay at home and become a pastor, that if they lack the dedication to be a pastor, they will no doubt serve as a doctor or a teacher, while those who end up in social work or the media or (worst of all) in politics are not far removed from serious backsliding!

It seems to me urgent to gain a truer perspective in this matter of vocation. Jesus Christ calls all his disciples to "ministry," that is, to service. He himself is the Servant par excellence, and he calls us to be servants too. This much then is certain: if we are Christians, we must spend our lives in the service of God and others. The only difference between us lies in the nature of the service we are called to render. Some are indeed called to be missionaries, evangelists or pastors, and others to the great professions of law, education, medicine and the social sciences. But others are called to commerce, to industry and farming, to accountancy and banking, to local government or parliament, and to the mass media, to homemaking and family building. In all these spheres, and many others besides, it is possible for Christians to interpret their life's work Christianly, and to see it neither as a necessary evil (necessary, that is, for survival), nor even as a useful place in which to evangelize or make money for evangelism, but as their Christian vocation, as the way Christ has called them to spend their lives in his service. Further, a part of their calling will be to seek to maintain Christ's standards of justice, righteousness, honesty, human dignity and compassion in a society that no longer accepts them.

When any community deteriorates, the blame should be attached where it belongs: not to the community that is going bad but to the church that is failing in its responsibility as salt to stop it from going bad. And the salt will be effective only if it permeates society, only if Christians learn again the wide diversity of divine callings, and if many penetrate deeply into secular society in order to serve Christ there.

To this end I would personally like to see the appointment of Christian vocation officers who would visit schools, colleges and churches not to recruit for the pastorate only but to set before young people the exciting variety of opportunities available today for serving Christ and their fellow human beings. I would also like to see regular vocation conferences, not *missionary* conferences only that accord the top priority to becoming a crosscultural missionary, nor *ministry* conferences that concentrate on the ordained pastorate, but *mission* conferences that portray the biblical breadth of the mission of God, apply it to today's world and challenge young people to give their lives unreservedly to service in some aspect of the Christian mission.

A second application concerns the local church. Here again our tendency has been to see the church as a worshiping and witnessing community. So we think that its responsibility to the parish or neighborhood is largely restricted to evangelistic witness. But if the local church is "sent" into its area as the Father sent the Son into the world, its mission of service is wider than evangelism. Once the local church as a whole recognizes and accepts this fuller dimension of its responsibility, it is ready for a further truth. Although all Christians are called in general terms to both kinds of service (to witness to Christ and to follow the example of the good Samaritan when the opportunity presents itself), not all Christians are called either to give their lives to both or to spend all their spare time in both.

It is clearly impossible for everybody to do everything that needs to be done. Therefore there must be specialization according to the gifts and calling of Christ. Some members of the local church are without doubt gifted for evangelism and called to evangelism. But can we now say with equal conviction that Christ's gifts and calling to others point rather in a social direction? Can we now liberate ourselves from the human-made bondage (for that is what it is) of supposing that every really keen Christian will devote all their spare time to some "soul-winning" enterprise? Surely the biblical doctrine of the body of Christ, with different members gifted to fulfill different functions, should be enough to give us this larger freedom?

Once this principle has been welcomed, it should be possible for groups of concerned Christians in every congregation to coalesce into a variety of "study and action groups." For example, one might concentrate on house-to-house visitation, another on the evangelistic penetration of some particular unreached section (for example, a hostel or youth club, a college or coffee shop), another on community relations among immigrants, another on setting up a housing association to help the homeless, another on visiting old folk or the sick, or helping the handicapped, while others might address themselves to wider socioethical or sociopolitical questions such as abortion (if there is an abortion clinic in the parish) or labor relations (if the parish is industrial) or sexual permissiveness (if local pornographic shops are an offense in the neighborhood). I have deliberately used the expression "study and action groups" because we Christians have a tendency to pontificate from a position of ignorance, and we need to grapple with the complexities of our subject before recommending some course of responsible action, whether evangelistic or social or both, to the church council.

If we can accept this broader concept of mission as Christian service in the world comprising both evangelism and social action—a concept that is laid on us by the model of our Savior's mission in the world—then Christians could under God make a far greater impact on society, an impact commensurate with our numerical strength and with the radical demands of the commission of Christ.

two

REFLECTIONS ON MISSION

Chris Wright

The theology and practice of mission was close to John Stott's heart, from the earliest days following his conversion as a schoolboy to the closing days of his ninetieth year on earth. The book in your hands emerged in the immediate aftermath of the First Lausanne Congress on World Evangelization in 1974, in which he played such a significant role as the architect of its defining document, the Lausanne Covenant. And in the closing months of his life, when his eyesight had completely failed, he insisted that the Cape Town Commitment, the statement of the Third Lausanne Congress in 2010, should be read to him, section by section over a period of several days. He rejoiced in it, endorsed it and was greatly encouraged by the continuing commitment of evangelicals globally to world mission as understood in all its wholeness and fullness in those great documents.

So it is not surprising that the themes of this 1975 book retained his attention for the following decades before his death in 2011. If, at some future date, we may hope to have access to a searchable, digitized, complete works of John Stott, the key words of this book, *mission, evangelism, dialogue, salvation* and *conversion*, will turn up a gold mine of references and quotations for any researcher. For that reason, I begin by noting some of the enduring affirmations that Stott makes in this chapter, and then in each case I reflect on some of the ongoing developments over the following years—some of them under Stott's own active leadership.

OUR MISSION FLOWS FROM THE MISSION OF GOD

When Stott seeks to move beyond the polarized extremes of seeing mission as either exclusively evangelism or almost wholly sociopolitical action, toward what he calls "a better way, a more balanced and more biblical way of defining the mission of the church," he rightly emphasizes a God-centered understanding of what mission is. "All of us should be able to agree," he hopes, "that mission arises primarily out of the nature not of the church but of God himself. The living God of the Bible is the sending God." This, of course, is a move that is characteristic of Stott's habitual turn of thought. Whatever the problem or issue that he was seeking to address, he would ask, "What does the Bible say?" and "How does this connect with what we know from the biblical revelation about the character, purposes and actions of God, especially as revealed in Christ?" John Stott had a Bible-saturated, God-centered, Christ-focused worldview. Those were the spectacles he put on before settling his gaze on any issue.

It is a refreshing and challenging thing to do. When we get exhausted and frustrated with the constant questions, "What is the essential mission of the church? What should the mission of the church legitimately include (and what does it not include)?" it is worth reminding ourselves that the key question is not so much "What kind of mission does God intend for his church?" as "What kind of church does God require for his mission?" The church exists, in its historical journey on earth, for the sake of God's mission in the world. So rather than asking only what the church should *do* (or not do), we should be asking what the church is *for*, and that drives us to consider the redemptive mission of God for all nations and all creation.

Now in this chapter Stott speaks of the mission of God only in terms of God as the *sending* God. That concept of "sending"—from the etymological root of the word *mission*, of course—dominates the meaning of mission here. When we "do mission," we send people out to do something. But Stott's point is, God was doing that long before we, the church, sent anybody anywhere. The "centrifugal" nature of God is seen in the way, in the three Persons of the Trinity, he is always "moving outward" toward his creation in self-giving love. And that then becomes historically rooted in a whole sequence of sendings throughout the Bible, beginning with Abraham and culminating in the sending of the Spirit, and of the disciples to the ends of the earth.

> All this is the essential biblical background to any under-standing of mission. The primal mission is God's, for it is God who sent his prophets, his Son, his Spirit. Of these missions the mission of the Son is central, for it was the culmination of the ministry of the prophets, and it embraced within itself as its climax the sending of the Spirit. And now the Son sends as he himself was sent.

Sending is certainly a very important component of a biblical the-ology of mission. And indeed there are many more examples of God sending people than Stott mentions.[1] However, a broader concept of mission includes not just the act of sending in itself, but the overall purpose, goal or plan within which those sendings take place and make sense. After all, merely sending somebody somewhere is meaningless unless there is some purpose behind it. A "mission" is not just the act of sending or the experience of being sent. It implies that the sender has a long-range purpose in mind, and that the one being sent participates in that wider purpose of the sender—whether or not they are conscious of the full extent of it.

So "the mission of God" has come to refer not merely to the God who sent and sends, but to the God who has an overarching purpose for his whole creation and is constantly "on mission" to accomplish it. When God sent people, in the Old or New Testament, it was in relation to this ultimate, universal purpose—at whatever specific point in the history of its outworking they happened to be at that point. Generally, God's sendings fall into two categories: God sends some people to *act*—to be agents of his will, in salvation or judgment. And God sends people to *speak*—to be heralds and messengers of his word. But all those sendings participate in the different phases of the mission of God as it plays out through the whole Bible narrative.

In other words, we have come to think of the mission of God in more comprehensive terms that embrace the whole Bible narrative, rather than solely as either multiple acts of sending or even a climactic single act such as the so-called Great Commission. To speak of God's mission is to speak of God's plan and purpose, or what Paul sometimes referred to as "the will of God" (*thelēma*; Ephesians 1:9-10), or "the whole counsel [*boulē*] of God" (Acts 20:27)—his ultimate goal of bringing the whole creation into reconciled unity in, through and under Christ.

Mission, then, is fundamentally the activity of God, driving this whole story forward and bringing it to its glorious conclusion. For this reason, when the Cape Town Commitment comes to define the mission to which we are committed, it begins by presenting a summary of the mission of God himself—in a paragraph full of biblical echoes.

> We are committed to world mission, because it is central to our understanding of God, the Bible, the Church, human history and the ultimate future. The whole Bible reveals the mission of

God to bring all things in heaven and earth into unity under Christ, reconciling them through the blood of his cross. In fulfilling his mission, God will transform the creation broken by sin and evil into the new creation in which there is no more sin or curse. God will fulfil his promise to Abraham to bless all nations on the earth, through the gospel of Jesus, the Messiah, the seed of Abraham. God will transform the fractured world of nations that are scattered under the judgment of God into the new humanity that will be redeemed by the blood of Christ from every tribe, nation, tongue and language, and will be gathered to worship our God and Saviour. God will destroy the reign of death, corruption and violence when Christ returns to establish his eternal reign of life, justice and peace. Then God, Immanuel, will dwell with us, and the kingdom of the world will become the kingdom of our Lord and of his Christ and he shall reign for ever and ever. [Genesis 1–12; Ephesians 1:9-10; Colossians 1:20; Revelation 21–22][2]

This has enabled a broader understanding of *our* mission, since it is wholly derived from God's mission. Once we grasp the comprehensiveness of God's great plan and purpose for all people and all creation, then there must be some analogous comprehensiveness to the way in which we are called by God to participate with him in that mission. *Not*, of course, in the sense that we do all that God does. God is God, and we (thank God) are not. We do not rule the world or save the world. As Stott puts it, "we cannot copy him in these things. We are not saviors." Rather, in the sense that when God calls us and sends us out to participate with God in fulfilling God's own great purpose for creation and humanity, he calls us into a very big agenda indeed. Or as Stott puts it in the opening statement of the following chapter: "The word *mission*, I have so far suggested, is properly a comprehensive word, embracing everything that God sends his people into the world to do." And that "everything" is indeed broad and inclusive, if we take account of what the whole Bible shows us concerning what God requires of his whole people in their engagement with the world around them.

So this "whole-story-of-the-Bible" understanding of the mission of God lays a strong foundation for the more holistic understanding of mission that Stott advocates (with careful clarifications) in this book.

But not only do we arrive at a more fully *biblical theology of mission*, we also gain a more *missional understanding of the Bible* itself.[3] "Missional hermeneutics" has become a serious discipline, with a community of scholars dedicated to exploring what it means to read the whole Bible from the perspective of God's mission and the mission of God's people. This movement has flourished particularly since the turn of the millennium, but just before that, Andrew Kirk had raised a significant question in his book *What Is Mission? Theological Explorations.* Speaking about the need for mission to inform the whole range of theological disciplines, he writes, "For example, what a difference it would make to biblical studies if full justice were done to the Bible as a book about mission from beginning to end, written by missionaries for missionaries! Given its content and intent, how could one study it in any other way?"[4]

This was the motivating question behind my own efforts to read the Bible from that perspective, leading to two books, *The Mission of God* and *The Mission of God's People.* The first of those had a very long gestation in thirteen years of teaching biblical courses at All Nations Christian College (ANCC), a training institution for a widely international and predominantly graduate, professional community of men and women called to various forms of crosscultural mission around the world. At ANCC we used to say that we did not teach "theology and mission," but rather "theology *for* mission." The whole curriculum of biblical, theological, historical, cultural, pastoral, religious and practical subjects was very consciously suffused with questions about how the material under study was relevant to, affected, challenged or illuminated by the realities of global mission. When David Bosch launched the 1990s with a call to transform the whole theological enterprise by recognizing its fundamentally missional nature, we at ANCC both welcomed his magisterial book and felt that we were already heeding its call!

> Just as the church ceases to be church if it is not missionary, theology ceases to be theology if it loses its missionary character. . . . We are in need of a missiological agenda for theology rather than just a theological agenda for mission, for theology, rightly understood, has no reason to exist other than critically to accompany the *missio Dei*.[5]

In my own Department of Biblical Studies at ANCC, that question haunted me, in a positive sense. I wanted to rename the course I taught from "The Biblical Basis of Mission" to "The Missional Basis of the Bible." I was striving for a thoroughgoing "missional hermeneutic" of Scripture—and *The Mission of God* was the end result of that.[6]

The impetus for a greater awareness of the centrality of mission, not only in biblical studies but in the whole theological enterprise, gathered strength throughout the decades following Lausanne 1974 and this book in 1975.[7]

Lesslie Newbigin, who returned to the United Kingdom in 1974 after a long missionary career in India and within the World Council of Churches, spoke and wrote prolifically for the next twenty years on the need for missional engagement with Western culture, and for a fully biblical, trinitarian understanding of mission itself. His most significant contributions include *Trinitarian Doctrine for Today's Mission*, *The Open Secret*, *Foolishness to the Greeks*, *The Gospel in a Pluralist Society* and *Truth to Tell*.[8] The influence of Newbigin has been immense, and many of those who are now involved in current efforts to develop a missional hermeneutic of

Scripture are consciously in his debt. He is the inspiration behind the Gospel and Our Culture network and the Newbigin House of Studies, under whose auspices a lot of missional study of the Bible along with biblical reflection on mission has taken place.[9]

That influence is seen in two outstanding contributions to the theology of mission in recent years—both of which comprehensively expound the essentially missional nature of the whole canon of Scripture, as the narrative of the mission of God, from which all human mission must be derived: Michael Goheen, *Introducing Christian Mission Today*, and Scott Sunquist, *Understanding Christian Mission*.[10] Sunquist combines a strong articulation and defense of a missional hermeneutic with an equally passionate trinitarian lens through which to see the whole Bible in relation to the person and mission of God.

So, then, the forty years since Stott wrote this book in the immediate aftermath of Lausanne 1974 have seen remarkable theological and biblical developments in the theology of mission—particularly in the evangelical community. This is something that I am quite certain he welcomed, both in the endeavor itself and in the broad direction in which it has moved.

EVANGELISM AND SOCIAL ACTION BELONG TOGETHER WITHIN OUR EXERCISE OF BIBLICAL MISSION

This book was not the first in which Stott expressed the conviction, which he sustained throughout his life, that Christian mission in obedience to the Great Commission could not be confined, in definition or in practice, to the verbal proclamation of the gospel (evangelism) alone, but that mission legitimately and biblically includes the practical involvement of Christians in society in the wide variety of good works that constitute social responsibility, service and action.[11] He insisted that both were inseparable partners in the task of Christian mission. Yet at the same time, he equally strongly affirmed (in the Lausanne Covenant, in this book and elsewhere) that evangelism has a certain "primacy" or "priority," for reasons that we shall come to shortly.

The first thing we observe is Stott's candid explanation that his own thinking on the matter had changed somewhat between the Berlin Congress of 1966 and the Lausanne Congress of 1974 ("Today, however, I would express myself differently"). One factor in this was his international travel in the 1960s and early 1970s to Majority World contexts where the realities of poverty and oppression were inescapable and could not be ignored by evangelicals committed to evangelism. Out of those travels developed close personal friendship with, and careful listening to, Majority World evangelicals such as René Padilla and Samuel Escobar—both of whom made significant presentations at the Lausanne Congress.[12] The impact is seen in Stott's writing of paragraph 5 of the Lausanne Covenant, on "Christian Social Responsibility," where we read "Evangelism and socio-political involvement are both part of our Christian duty. For both are necessary expressions of our doctrines of God and humankind, our love for our neighbour and our obedience to Jesus Christ."[13]

But in this book he characteristically argues not from experience but from the Bible. He had come to a fuller understanding of the Great Commission from all four Gospels.

> It is not just that the Commission includes a duty to teach baptized disciples everything Jesus had previously commanded (Matthew 28:20), and that social responsibility is among the things that Jesus commanded. I now see more clearly that not only the consequences of the Commission but the actual Commission itself must be understood to include social as well as evangelistic responsibility, unless we are to be guilty of distorting the words of Jesus.

Those two sentences are very significant and could do with a lot of unpacking, but they have not found universal agreement by any means. The question of how evangelism and social responsibility are to be related to each other continued to be a divisive issue among evangelicals, from the years immediately following Lausanne until today. For example, in their book *What Is the Mission of the Church?* Kevin DeYoung and Greg Gilbert quote John Stott in his use of the Johannine form of the commission ("As the Father has sent me, even so I send you," John 20:21, along with John 17:18), but they disagree with his view that it means our mission (like Christ's) must be characterized by serving (not just evangelizing), with an "incarnational" model of costly involvement in people's lives. In their view, the Great Commission is narrower and does not include or imply good works and social action *as part of the mission of the church* (though they do insist strongly that such practical works of love and compassion are indeed very important as part of our Christian obedience). "The mission consists of preaching and teaching, announcing and testifying, making disciples and bearing witness. The mission focuses on the initial and continuing verbal declaration of the gospel, the announcement of Christ's death and resurrection and the life found in him when we repent and believe."[14]

During the 1980s, the Lausanne movement continued to debate and explore what the Lausanne Covenant had affirmed, in an effort to sustain its commitment to a holistic understanding of mission on a firm biblical and theological foundation. John Stott, as chair of Lausanne's Theology Working Group, and as one who was deeply supportive across the spectrum of evangelical mission agencies involved in both evangelism (such as the International Fellowship of Evangelical Students and Scripture Union) and social action (such as Tear Fund), convened a landmark International Consultation on the Relationship between Evangelism and Social Responsibility, under the auspices of both Lausanne and the World Evangelical Alliance.[15] It met in Grand Rapids, Michigan, in 1982.

The lengthy report of that event speaks of three kinds of rela-

tionship (which in some ways echo the terms Stott uses in this
book) between social action and evangelism. Social activity can be,
first, a *consequence* of evangelism, and second, a *bridge* to evangelism. But the third, and most important, point of the report is the
one Stott makes in this book. They are *partners.*

> They are like the two blades of a pair of scissors or the two
> wings of a bird. This partnership is clearly seen in the public
> ministry of Jesus, who not only preached the gospel but fed
> the hungry and healed the sick. In his ministry, *kerygma*
> (proclamation) and *diakonia* (service) went hand in hand. . . .
> His words explained his works, and his works dramatized his
> words. Both were expressions of his compassion for people,
> and both should be of ours. . . . Indeed, so close is this link
> between proclaiming and serving, that they actually overlap.
>
> This is not to say that they should be identified with each
> other, for evangelism is not social responsibility, nor is social
> responsibility evangelism. Yet, each involves the other.
>
> To proclaim Jesus as Lord and Saviour (evangelism) has
> social implications, since it summons people to repent of social
> as well as personal sins, and to live a new life of righteousness
> and peace in the new society which challenges the old.
>
> To give food to the hungry (social responsibility) has evan-
> gelistic implications, since good works of love, if done in the
> name of Christ, are a demonstration and commendation of
> the gospel. . . .
>
> Thus, evangelism and social responsibility, while distinct
> from one another, are integrally related in our proclamation
> of and obedience to the gospel. The partnership is, in reality,
> a marriage.[16]

The report immediately goes on to reaffirm the "primacy" of evangelism within this partnership, in the same terms as the Lausanne

Covenant. This is partly a matter of logical priority: "The very fact of Christian social responsibility presupposes socially responsible Christians, and it can only be by evangelism and discipling that they have become such." But it is also because,

> Evangelism relates to people's eternal destiny, and in bringing them Good News of salvation, Christians are doing what nobody else can do. Seldom if ever should we have to choose between satisfying physical hunger and spiritual hunger, or between healing bodies and saving souls, since an authentic love for our neighbour will lead us to serve him or her as a whole person. Nevertheless, if we must choose, then we have to say that the supreme and ultimate need of all humankind is the saving grace of Jesus Christ, and that therefore a person's eternal, spiritual salvation is of greater importance than his or her temporal and material well-being. . . . The choice, we believe, is largely conceptual. In practice, as in the public ministry of Jesus, the two are inseparable. . . . Rather than competing with each other, they mutually support and strengthen each other in an upward spiral of increased concern for both.

At the end of the decade, the Second Lausanne Congress in Manila, in 1989, made essentially the same affirmations as the Consultation on the Relationship between Evangelism and Social Responsibility report on this matter:

> The authentic gospel must become visible in the transformed lives of men and women. As we proclaim the love of God we must be involved in loving service, as we preach the Kingdom of God we must be committed to its demands of justice and peace.
>
> Evangelism is primary because our chief concern is with the gospel, that all people may have the opportunity to accept Jesus Christ as Lord and Saviour. Yet Jesus not only proclaimed the

Kingdom of God, he also demonstrated its arrival by works of mercy and power. We are called today to a similar integration of words and deeds. In a spirit of humility we are to preach and teach, minister to the sick, feed the hungry, care for prisoners, help the disadvantaged and handicapped, and deliver the oppressed. While we acknowledge the diversity of spiritual gifts, callings and contexts, we also affirm that good news and good works are inseparable. It has been said, therefore, that evangelism, even when it does not have a primarily social intention, nevertheless has a social dimension, while social responsibility, even when it does not have a primarily evangelistic intention, nevertheless has an evangelistic dimension.[17]

The language of "dimension" and "intention" is significant here, and almost certainly (since the Manila Manifesto was drafted by John Stott) reflects Stott's awareness of the origin of that distinction in a 1959 book by Lesslie Newbigin, whose writings on mission Stott admired. The distinction helps to protect us from Stephen Neill's famous (and much quoted) warning that if everything is mission, then nothing is mission. Simply put, everything the church does has a missional dimension, since the church exists for the sake of God's mission, but some things the church does have specific missional intention. Michael Goheen summarizes Newbigin's point as follows, and then goes on to discuss its implications more fully:

An important distinction emerged between missional dimension and missional intention. Lesslie Newbigin observes that this distinguishes "between mission as a *dimension* of the Church's whole life, and mission as the primary *intention* of certain activities. Because the Church *is* the mission there is a missionary dimension to everything that the Church does. But not everything the Church does has a missionary intention"; certain activities can be considered to have a missional intention when they are "an action of the Church in going out beyond the frontiers of its own life to bear witness to Christ as Lord among those who do not know Him, and when the overall *intention* of that action is that they should be brought from unbelief to faith."[18]

In personal correspondence on this distinction, Michael Goheen wrote to me, concerning the life of Christians within the church and the world:

> What Newbigin was trying to do was to affirm the growing consensus that mission was all of life, that is, every part of a Christian's human life witnesses to the renewing work of God. But he wanted to protect certain activities that had as their specific and deliberate intention the purpose of sharing the gospel with folk to invite them to respond in faith. I believe the distinction is way more important than most people realise. It would clear up so much confusion around mission.

Both of those documents (the CRESR Report and the Manila Manifesto) owe a lot, of course, to Stott's own drafting skills. But his most worked-out defense of a holistic understanding of Christian mission followed a few years later, in 1992, in his chapter "Holistic Mission" in *The Contemporary Christian*.[19] There, he explains the context, surveys the biblical foundations for his position, answers some common objections and gives some historical examples.

By the time of the Third Lausanne Congress in Cape Town in 2010, the phrase "holistic mission" was already being somewhat overtaken by the phrase "integral mission." The shift in emphasis picks up on the language of "integrally related" (CRESR), and "integration of words and deeds" (Manila). So, rather than seeing the two activities (evangelism and social action) as simply partners that happen to stand or work alongside each other, this conception sees mission as an integrated system of interrelated activities—in which the proper functioning of each is essential to the functioning of the others, and to the health and "success" of the whole enterprise.

The human body is an integrated system. There is the respiratory system, the digestive system, the circulation of the blood and so on. Now these are separate and distinguishable "activities"; they are not just different words for the same thing. But in a normal, living human body they have to function integrally, essentially and inseparably. It makes little sense to talk about the primacy or priority of one over another, except in extreme circumstances where one has to pay attention to one above another, such as a near-drowning or a serious road accident, where breathing, blood loss or heart failure would take priority over giving somebody food or drink. But in everyday life, all the bodily functions are necessary, are integrated and contribute each in their own way to what it means to be a living human being. Likewise, integrated mission binds together all the dimensions of our Christian obedience to Christ to serve God's purposes in the world. Evangelism and social action are thus integral to each other—different, but necessary, functions within the total life of mission.[20]

The Micah Declaration on Integral Mission (2001) put it like this:

Integral mission is the proclamation and demonstration of the gospel. It is not simply that evangelism and social involvement are to be done alongside each other. Rather, in integral mission our proclamation has social consequences as we call people to love and repentance in all areas of life. And our social involvement has evangelistic consequences as we bear witness to the transforming grace of Jesus Christ. If we ignore the world, we betray the Word of God which sends us out to serve the world. If we ignore the Word of God, we have nothing to bring to the world.[21]

But integration requires a "something" within which, or around which, everything is integrated. All the systems of my body are integrated within the person that I am. *What is the integrating center of mission that binds together evangelism and social action?* It is surely the gospel itself—meaning the gospel as the biblical good news of all that God has done in Christ to save the world and inaugurate the kingdom of God under Christ's lordship. In other words, "the gospel" is not merely the mechanism by which individuals can be saved, but the story, the facts, the saving acts of God—and their implications for us when we respond to hearing about them.

The Cape Town Commitment integrates mission around that gospel core.

> *The integrity of our mission.* The *source* of all our mission is what God has done in Christ for the redemption of the whole world, as revealed in the Bible. Our evangelistic task is to make that good news known to all nations. The *context* of all our mission is the world in which we live, the world of sin, suffering, injustice, and creational disorder, into which God sends us to love and serve for Christ's sake. All our mission must therefore reflect the integration of evangelism and committed engagement in the world, *both being ordered and driven by the whole biblical revelation of the gospel of God.*[22]

That final phrase in (added) italics is crucial. It evokes the image of a wheel. The driving wheel of a car is an integrated object in which the hub (which is connected to the source of power, the engine), is integrated with the rim or tire (which is connected to the road). Every point of connection with the road (the context) has to be energized by the power transmitted from the engine through the hub (the gospel). The hub and the rim must be integrated with each other, and through their integration both are connected to, and driven by, the engine.[23]

Thinking of the whole task of mission with this analogy, I find myself preferring to speak of the *centrality of the gospel* rather than the *primacy of evangelism*. If we do still wish to speak of the centrality of evangelism (at the *heart* of mission, as some have said), it would be not primarily (though of course truly) because it addresses the greatest and most ultimate need of human beings (being lost in sin and alienated from God), but because it connects everything that we do to *what God has done in Christ*. We are gospel-centered because we are God-centered, not merely as another way of being human-centered.

Thus, again, Cape Town, in its section on evangelism, says, "Let us keep evangelism at the centre of the fully-integrated scope of all our mission, inasmuch as *the gospel itself is the source, content and authority of all biblically-valid mission*. All we do should be both an embodiment and a declaration of the love and grace of God and his saving work through Jesus Christ."[24] Although, as noted above, there is still a strong case being argued by some for confining the definition of the word *mission* (and therefore the missional task of the church) to a narrower interpretation of the Great Commission, as solely the preaching and teaching work involved in making disciples (for example, Kevin DeYoung and Greg Gilbert's book), this more integrated understanding seems to have convinced many within the evangelical community who are equally as committed to biblical authority and the truth and centrality of the gospel. We have seen that such an integrated and holistic understanding permeates the mission theology (and practice) of the Lausanne Movement.[25] It is also the understanding of mission adopted by the World Evangelical Alliance, through both its Mission Commission and its Theological Commission.[26] It has been at the heart of the International Fellowship for Mission as Transformation since its beginnings in 1980 and its official formation in 1987.[27]

Among those who conceive the mission of the church in this holistic or integrated way are some with outstanding qualifications in both practical missionary experience and extensive missiological reflection and teaching, both in the West and the Majority World. To mention but a few, these would include Dean Flemming, Michael Goheen, Scott Sunquist, Samuel Escobar, René Padilla, Rosemary Dowsett, John Dickson, Vinay Samuel and Chris Sugden.[28]

An interesting point that both Goheen and Sunquist make is that the effort expended in struggling to relate or integrate the two aspects of Christian mission (evangelism and social engagement) would have been unnecessary if we had not pulled them apart in the first place. The hostile dichotomy that Stott laments in this book, as between the ecumenical emphasis on the sociopolitical realm (to the neglect of evangelism), and the evangelical emphasis on evangelism (to the neglect of social engagement—at least in the first half of the twentieth century), may owe its power and longevity to the dominance of Enlightenment dualism—in *both* camps. That is, we have imported into our thinking distinctions and rankings that do not really reflect the wholeness of the biblical worldview and teaching. We insist on taxonomies where the Bible calls for simple obedience to the totality of its mandates on the lives of God's people—or in Jesus' simpler words, "to obey *all that I have commanded you.*"[29] Goheen writes,

> The original split between the fundamental[ist] and liberal traditions was born of a shared dualism. When the imbalance was recognized, the two parts were artificially joined together. Two dimensions of the church's mission—word and deed— were abstracted from their original context of the full-orbed mission of the church. Each was given a life of its own. This forced a choice about which of the two has priority, and that was given to the word because (in keeping with a deeper dualism) the eternal had priority over the temporal.[30]

Sunquist takes the integration back to Christ himself, and deplores the kind of approach that injects a division between Christ's words and deeds as a basis for creating a dichotomy between evangelism and social justice (whichever way we prioritize the dichotomy thus created). It seems to me that Sunquist agrees with the thrust of what John Stott says (while rejecting his "partners" metaphor), but urges us to go back behind the "dichotomy problem" to a more fundamental integration.

> In evangelism, we start with a single quality of God in Jesus Christ—love—rather than starting with a dichotomy of word and works, or evangelism and justice, or preaching and social justice [a dichotomy assumed in the Lausanne Covenant, paragraph 5].
>
> We should be a little suspicious if a person talks about "both sides" of the life of Jesus. In the past it was common to use such language, to talk about the mission of God as two dance partners (evangelism and social justice) or as two sides of the same coin. But these analogies are not just inadequate, they are misleading. Jesus was a whole person, filled to overflowing with the kenotic, self-emptying love of God.[31]

Before leaving this section we should take note of one further area of integration in evangelical theology of mission that has developed since the publication of this book in 1975. That is the embracing of *creation care* as a dimension of Christian responsibility, and something that can legitimately be included in the overall category of Christian mission. There is still, of course, a wide variety of opinion on this, amounting to rejection of the whole environmental agenda in some evangelical quarters. But increasingly evangelicals are realizing that the Bible itself includes creation (here meaning specifically the earth in which we live) in the consequences of sin, in the redemptive purposes of God and in the reconciling accomplishment of the cross.

The earliest hint of awareness of the ecological dimension that I can find in the Lausanne documents is in the Manila Manifesto

(1989), where, in paragraph 4 on "The Gospel and Social Responsibility," we read that "among the evils we deplore are . . . all forms of exploitation of people *and of the earth*" (italics added).[32] Already, however, evangelicals were responding to the growing awareness of ecological crisis through humble but prophetically significant organizations such as the Au Sable Institute (founded in 1979) and A Rocha (founded in 1983).[33] The Evangelical Environmental Network was founded in 1993 and later published the Evangelical Declaration on the Care of Creation.[34] Indeed, since Lausanne 1974 there has been steady and increasing flow of serious evangelical and biblical writing on the issue, to which John Stott and I have both contributed.[35] In fact, Stott included a chapter on creation care in the very last book he wrote—*The Radical Disciple.*[36] So I know that he endorsed the way the Cape Town Commitment went beyond the integration of only the two spheres of evangelism and social concern to embrace creation as well. Notice, in the following quote, how the integration is once again clearly done around the centrality of the gospel, focusing on the lordship of Jesus Christ—the first and crucial affirmation of the Great Commission itself.

> "The earth is the Lord's and everything in it." The earth is the property of the God we claim to love and obey. We care for the earth, most simply, because it belongs to the one whom we call Lord [Psalm 24:1; Deuteronomy 10:14].
>
> The earth is created, sustained and redeemed by Christ [Colossians 1:15-20; Hebrews 1:2-3]. We cannot claim to love God while abusing what belongs to Christ by right of creation, redemption and inheritance. We care for the earth and responsibly use its abundant resources, not according to the rationale of the secular world, but for the Lord's sake. If Jesus is Lord of all the earth, we cannot separate our relationship to Christ from how we act in relation to the earth. For to proclaim the gospel

that says "Jesus is Lord" is to proclaim the gospel that includes
the earth, since Christ's Lordship is over all creation. Creation
care is thus a gospel issue within the Lordship of Christ. . . .

The Bible declares God's redemptive purpose for *creation*
itself. Integral mission means discerning, proclaiming, and
living out, the biblical truth that the gospel is God's good
news, through the cross and resurrection of Jesus Christ, for
individual persons, *and* for society, *and* for creation. All three
are broken and suffering because of sin; all three are included
in the redeeming love and mission of God; all three must be
part of the comprehensive mission of God's people.[37]

MISSION AND MINISTRY ARE FOR ALL DISCIPLES IN ALL AREAS OF LIFE

My third and final reflection on Stott's chapter on mission picks up
comments he makes in the first part of the section on practical implications. He affirms that mission and ministry are the privilege and
responsibility of all believers, not only for those called into crosscultural missionary work or ordained pastoral ministry. He argues that
we need "to gain a truer perspective in this matter of vocation," and
of ministry. All Christians are called into ministry, and for some that
will mean crosscultural missionary service or ordained pastoral ministry. But ministry—serving God and others—applies to all forms of
work and service that a Christian may be engaged in, whether in an
employed capacity or not. Although Stott had a very serious personal
commitment to the biblical validity of ordained pastoral/teaching
ministry within the church, he passionately believed that it was dam-
agingly unbiblical to confine the concept of "ministry" to the clergy.
He affirmed that ministry and mission were the calling of all disciples
of Christ—in all their varied vocations.

He was calling, though not in so many words at the time, for the eradication of that toxic sacred-secular dichotomy that has so infected Christian thinking, namely the view that God is interested in the religious area of life (church, worship, prayer, evangelism and so on), whereas the rest of life as it is lived in the "secular" world of work and leisure is of little or no relevance to God or to the mission of the church. In place of that he wanted a return to the strong theology of work and vocation found in the Reformers and Puritans, in which every kind of honest work can be done for the service of others, for the benefit of the community *and for the glory of God and in a way that "adorns the gospel"*—which of course is the clear teaching of the apostle Paul (Ephesians 6:5-8; Colossians 3:22-24; Titus 2:9-10).

Stott expanded on this theme in *The Contemporary Christian* (1992). It is worth quoting some sections at length, to sense the passion of Stott's conviction on this point. I quote the first paragraph with some nostalgia, having heard him say these words on many occasions, more or less verbatim, in one of his favorite addresses.

We do a great disservice to the Christian cause whenever we refer to the pastorate as "the ministry," for by our use of the definite article we give the impression that the pastorate is the only ministry there is. . . . I repented of this view, and therefore of this language, about twenty-five years ago, and now invite my readers, if necessary, to join me in penitence. Nowadays, whenever somebody says in my presence that "So-and-so is going into the ministry," I always ask innocently, "Oh really? Which ministry do you mean?" And when my interlocutor probably replies, "The pastoral ministry," I come back with the gentle complaint, "Then why didn't you say so?!" The fact is that the word "ministry" is a generic term; it lacks specificity until we add an adjective. . . .

There is a wide variety of Christian ministries. This is because "ministry" means "service," and there are many different ways in which we can serve God and people. [There follows a discussion of the events in Acts 6] . . . It is essential to note that both distributing food and teaching the word were referred to as ministry (*diakonia*). Indeed, both were Christian ministry, could be full-time ministry, and required Spirit-filled people to perform them. The only difference between them was that one was pastoral ministry, and the other social. It was not that one was "ministry" and the other not; nor that one was spiritual and the other secular; nor that one was superior and the other inferior. It was simply that Christ had called the Twelve to the ministry of the word and the Seven to the ministry of tables. . . .

It is a wonderful privilege to be a missionary or a pastor, *if God calls us to it.* But it is equally wonderful to be a Christian lawyer, industrialist, politician, manager, social worker, television script-writer, journalist, or home-maker, *if God calls us to it.* According to Romans 13:4 an official of the state (whether legislator, magistrate, policeman or policewoman) is just as much a "minister of God" (*diakonos theou*) as a pastor. . . .

There is a crying need for Christian men and women who see their daily work as their primary Christian ministry and who determine to penetrate their secular environment for Christ.[38]

It was precisely this conviction about the missional importance of lay Christians in their everyday workplaces that led Stott to found the London Institute for Contemporary Christianity, in 1982, "with the core belief that every part of our lives comes under the Lordship of Christ, and that all of life is a context for worship, mission, ministry and active Christian engagement."[39] The present director of the institute is Mark Greene, who emulates John Stott in his passion for equipping Christians to be committed and fruitful in the ministry and mission God has for them in the world of work and all the rest of our surrounding culture. In addition to his books, Greene was on the team that led workshops on the workplace at Lausanne, Cape Town 2010, and contributed to the section on "Truth and the Workplace" in the Cape Town Commitment.[40]

> The Bible shows us God's truth about human work as part of God's good purpose in creation. The Bible brings the whole of our working lives within the sphere of ministry, as we serve God in different callings. By contrast, the falsehood of a "sacred-secular divide" has permeated the Church's thinking and action. This divide tells us that religious activity belongs to God, whereas other activity does not. Most Christians spend most of their time in work which they may think has little spiritual value (so-called secular work). But God is Lord of *all* of life. "Whatever you do, work at it with all your heart, as working for the Lord, not for men," said Paul, to slaves in the pagan workplace [Colossians 3:23].[41]

I have no doubt that John Stott endorsed the robust missional theology and practical relevance of this paragraph, and would have seen it as entirely in line with, and the fruition of, the insights and summons he put forward in this book in 1975.

three

EVANGELISM

John Stott

The word *mission*, I have so far suggested, is properly a comprehensive word, embracing everything that God sends his people into the world to do. It therefore includes evangelism and social responsibility, since both are authentic expressions of the love that longs to serve others in their need.

THE PRIORITY OF EVANGELISM

Yet I think we should agree with the statement of the Lausanne Covenant that "in the church's mission of sacrificial service evangelism is primary."[1] Christians should feel an acute pain of conscience and compassion when human beings are oppressed or neglected in any way, whether what is being denied them is civil liberty, racial respect, education, medicine, employment, or adequate food, clothing and shelter. Anything that undermines human dignity should be an offense to us. But is anything so destructive of human dignity as alienation from God through ignorance or rejection of the gospel? And how can we seriously maintain that political and economic liberation is just as important as eternal salvation? Both are certainly challenges to Christian love. But listen to the apostle Paul when he writes with solemn emphasis about his concern for his fellow Jews: "I am speaking the truth in Christ, I am not lying; my conscience bears me witness in the Holy Spirit, that I have great sorrow and unceasing anguish in my heart. For I could wish that I myself were accursed and cut off from Christ for the sake of my brethren, my kinsmen by race" (Romans 9:1-3). What was the cause of his anguish? That they had lost their national Jewish independence and were under the colonial heel of Rome? That they were often despised and hated by Gentiles, socially boycotted and deprived of equal opportunities? No. "Brethren, my heart's desire and prayer to God for them is that they may be saved" (Romans 10:1), and the context makes it plain beyond doubt that the "salvation" Paul desired for them was their acceptance with God (Romans 10:2-4). That few if any of us feel this inward agony is a mark of our spiritual immaturity.

Moreover, in our evangelistic concern our chief burden should be for those millions of unreached peoples of the world. In relation to them the Lausanne Covenant stresses the urgency of the evangelistic task in the following way:

> More than two-thirds of all humanity have yet to be evangelized. We are ashamed that so many have been neglected; it is a standing rebuke to us and to the whole church. . . . We are convinced that this is the time for churches and para-church agencies to pray earnestly for the salvation of the unreached and to launch new efforts to achieve world evangelization. A reduction of foreign misisonaries and money in an evangelized country may sometimes be necessary to facilitate the national church's growth in self-reliance and to release resources for unevangelized areas. Missionaries should flow ever more freely from and to all continents in a spirit of humble service. The goal should be, by all available means and the earliest possible time, that every person will have the opportunity to hear, to understand, and to receive the good news.[2]

THE MEANING OF EVANGELISM

Granted, then, the priority of evangelism, how is it to be defined? In a few words, *euangelizomai* means to bring or to announce the *euangelion*, the good news. Once or twice in the New Testament it is used of ordinary, one might almost say "secular," news items, as when the angel Gabriel told Zechariah the good news that his wife Elizabeth was to have a son (Luke 1:19), and when Timothy brought Paul the good news of the Thessalonians' faith and love (1 Thessalonians 3:6). The regular use of the verb relates, however, to the *Christian* good news. It is the spread of the gospel that constitutes evangelism, and this fact enables us to begin negatively by stating what evangelism is not.

First, evangelism must not be defined in terms of *results*, for this is not how the word is used in the New Testament. Normally the verb is in the middle voice. Occasionally it is used absolutely, for example "there they evangelized," meaning "there they preached the gospel" (Acts 14:7; compare Romans 15:20). Usually, however, something is added. Sometimes it is the message they preached, for example, they "went about evangelizing the word" (Acts 8:4, my translation), while Philip in Samaria "evangelized concerning the kingdom of God and the name of Jesus Christ" (Acts 8:12, my translation). Sometimes, however, what is added is the people to whom or the places in which the gospel was preached. For example, the apostles "evangelized many villages of the Samaritans" and Philip "evangelized all the towns" along the Palestinian coast (Acts 8:25, 40, my translation). There is no mention in these verses whether the word that was "evangelized" was believed, or whether the inhabitants of the towns and villages "evangelized" were converted. To "evangelize" in New Testament usage does not mean to win converts, as it usually does when we use the word. Evangelism is the announcement of the good news, irrespective of the results.

So although the word is often defined in popular missionary

writing and speaking as bringing people to conversion, that result is not included in its New Testament meaning. Evangelism is neither to convert people, nor to win them, nor to bring them to Christ, though this is indeed the first *goal* of evangelism. Evangelism is to preach the gospel.

Dr. J. I. Packer justly criticized the famous definition of evangelism first formulated in England in 1919 by the Archbishops' Committee of Enquiry into the Evangelistic Work of the Church. It begins, "To evangelize is so to present Christ Jesus in the power of the Holy Spirit that men shall come to put their trust in God through him." Dr. Packer draws attention to the form of the sentence "*so* to present Christ Jesus . . . that men *shall* . . ." This is to define evangelism in terms of success. But to evangelize is not *so* to preach that something happens. "The way to tell whether in fact you are evangelizing is not to ask whether conversions are known to have resulted from your witness. It is to ask whether you are faithfully making known the gospel message."[3] He adds that "the results of preaching depend not on the wishes and intentions of men, but on the will of God Almighty." Now of course our objective is that something *will* happen, namely, that people will respond and believe. That is why we plead with them to "be reconciled to God" (2 Corinthians 5:20). At the same time we must not confuse an objective (what we want to happen) with a consequence (what actually does happen). If we want to be biblically accurate we must insist that the essence of evangelism lies in the faithful proclamation of the gospel. It is with a view to persuasion indeed. We are not indifferent to results. We long for people to be converted. But it is still evangelism whether in fact people are persuaded to embrace it or not. I shall say more about the element of persuasion later.

Second, evangelism must not be defined in terms of *methods.* To evangelize is to announce the good news, however the announcement is made. It is to bring the good news, by whatever means it is brought. In different degrees we can evangelize by word of mouth (whether to individuals, groups or crowds); by print, picture or screen; by drama (whether what is dramatized is fact or fiction); by good works of love (Matthew 5:16); by a Christ-centered home; by a transformed life; and even by an almost speechless excitement about Jesus. Nevertheless, because evangelism is fundamentally an announcement, some verbalization is necessary if the content of the good news is to be communicated with any precision.

After these negatives, we come back to the positive statement that evangelism may and must be defined only in terms of *the message*. Therefore biblical evangelism makes the biblical evangel indispensable. Nothing hinders evangelism today more than the widespread loss of confidence in the truth, relevance and power of the gospel. Paul said he was "eager" to preach the gospel in Rome. But then he was convinced that it was God's power for salvation (Romans 1:14-16).

IS THERE A NEW TESTAMENT GOSPEL?

What, then, is the New Testament gospel? Before we are in a position to answer this question, two preliminary problems stand in our way.

First, is there in fact one New Testament gospel? The New Testament certainly presents us with no wooden and unbending stereotype. There are clear differences of emphasis, owing to the author's own background and temperament, and to the Holy Spirit's revelation, so that the apostle Paul can dare to write of "my gospel" when he is referring to the particular "mystery" that has been disclosed to him.

There is also some historical development, even in the same author, so that what Paul writes in his later letters is recognizably different from what he has written earlier. Different situations also called forth different treatments. The apostolic approach was "situational," that is, a sensitive response to each particular challenge. Paul's synagogue sermon in Antioch diverged widely from his Areopagus address in Athens; so did his letter to the Romans from those to the Corinthians. Nevertheless, having allowed for all these variations, and despite all the rich diversity of theological formulation in the New Testament, there was only one basic apostolic tradition of the gospel. Paul insists to the Galatians that the Jerusalem apostles had given him "the right hand of fellowship" as a sign of their acknowledgment of his mission and message (Galatians 1–2, especially Galatians 2:9). In the same chapters he affirms vehemently that there is no other gospel, and calls down the curse of God on anybody, angelic or apostolic—indeed even himself—who should presume to preach a different gospel. Later, in 1 Corinthians, after summarizing the gospel and listing the resurrection appearances, he concludes: "Whether then it was I or they, so we preach and so you believed" (1 Corinthians 15:11). This cluster of personal pronouns—*I, they, we* and *you*—is very impressive. It is an assertion that he and the Jerusalem apostles were agreed about the gospel, that together the whole apostolic band proclaimed it, and that together the whole Christian church received and believed it. There is only one gospel.

The second preliminary question is whether the one New Testament gospel is transient because it was culturally conditioned, or whether it is changeless. There can be no gainsaying the fact that in the purpose of God his revelation reached its culmination in the first century A.D., in Christ and in the apostolic witness to Christ, and therefore in what to us is an ancient culture of mixed Hebrew, Greek and Roman ingredients. Nor can there be any doubt that, in order to grasp his revelation, we have to think ourselves back into that culture. But the fact that God disclosed himself in terms of a particular culture gives us not a justification for rejecting his revelation, but rather the right principle by which to interpret it, and also the solemn responsibility to reinterpret it in terms meaningful to our own culture. But there is only one gospel, and in its essence it never changes.

Let me say something more about revelation and culture. I am arguing that evangelism must be defined in terms of the message that we share with others. We have good news to communicate. So if evangelism is to take place, there must be communication—a true communication between ancient revelation and modern culture. This means that our message must be at the same time faithful and contemporary. First it must be faithful—faithful, that is, to Scripture. We find our message first and foremost not in any existential situation, but in the Bible. As Dr. Visser 't Hooft wrote, "I do not believe that evangelism is adequately described as answering the questions which men are asking, however deep those questions may be. For evangelism is in the first place the transmission of God's question to man. And that question is and remains whether we are willing to accept Jesus Christ as the one and only Lord of Life." But he goes on to say that we must "try to relate God's question to the existential situation of men and show that as they answer God's question they find at the same time the answer to their deepest concerns."[4]

Now it is comparatively easy to be faithful if we do not care about being contemporary, and easy also to be contemporary if we do not bother to be faithful. It is the search for a combination of truth and relevance that is exacting. Yet nothing else can save us from an insensitive loyalty to formulas and shibboleths on the one hand, and from a treasonable disloyalty to the revelation of God on the other. We need both to be true to the Bible, and also to be timely in our culture.

We come back now to our earlier question: what is the one, the changeless New Testament gospel? And in stating it can we indicate at all its contemporary power? The first and best answer would be to say that the whole Bible is God's good news in all its astonishing relevance. *Bible* and *gospel* are almost alternative terms, for the major function of the Bible in all its length and breadth is to bear witness to Jesus Christ. Nevertheless, God's revelation recorded in Scripture has been distilled for us in the good news the apostles proclaimed. What is it?

C. H. Dodd produced a seminal analysis of the sermons of the apostles.[5] He made a distinction between *kerygma* and *didachē*, that is, between the proclamation of the gospel and the ethical instruction of converts. Then he presented systematic reconstructions of the *kerygma* as preached by Paul, and as seen in the speeches attributed to Peter in Acts—showing the remarkable amount of common structure and content that they exhibit. The points below build on Dodd's helpful analysis.

In a single word, God's good news is Jesus. On the day of Pentecost, after quoting from Joel, Peter began his sermon proper: "Men of Israel, hear these words: Jesus . . ." (Acts 2:22). His first word was Jesus, and Jesus must be our first word too. Jesus Christ is the heart and soul of the gospel. When Philip sat down beside the Ethiopian, we are told literally that "he evangelized to him Jesus," that is, he shared with him the good news of Jesus (Acts 8:35, my translation). Similarly, Paul began his great manifesto to the Romans by describing himself as "set apart for the gospel of God . . . concerning his Son . . . Jesus Christ our Lord" (Romans 1:1-4). And we must all be profoundly thankful that the personality of Jesus retains its powerful hold over human minds. When people take any serious interest in Jesus, whether they come from a background of other faiths, or secularism, or youthful counterculture, they often feel his fascination.

But how did the apostles present Jesus? Their good news contained at least five elements.

THE GOSPEL EVENTS

First, of course, there were *the gospel events.* For certain "things" had "happened" in Jerusalem and "been accomplished" among them (Luke 1:1; 24:14, 18), which nobody could deny. In particular, Jesus of Nazareth had been crucified and resurrected. So Paul summarizes the gospel tradition: "I delivered to you as of first importance what I also received, that Christ died for our sins . . . , that he was buried, that he was raised on the third day . . . , and that he appeared" (1 Corinthians 15:3-5). He actually mentions four events—the death, burial, resurrection and appearance of Jesus. Yet it is clear that his emphasis is on two, namely, that Christ died (and was buried in order to prove it) and that Christ rose (and was seen in order to prove it). The appearance attested the reality of his resurrection, as the burial attested the reality of his death.

The same stress on the resurrection of Jesus is clear in the speeches of the Acts. Sometimes the apostle Peter would begin with a reference to the life and ministry of the man Jesus (Acts 2:22; 3:22; 10:36-39; compare Acts 13:23-25), and sometimes he went on to his exaltation, reign and return. But Peter's message, like Paul's, focused on Jesus' death and resurrection. Both events were real, objective and historical. And surely the right response to the existential mood of today is not to create a parallel Christian existentialism that despises history in favor of experience, and demythologizes the resurrection into an inward encounter with reality, but rather to offer to the modern mind as it flounders in the quicksand of subjectivity the objective bedrock of Jesus Christ whose death and resurrection are solid historical events.

The apostles did not present their Lord's death and resurrection merely as historical events, however, but as significant events, as saving events. Paul was clear that he "died for our sins" (1 Corinthians 15:3; compare Galatians 1:4) and was "raised for our justification" (Romans 4:25). It is sometimes said that, by contrast, the apostle Peter in his early Acts speeches had no doctrine of the cross, but proclaimed it as untheological history. This is C. H. Dodd's position, for example.[6] Yet one wonders whether he allows sufficiently for the implications of what Peter said. First, he attributed the cross as much to "the definite plan and foreknowledge of God" as to "the hands of lawless men" (Acts 2:23), and if the cross was part of a divine purpose, it must have had a meaning. Second, he designated Jesus God's "servant," which must be an allusion to the Suffering Servant who bore the sins of many (Acts 3:13; 4:27; compare Acts 8:32-33). Third, there is the surprising description of the crucifixion as a "hanging" of Jesus on a "tree" (Acts 5:30; 10:39; compare Acts 13:29). This example of apostolic shorthand looked back to Deuteronomy 21:23, which said that any man hanged on a tree was under the curse of God, and so also anticipated the developed doctrine of Christ bearing our sin and even the curse of the law, which we find later in the letters of both Paul and Peter (Galatians 3:10, 13 and 1 Peter 2:24).

Certainly too the resurrection was more than a historical event. It was a divine vindication of Jesus. "You killed him," Peter repeated several times (Acts 2:23; 3:15; 5:30-31), "but God raised him," thus reversing the verdict of men, snatching him from the place of a curse and exalting him to his own right hand as Lord, Christ and Savior (Acts 2:24; 3:13-15; 5:30-31).

THE GOSPEL WITNESSES

The second element in the apostles' message is *the gospel witnesses*, by which I mean the evidence to which they appealed for its authentication. This was twofold, in order that in the mouth of two witnesses the truth of the testimony might be established.

The first witness was the Old Testament Scriptures. Paul emphasized this by repetition in his succinct statement of the gospel (1 Corinthians 15:3-4): "Christ died for our sins in accordance with the scriptures" and "was raised on the third day in accordance with the scriptures." And Peter kept quoting Scripture in his Acts speeches, to demonstrate that the Christ of Old Testament expectation was Jesus. We can say with confidence that the apostles had learned from Jesus himself this truth of the fulfillment of Scripture in his death and resurrection. They learned it partly during his public ministry, but especially after his resurrection, as Luke records. They would never forget his words, that "'everything written about me in the law of Moses and the prophets and the psalms must be fulfilled.' Then he opened their minds to understand the Scriptures and said to them, 'Thus it is written, that the Christ should suffer and on the third day rise from the dead'" (Luke 24:46). In this way the apostles urged that they were not innovators. They had not invented their message. As Paul was to claim later, when standing on trial before Agrippa: "So I stand here testifying both to small and great, saying nothing but what the prophets and Moses said would come to pass: that the Christ must suffer, and that, by being the first to rise from the dead, he would proclaim light both to the people and to the Gentiles" (Acts 26:22-23).

The emphasis on Scripture had another significance. Since the death of Jesus, his resurrection and his subsequent outpouring of the Spirit were all in fulfillment of messianic prophecy, it was evident that the new age had dawned and that Christ had ushered it in. As C. H. Dodd puts it, "The Pauline *kerygma* . . . is a proclamation of the facts of the death and resurrection of Christ in an eschatological setting which gives significance to the facts," indeed a "saving significance."[7]

The second witness was the evidence of the apostles' own eyes. Jesus himself had linked the forthcoming apostolic witness to the prophetic witness of the Old Testament when he added to his reference to Scripture "you are witnesses of these things" (Luke 24:48). He did it again before the ascension: "you shall be my witnesses" (Acts 1:8). They knew they were uniquely qualified to witness to Christ, not just because they had been "with him from the beginning" (compare Mark 3:14; John 15:27; Acts 1:21-22), but especially because they had seen the cross and the risen Christ with their own eyes. So Peter regularly included in his sermons a reference to the apostolic witness:

This Jesus God raised up, and of that we all are witnesses. (Acts 2:32)

You . . . killed the Author of life, whom God raised from the dead. To this we are witnesses. (Acts 3:15)

And we are witnesses to these things. (Acts 5:32)

To Cornelius, Peter was even more explicit:

And we are witnesses to all that he did both in the country of the Jews and in Jerusalem. They put him to death by hanging him on a tree; but God raised him on the third day and made him manifest; not to all the people but to us who were chosen by God as witnesses, who ate and drank with him after he rose from the dead. And he commanded us to preach to the people, and to testify. (Acts 10:39-42)

Thus the apostles joined together the witness of the Old Testament prophets and their own witness, which came later to be recorded in the New Testament.

This double authentication is important for our own day. We have already noted the fascination that the person of Jesus has for our contemporaries, and that this often gives us a meeting point with them. But which Jesus are we talking about? Even Paul in his day recognized the possibility of teachers proclaiming "another Jesus" than the Jesus he preached (2 Corinthians 11:4). And there are many "Jesuses" abroad today. There is Jesus whom some scholars treat as a myth. There is Jesus the tragic, failed revolutionary. There is Jesus as portrayed in musicals and movies. It is over against these human reinterpretations that we need urgently to recover and reinstate the authentic Jesus, the Jesus of history who is the Jesus of Scripture.

This means, further, that we have no liberty to preach Jesus Christ according to our own fantasy, or even according to our own experience. Our personal witness does indeed corroborate the witness of the biblical authors, especially that of the apostles. But theirs is the primary witness, for they were "with Jesus" and knew him, and they have borne witness to what they heard with their ears and saw with their eyes. Our witness is always secondary and subordinate to theirs. So there is no escape from the continuing work of conservative scholars who are seeking to defend the reliability of the gospel portrait of Jesus and to reestablish public confidence in the apostolic witness. Our responsibility in evangelism is neither to create a Christ of our own who is not in Scripture, nor to embroider or manipulate the Christ who is in Scripture, but to bear faithful witness to the one and only Christ there is as God has presented him to the world in the remarkably unified testimony of both the Old and the New Testament Scriptures.

THE GOSPEL AFFIRMATIONS

Third, there were and still are *the gospel affirmations.* As we have seen, they center on Jesus Christ. They concern not simply what he *did* more than nineteen centuries ago, however, but what he *is* today in consequence. The historical Christ is the contemporary Christ. In New Testament terms, the fundamental affirmation is that "Jesus is Lord." If we confess with our lips that "Jesus is Lord," Paul wrote, and believe in our heart that God raised him from the dead, we will be saved (Romans 10:9). Indeed, the end for which Christ died and rose again was "that he might be Lord both of the dead and of the living" (Romans 14:9). For God has highly exalted Jesus and bestowed on him the name above every name that every knee should bow to him and every tongue confess that "Jesus Christ is Lord" (Philippians 2:9-11). It is an essentially Christian affirmation, for no one can make it but by the illumination of the Holy Spirit (1 Corinthians 12:3).

What Paul insists on in these texts is that the lordship or sovereignty of Jesus is a direct consequence of his death and resurrection.

Peter taught the same in his Acts speeches. It is the Jesus who died and whom God raised up who is now "exalted at the right hand of God" (Acts 2:32-33; compare Acts 3:13; 4:11). This was in fulfillment of the great messianic promise "Sit at my right hand, till I make your enemies your footstool" (Psalm 110:1), which not only looked back to the Savior's completed work from which he was now resting, as the writer to the Hebrews shows (Hebrews 10:12), but also looks on to the final triumph for which he is now waiting. Yet this is assured. Already in anticipation, Peter could say to Cornelius, albeit in a parenthesis, "he is Lord of all" (Acts 10:36).

The "right hand of God" at which Christ "sits" is then symbolic of his universal authority, because of which he is able both to bestow blessing and to require submission. First, the blessing. It was after his exaltation to God's right hand that he "received from the Father the promise of the Holy Spirit" and poured out on his church this distinctive blessing of the new age (Acts 2:33). According to the Joel prophecy that Peter said had been fulfilled, it was God himself who had promised "I will pour out my Spirit upon all flesh" (Acts 2:17). Yet, knowing this, Peter does not hesitate to attribute the outpouring to Jesus, who occupies the position of supreme honor and authority at the Father's right hand.

If from the throne Jesus bestows blessing on his people, he also expects them to submit to him, to bow their knee to him. "Let all the house of Israel therefore know assuredly that God has made him both Lord and Christ, this Jesus whom you crucified" (Acts 2:36). These words formed the climax of Peter's sermon. They cut his listeners to the heart and made them cry out for instruction on what to do. They must repent, Peter said. God had reversed their verdict on Jesus, for they had killed him but God had raised him. Now they must reverse their verdict too. They must bring the whole of life, individual and social, under the sovereign lordship of Jesus. To be in his kingdom or under his rule brings both total blessing and total demand.

Thus the symbolic statement that Jesus is "at God's right hand" comprises the two great gospel affirmations that he is Savior (with authority to bestow salvation) and that he is Lord (with authority to demand submission). The two are joined by Peter in his second speech to the Sanhedrin: "God exalted him at his right hand as Leader and Savior, to give repentance to Israel and forgiveness of sins" (Acts 5:31).

Moreover, both affirmations are part of the absolute uniqueness of Jesus Christ. If we are asked in today's increasingly syncretistic culture wherein lies the uniqueness of Jesus, I think we should have to answer "Jesus is Lord" and "Jesus is Savior." Theologically speaking, these affirmations express the great doctrines of incarnation and atonement, and there is nothing comparable to them in other religions. The claimed "avatars" ("descents" or so-called incarnations) of Hinduism not only lack historical foundation, but their incidental nature and their plurality set them apart from the central Christian claim that once only and in verifiable history God became man in Jesus. And the repeated promises in the Qur'an of the forgiveness of a compassionate and merciful Allah are all made to the meritorious, whose merits have been weighed in Allah's scales, whereas the gospel is good news of mercy to the undeserving. The symbol of the religion of Jesus is the cross, not the scales. The world is still waiting to hear these gospel affirmations, and to hear them in the present tense that speaks to people today, namely, "Jesus is Lord" and "Jesus is Savior."

THE GOSPEL PROMISES

Fourth, we turn logically from the gospel affirmations to *the gospel promises*, to what Christ now offers and indeed promises to those who come to him. For the good news concerns neither just what Jesus once *did* (he died and rose again), nor just what he now *is* (exalted to God's right hand as Lord and Savior), but also what he now *offers* as a result. What is this? At the end of his Pentecost sermon Peter promised the crowd with great assurance that if they repented and were baptized they would receive two free gifts of God, namely, "the forgiveness of sins" and "the gift of the Holy Spirit."

Forgiveness is an essential ingredient of the salvation offered in the gospel. The risen Lord had commanded that "forgiveness of sins" be proclaimed to all nations on the basis of his name (Luke 24:47), and the Reformed understanding of his statement "if you forgive the sins of any, they are forgiven" (John 20:23) has always been that he was telling them to preach the terms of the divine forgiveness with boldness and authority. Certainly this is what the apostles did. "Repent," cried Peter, "and turn again that your sins may be blotted out" (Acts 3:19). And he assured Cornelius: "Every one who believes in him receives forgiveness of sins through his name" (Acts 10:43). Similarly, Paul declared in the synagogue in Antioch, "Through this man forgiveness of sins is proclaimed to you" (Acts 13:38). However unpopular this message may be today, forgiveness remains humanity's chief need and an indispensable part of the good news.

But Christ offers more than the forgiveness of our past. He offers too a new life in the present through the regeneration and indwelling of the Holy Spirit, who is also the guarantee of our future inheritance in heaven. We must not separate the two gospel promises that God has joined together, forgiveness and the Spirit. Both belong to the "salvation" that Peter insisted was in Jesus Christ alone (Acts 4:12), and both are part of the "liberation" that so many people seek. True freedom is more than deliverance from guilt; it is deliverance also from self, from what Malcolm Muggeridge once called "the dark little dungeon of my own ego." Once rescued from guilt and self-centeredness, we can give ourselves to the service of God and others. And only in this servitude is true freedom to be found.

THE GOSPEL DEMANDS

Fifth, we come to *the gospel demands.* We move from what Jesus did, who Jesus is and what Jesus promises, to what Jesus requires

of us today. We have already seen that Peter's first word in answer
to the crowd's conscience-stricken question of what they should do
was repent. It was his first word again at the conclusion of his
second sermon: "Repent therefore" (Acts 3:19). And Paul ended his
sermon to the Athenians with the statement that God "now commands all men everywhere to repent" (Acts 17:30).

To repent was to turn from their sin, and in particular their
grievous sin of rejecting Jesus. Their *metanoia* or "change of mind"
was, then, a reversal of their opinion of Jesus and of their attitude
toward him. They had repudiated him and expressed their rejection
in the crucifixion; now they were to believe in him as Lord, Christ
and Savior, and express their acceptance in their baptism. For, although baptism no doubt means more than this, it cannot mean
less. They were to be baptized "in the name of Jesus Christ." That is,
they were to submit humbly to baptism in the name of the very
person they had previously sought to destroy. Nothing could indicate more clearly than this their public and penitent faith in him.
Further, their repentance and baptism introduced them into the
new community of Jesus. There was no conversion without church
membership, as I shall argue at greater length later.

At the Lausanne Congress in 1974, the speaker who laid greatest
emphasis on the indispensable necessity of repentance was Dr.
René Padilla from Argentina. He also insisted on the social dimension of repentance. In that section of his pre-Congress paper
that was titled "Evangelism and Repentance Ethics," he wrote, "This
new reality (sc. the arrival of the Kingdom) places men in a position
of crisis—they cannot continue to live as if nothing had happened;
the Kingdom of God demands a new mentality, a reorientation of
all their values, repentance." Also, "the change imposed involves a
new life-style. . . . Without ethics there is no real repentance. . . .
And without repentance there is no salvation." Further, "Repentance is much more than a private affair between the individual and

God. It is the complete reorientation of life in the world—among men—in response to the work of God in Jesus Christ."[8]

Thus social responsibility becomes an aspect not of Christian mission only, but also of Christian conversion. It is impossible to be truly converted to God (as we shall consider in the last chapter) without being thereby converted to our neighbor.

Conversion includes faith as well as repentance. It is true that Peter's command to the crowd was to "repent" rather than to "believe." Yet, those who received Peter's word, repented and were baptized are a few verses later referred to as "believers" (Acts 2:44). "Every one who believes in him receives forgiveness," Peter said to Cornelius (Acts 10:43). "Believe in the Lord Jesus, and you will be saved," Paul said to the jailer at Philippi (Acts 16:31).

So the gospel demands are repentance and faith—and (in public) baptism. This leads me to mention a controversy in certain evangelical circles. Some have been so determined to maintain the doctrine of justification by faith alone that they have not been able to accommodate themselves to the addition of repentance. They distinguish sharply between the acceptance of Jesus as Savior and the surrender to him as Lord, and they even promulgate the grotesque notion that to insist on surrender in addition to acceptance is to distort the gospel. Well, I honor their conscientious desire to protect the gospel from all perversions. And certainly justification is by grace alone in Christ alone through faith alone. Further, we must be careful never to define faith in such a way as to ascribe to it any merit. The whole value of faith lies in its object (Jesus Christ), not in itself. Nevertheless, saving faith is not an "acceptance of Jesus Christ as Savior" within a kind of mystical vacuum and without any awareness either of the Christ being "accepted" or of the concrete implications of this acceptance. Saving faith is a total, penitent and submissive commitment to Christ, and it would have been inconceivable to the apostles that anybody could believe in Jesus as Savior without submitting to him as Lord. We have already seen that the one exalted to God's right hand is Jesus the Lord and Savior. We cannot chop this Jesus into bits and then respond to only one of the bits. The object of saving faith is the whole and undivided person of our Lord and Savior, Jesus Christ.

One other point before I leave the gospel demands. We must not miss the note of urgency as well as authority in which the apostles issued their call to repent and believe. They were conscious not only that the summons came from the throne where Jesus reigned but also that this same Jesus would return as Judge. The God who "now . . . commands all men everywhere to repent" had already fixed the judgment day and appointed the Judge. He is Jesus, the same one who had died and been resurrected (Acts 17:30-31; compare Acts 3:20-21; 10:42; 13:40-41).

THE CONTEXT OF EVANGELISM

Evangelism, then, is sharing the good news with others. The good news is Jesus. And the good news about Jesus that we announce is that he died for our sins and was raised from death, and that in consequence he reigns as Lord and Savior at God's right hand, and has authority both to command repentance and faith, and to bestow forgiveness of sins and the gift of the Spirit on all those who repent, believe and are baptized. And all this is according to the Scriptures of the Old and New Testaments. It is more than that. It is precisely what is meant by "proclaiming the kingdom of God." For in fulfillment of Scripture God's reign has broken into the life of humanity through the death and resurrection of Jesus. This reign or rule of God is exercised from the throne by Jesus, who bestows salvation and requires obedience. These are the blessing and the demand of the kingdom. As Jesus himself had put it at the very beginning of his public ministry, "The time is fulfilled, and the kingdom of God is at hand; repent, and believe in the gospel" (Mark 1:15).

Finally, having tried to define evangelism in terms of the evangel,

I think I need to say something about its context, for the proclamation of the gospel cannot be seen as an activity in isolation. Something precedes it and something follows it. What precedes it may justly be called "presence" and what follows it "persuasion."

The first word is *presence*. The notion of the "Christian presence" has not always commended itself because its advocates have sometimes spoken of a "silent presence" or an "authentic silence." No doubt there are occasions when it is more Christian to be silent than to speak. Yet the Christian presence in the world is intended by God to lead to the Christian proclamation to the world. On the other hand, we can accept that those who advocate a degree of "silent presence" may be reacting justifiably against some of our brash and aggressive evangelical forms of evangelism. If, however, generally speaking, there should be no presence without proclamation, we must equally assert that there should be no proclamation without presence. The risen Lord's first word of commission was not preach but go. And going into the world means presence.

Moreover, it is to be the visible presence of a church that bears an attractive aspect. As Samuel Escobar wrote in his paper for the 1974 Lausanne Congress, "The primitive church was not perfect, but evidently it was a community that called the attention of men because of the qualitative differences of its life. The message was not only heard from them, it was also seen in the way they lived."[9] There can be no evangelism without the church. The message comes from a community that embodies it and that welcomes into its fellowship those who receive it.

The second word is *persuasion*. I mentioned earlier J. I. Packer's criticism of the archbishops' definition of evangelism. I have argued that we should not *define* evangelism in such a way as to include the element of persuasion within that definition of the activity itself. Evangelism is to share the good news of the facts of what God has done through Christ for the salvation of the world. Of course, we must certainly accept that Paul described his evangelistic preaching by the statement "we persuade men" (2 Corinthians 5:11), and that many times in the Acts Luke describes him doing so, adding that many were "persuaded." This is not in dispute; but to make the persuasion of our hearers a part of our definition of evangelism is to confuse the activity itself with its goals. Our goal is indeed to persuade people to repent and trust in Christ. We have this liberty to state our *purpose*: yet it is not for us to determine the *result*. Some speak of "persuasion" as if the outcome could be secured by human effort, almost as if it were another word for "coercion." But no. Our responsibility is to be faithful; the results are in the hand of Almighty God.

I do not think I can conclude more appropriately than by quoting paragraph 4 of the Lausanne Covenant, which is titled "The Nature of Evangelism":

> To evangelize is to spread the good news that Jesus Christ died for our sins and was raised from the dead according to the Scriptures, and that as the reigning Lord he now offers the forgiveness of sins and the liberating gift of the Spirit to all who repent and believe. Our Christian presence in the world is indispensable to evangelism, and so is that kind of dialogue whose purpose is to listen sensitively in order to understand. But evangelism itself is the proclamation of the historical, biblical Christ as Saviour and Lord, with a view to persuading people to come to him personally and so be reconciled to God. In issuing the gospel invitation we have no liberty to conceal the cost of discipleship. Jesus still calls all who would follow him to deny themselves, take up their cross, and identify themselves with his new community. The results of evangelism include obedience to Christ, incorporation into his church and responsible service in the world.[10]

four

REFLECTIONS ON EVANGELISM

Chris Wright

J ohn Stott was an evangelist at heart, from the earliest days following his spiritual birth as a Christian to the latest days of his life on earth. Led to faith in Christ as a seventeen-year-old schoolboy by the remarkable evangelist E. J. H. Nash (affectionately known as "Bash"), he quickly became a leader in the evangelistic camps for boys at Iwerne Minster.[1] He became a renowned university evangelist, first in his own alma mater, Cambridge University, then on campuses in the United States, Canada and internationally. He led his church, All Souls Church, Langham Place, London, to be a model of parish evangelism, mobilizing an army of laypeople in the skills of personal witnessing and systematic discipling of new believers. And on one occasion when I visited him at the care home where he spent his last four years in increasing incapacity, his face lit up as he told me how he had shared the way of salvation with one of the staff in response to a question, as she wheeled him back from the dining room to his own small apartment.

So it is not at all surprising that he begins his chapter on evangelism by repeating the statement of the Lausanne Covenant paragraph 6 (which he himself had drafted), "In the church's mission of sacrificial service evangelism is primary." He has already made it clear that he does not mean by this that evangelism is the *only* task of the church. Rather, in his opening words, "the word *mission* . . . is a properly comprehensive word, embracing everything that God sends his people into the world to do. It therefore includes evangelism and social responsibility." Nevertheless, within this nonnegotiable breadth and wholeness of the church's missional task (which Stott staunchly upheld all his life), evangelism has priority. How that double commitment *both* to the intrinsically holistic nature of mission *and* to the primacy of evangelism within that holism was to be worked out in theory and practice was something to which he devoted a lot of attention in consultations and writing over the following decades.

As I argued above, I myself would prefer to speak of the centrality of the gospel, rather than the primacy of evangelism, in seeking to define what is meant by holistic and integrated mission. And I do so with a subtle change of emphasis from the way Stott (along with many others) justifies the assertion of the primacy of evangelism on the basis of what constitutes humanity's greatest need. I do not, of course, in any way question the radical biblical diagnosis of the human condition as one of fundamental alienation from God, lost in rebellion and sin and facing God's judgment. People need to hear the good news that addresses that reality. But to speak of the centrality of the gospel points us not first of all to humans in their need, but to God in his grace and to the biblical story of what God has done in Christ to save the world. And by pointing us to the great biblical narrative as constitutive of the gospel, it necessarily integrates into that good news all the biblically revealed dimensions of God's good purposes for human life, recognizing but not dichotomizing spiritual and material, eternal and earthly, and so on, dimensions thereof.

I think there is very little difference in practice between this way of expressing the point and how Stott actually does work out his balance of "holism with priority." For in this chapter, after his short discussion of how evangelism should be defined, he immediately goes on to his majestic exposition of the gospel that forms the bulk of the chapter (the gospel events, witnesses, affirmations, promises and demands). One might say that for Stott, it was the centrality of the gospel that generated the primacy of evangelism, whereas for me the centrality of the gospel generates the *ultimacy* and necessity of evangelism within an integrated understanding of mission as a whole.[2] This kind of centrality is not such as makes everything else merely peripheral, marginal and unimportant, but rather the centrality around which everything else is integrated, held together and given direction and meaning.

Two of Stott's points in this chapter seem to me to deserve further reflection and greater expansion—in ways that, again, I believe he would have approved. In each case they can be introduced by a quotation from the chapter itself.

"THE WHOLE BIBLE IS GOD'S GOOD NEWS"

In a few powerful sentences, Stott articulates a view of the gospel that remarkably foreshadows recent efforts to call evangelicals back from using the term *gospel* as if it meant only a "plan of salvation," or a few spiritual laws that provide a mechanism for individuals to ensure their place in heaven when they die. Rather, we need to speak about the gospel in the way the New Testament itself does, as fundamentally the good news constituted by the whole-Bible story of all that God both promised and accomplished and will bring to completion through Jesus of Nazareth, as promised Messiah, atoning Savior and returning King.[3]

What is the gospel? Stott writes, "The first and best answer would be to say that the whole Bible is God's good news in all its astonishing relevance. *Bible* and *gospel* are almost alternative terms, for the major function of the Bible in all its length and breadth is to bear witness to Jesus Christ. . . . In a single word, God's good news is Jesus."

Working backwards through Stott's concise logic, his point is this:

- The gospel is centered on Jesus Christ. Jesus himself is the good news that God declares to us.

- It is the Bible that "gives" us Jesus, for the whole Bible bears witness to him in one way or another.

- Therefore *the Bible as a whole* constitutes "gospel," for it is what God has given us to be able to know and understand the person and work of Jesus as "God's good news."

Now all this is incontrovertibly true, and just as it stands it counteracts the tendency to reduce the gospel to a few extracted biblical verses, arranged in a sequence that focuses first on my personal sin problem, and then on the death of Jesus bearing my sin in my place, and finally on the promise of forgiveness and eternal life—for me. I do not for one moment deny the glorious truth of those verses and the eternal consequences they generate for those who are led to put their faith in Christ through them, including myself. But this personalized salvation plan, though it is accomplished and guaranteed within the gospel, is not the whole story. Or to be more precise, it is not the whole story that the gospel fundamentally is and tells.

When Stott goes on to support his claim that the gospel involves the whole Bible, he does it in two ways. First (in "The Gospel Events"), he points to the biblical record of historical events—the things that actually happened in Jerusalem: the crucifixion and resurrection of Jesus of Nazareth. But these events, he points out, are given their saving significance because of the scripturally revealed plan and purpose of God and the interpretation of the Messiah's death already provided in the Old Testament. And second (in "The Gospel Witnesses"), he emphasizes the fulfillment of Old Testament prophecies, as highlighted by Jesus himself when he said to his disciples, "This is what is written: The Messiah will suffer and rise from the dead on the third day, and repentance for the forgiveness of sins will be preached in his name to all nations" (Luke 24:46-47 NIV).

These two points are, of course, true, but they do not quite go far enough in clarifying the relationship of the Old Testament to the gospel. For it is not just a book of prophecies about Christ. Rather, it tells the first part of the *overarching biblical story* that establishes the whole framework within which the identity and work of Jesus Christ make sense and constitute good news for all nations. The gospel is good news *within* an understanding of the world and humanity and the future of both that is rendered to us by the whole Bible story. Without the biblical worldview, constituted by the biblical story, our understanding and presentation of the gospel will be deficient.

When Jesus referred his disciples to "the law of Moses and the prophets and the psalms" (Luke 24:44), he was specifying not merely the predictive prophecies but the whole canon of what we now call the Old Testament, in the full sweep, direction and flow of its grand narrative. The Torah includes the story of creation, the fall, God's covenant promise to Abraham with its universal vision, the exodus redemption of Israel, the Sinai covenant, and the anticipation of a future that would see the ultimate triumph of the faithfulness and grace of God over the rebellion and judgment of his people. "The Prophets," in the Hebrew canon, include the Former Prophets (the so-called Deuteronomic History from Joshua to 2 Kings), telling the story of the gift of the land, the emergence of monarchy and the covenant with David, the long decline into the death of exile, and the "resurrection" of the return from exile. And in the course of this great story, in passages drawn from all three sections (Law, Prophets and Psalms ["Writings"]), we find again and again the note of God's universal purpose for all nations. We are reminded often that this story is ultimately one that will embrace all nations and indeed all creation within God's redemptive covenant blessing.[4] The Old Testament is, in fact, a good news story, even if the good news has not arrived yet.

Sadly, the Old Testament is often presented as a kind of negative backdrop, a contrasting foil for the gospel—something *from which* the gospel actually rescues us. We easily treat the *distortion* of the Old Testament by the apostle Paul's opponents as if it were what the Old Testament itself taught. Now of course, as Paul fully acknowledged (in company with Jesus, Moses and all the prophets), the *people of Israel* failed miserably, proving themselves to be just as much sin-laden, fallen rebels as the rest of the human race. But the *purposes of God* were not nullified by the failure of Israel. On the contrary, the *good news* of the Old Testament is precisely the promise and undying hope that Yahweh, the God of Israel, would triumph over evil, would reign as king and would bring salvation to the ends of the earth. That "gospel" was first announced to Abraham, says Paul, quoting Genesis 12:3 (Galatians 3:8).[5] And even the key New Testament gospel words *euangelion,* and *euangelizomai* come from the Greek translations of Old Testament "good news" texts about the reign of God among the nations, such as Psalm 96:1-3 and Isaiah 52:7-10.

So when Jesus came announcing that the kingdom of God was breaking into history in his own person, people did not need to check a dictionary to find out what he meant by "believe in the *gospel*" (Mark 1:15). They knew the story they were in. They knew their God (Yahweh the Holy One of Israel) and his promises. They may have had many confused ideas about what it would mean when their God fully established his reign (which Jesus spent a lot of time correcting), but they knew that only when "our God reigns" would there be good news for the celebration of "the ruins of Jerusalem," for all nations and the ends of the earth—and indeed for the rejoicing of all creation (Isaiah 52:9-10; Psalm 96:10-13). The good news was that God had kept his promise to Abraham, though he had done so through the paradoxical path of the incarnation, life, rejection, suffering, death and resurrection of Jesus of Nazareth. So to those who joined themselves to Christ in repentance, faith and obedient discipleship, there comes the further good news of the assurance of future participation in the "good ending" of the story, in the resurrection of the dead and eternal life in the new creation.

In other words, although we must agree and insist with Stott that the gospel is indeed constituted by Jesus Christ himself, and centers on his atoning death and victorious resurrection, we must also see that "Christ-story" within the framework of the whole-Bible story, from creation to new creation—which I think is probably what Paul meant when he refers to "the whole counsel/plan/will of God" (Acts 20:27; compare Ephesians 1:9-10; Colossians 1:15-23). Ben Witherington III has explored in great depth how Paul's whole thinking, preaching and teaching was shaped by that scriptural story—including the way he understood and preached the gospel itself.

> Paul's thought, including both theology and ethics, is grounded in the grand narrative and in a story that has continued to develop out of that narrative.
>
> This Story is a tale as large as the universe yet as small as an individual human being. It is, however, not a Story about everything, not even about all of human history. It is a Story that focuses on God's relationship to humankind, from the beginning of the human race in Adam to its climax in the eschatological Adam, and beyond. It is a Story about creation and creature and their redemption by, in, and through Jesus Christ. It is a Story about a community of faith created out of the midst of fallen humanity. It involves both tragedy and triumph, both the lost and the saved, both the first and the last. Its focus is repeatedly on divine and human actions on the stage of human history. It is out of this Story, which Paul sees as involving both history and His story (i.e. Christ's), that he argues, urges, encourages, debates, promises and threatens.[6]

That great story as a whole—Bible-revealed, God-driven, Christ-centered and hope-filled—constitutes the good news that we are called first to participate in by faith and life, and then to share in the "gospeling" work of evangelism.[7]

At one point, Stott laments the loss of urgency in evangelism, which he attributes to our loss of confidence in the gospel itself. "Nothing hinders evangelism today more than the widespread loss of confidence in the truth, relevance and power of the gospel." I agree. But I would add that one reason for that loss of confidence in the gospel is that so many Christians, including evangelicals, have simply forgotten the story we are in (or never really learned it)—the story within which the gospel is constituted. They have accepted the gospel as an individualized guarantee of a future "in heaven" through faith in the atoning work of the cross. But then they continue to live in this world by this world's story—whatever story that happens to be in their particular cultural milieu. They have not allowed the gospel to transform their worldview at its deepest level, as the true story of the universe and the stance from which to interpret history, the present and the future. Basically, they have "added Jesus" to provide a happy ending to an otherwise unaltered personal and cultural story.

How else can we explain the massive syncretism of Western Christianity, for example, in which there seems so little difference between even evangelical Christians and the ambient idolatrous consumerism with its underlying myths of progress and "growth"? Even those who claim to "believe the gospel" show few signs of knowing, believing and living by the only story, the biblical story, that makes the gospel to be good news at every level, from personal to cosmic.[8] For that reason, we should welcome every effort and every publication or course that helps Christians to know the story they are in—that is to say, to have an overarching understanding of the Bible as a whole story (which is not the same thing as comprehensively knowing all the details of the Bible—as if our salvation or our sanctification depended on passing a trivia competition on Bible knowledge).[9]

In 2004 I was invited by the board of directors of the Lausanne Movement to take the chair of the Lausanne Theology Working Group—a position that John Stott had occupied in the years of theological wrestling that followed the first Lausanne Congress in 1974. In the years immediately prior to the third Congress in Cape Town 2010, we embarked on a series of consultations on the Lausanne slogan, "the whole church taking the whole gospel to the whole world." What does each phrase actually mean, in biblical and missiological perspective?

The first consultation, in Chiang Mai in 2008, was on "The Whole Gospel." The statement issued from that event identified several ways in which the apostle Paul uses the *euangel-* words, as noun or verb.[10] The first point of the statement expresses the narrative nature of the gospel:

A. *The gospel tells the story of Jesus in the light of the whole Bible.*

1. The gospel for Paul is above all else the historical facts about Jesus of Nazareth through whom God has accomplished salvation. The gospel is an account of the events of Jesus' death and resurrection, understood in the light of the scriptures of the Old Testament. . . . "According the Scriptures" means "in accordance with the Old Testament"—i.e. with the narrative of all that God had done and had promised in Old Testament Israel that had now been fulfilled in the Messiah Jesus (Acts 13:32-39). . . .

2. Paul's definition of the gospel, then, includes both the central historical facts (Christ died for our sins, was buried and was raised on the third day), *and* their scriptural context and frame of meaning. . . .

3. Drawing our understanding of the whole gospel from the whole Bible will protect us from a reductionism that shrinks the gospel to a few formulae for ease of communication and "marketing."[11]

The Chiang Mai statement goes on to summarize Paul's use of the term *gospel* in the following terms (in each case a short extract from the full statement is quoted):[12]

B. The gospel creates a new reconciled humanity in the one family of God.

1. For Paul, as "apostle to the Gentiles," clearly the good news about Jesus was a universal message for all the nations. And that too had deep Old Testament roots. God's plan, announced to Abraham, had always been to bring blessing through Israel to all the nations of the world. But the nations were utterly outside and alienated from the covenantal grace of God and membership in God's household (Eph. 2:11-12). The gospel transforms this situation. . . .

2. It is important to see how this "peace-making" work of the cross—reconciling Jews and Gentiles, and creating one new humanity—is *not just a by-product* of the gospel, but is *of the essence* of the gospel itself (Eph. 3:6). Paul includes it in the work of the cross. . . .

C. The gospel proclaims the saving message of the cross.

1. The very nature of "gospel" is that it is good news that has to be announced (as the biblical roots of the word show, Isa. 52:7). For Paul, the gospel must be heard as "word of truth" (Eph. 1:13; Col. 1:5, 23), and on being heard, it needs to be received and believed for what it is (1 Thess. 2:13). This message is to be preached to all nations in fulfilment of God's promise to Abraham. . . .

D. The gospel produces ethical transformation.

1. "*Repent* and believe the gospel," said Jesus (Mk. 1:15). Radical change of life goes along with faith in the good news. They cannot be separated. For Paul, the gospel involved putting off the filthy clothes of the old humanity and putting on the clothes that bore the aroma of Christ-likeness. . . . It is not the case that one is "gospel" and the other is "ethics." This common way of summarizing the two "halves" of Ephesians is vulnerable to misunderstanding—as if one could separate doctrinal believing from ethical living. The belief of faith and the life of faith cannot be separated. Both are intrinsic to the gospel itself.

"Although we cannot be saved by good works, we also cannot be saved without them. Good works are not the way of salvation, but its proper and necessary evidence. A faith which does not express itself in works is dead,"[13] Stott says.

E. The gospel declares truth and exposes evil before God's judgment.

1. According to Paul, the gospel is also truth that needs to be defended, against denial or perversion. So there is a polemical dimension to the gospel. . . .

F. The gospel has cosmic power through the mighty working of the Holy Spirit.

1. The gospel is the power of God at work in history and creation. For Paul this was something to marvel at and celebrate. The gospel seemed to have life of its own, such that Paul could personify it as being at work, active, spreading and bearing fruit all over the world (Col. 1:6). . . .

2. In Paul's most eloquent summary of the gospel, he proclaims that all things in the universe have been created by

Christ, and are being sustained by Christ, and will be reconciled to God by Christ through the blood of his cross. That is the breathtakingly universal scope of the gospel (Col. 1:15-23). And only after that survey of the cosmic significance of Christ, his church, and his cross, does Paul move to the personal reconciliation of believers.

"THE BLESSING AND THE DEMAND OF THE KINGDOM"

Stott's short section "The Gospel Demands" is very much in line with point D above—*The gospel produces ethical transformation.* Or, to be more precise, it does so when it meets with the response of repentance and faith.

At the beginning of the chapter, Stott stresses that, in his definition, evangelism is simply the faithful presentation of the gospel. While evangelism has as its *goal* the desire that people should be persuaded of the truth of the gospel and respond to it in saving faith, such *results* are not intrinsic to the definition of evangelism itself. Nevertheless, having made that clarifying point about the nature of evangelism (as something we humans do), he expounds *the gospel* (as the good news of what God has done) to show that it comes to us not only as affirmation, but also as promise and demand. Precisely because the gospel tells the story of what *God has done*, it cannot confront us merely as a record of objective facts, even though they are intrinsic to it. The gospel is indicative, promissory and imperative simultaneously. It affirms, it promises and it commands. Such is its very nature, for it addresses us as the voice of our Creator.

That is why Stott can correctly say that preaching the gospel is *proclaiming the kingdom of God*—since the two are equated in the mouth of Jesus, according to the Gospels themselves. Once again, Stott manages to condense into a few prime sentences a perception that has come to prominence decades later—the recognition of the importance of the kingdom of God as "gospel," and the extent to which that connection has been overlooked among evangelicals particularly, and is strangely lacking in much evangelism.[14]

> Evangelism, then, is sharing the good news with others. The good news is Jesus. And the good news about Jesus that we announce is that he died for our sins and was raised from death, and that in consequence he reigns as Lord and Savior at God's right hand, and has authority both to command repentance and faith, and to bestow forgiveness of sins and the gift of the Spirit on all those who repent, believe and are baptized. And all this is according to the Scriptures of the Old and New Testaments. It is more than that. *It is precisely what is meant by "proclaiming the kingdom of God."* For in fulfillment of Scripture God's reign has broken into human life through the death and resurrection of Jesus. This reign or rule of God is exercised from the throne by Jesus, who bestows salvation and requires obedience. These are the blessing and the demand of the kingdom. As Jesus himself had put it at the very beginning of his public ministry, "The time is fulfilled, and the kingdom of God is at hand; repent, and believe in the gospel" (Mark 1:15). (italics added)

At a theological conference I recently heard a renowned evangelical leader say, "The kingdom of God is *not* the gospel." My first instinct was to retort that Jesus would have disagreed (compare "this gospel of the kingdom will be preached throughout the whole world," Matthew 24:14). But I knew what he meant. The mere declaration that God is king is not good news *for individuals*, unless and until they respond in repentance and faith, as Jesus called for. Nevertheless it *is* good news that God reigns and that his reign will ultimately extend over all creation and all nations. It *is* good news that evil will not have the last word in the cosmos. It *is* good news that God's reign will usher in a new creation of justice and peace from which all evil, suffering, death and curse will be banished eternally. In these senses, unquestionably the proclamation of the kingdom of God *is* gospel.

But when the message of the reign of God confronts people (as a community or as individuals), it necessarily demands a response. That is unavoidable, because the Bible has shown ever since the Garden of Eden that human beings cannot encounter God without responding. Even Cain, in denying that he had any accountability for his brother, still had to *answer God* in doing so. And since any person or persons may respond with continued rejection and rebellion, *for them* the reign of God is very bad news indeed. For the God who is king is the God who is judge—the whole Bible affirms that and anticipates it. Not only so, but it affirms that the future reality of God's judgment is actually part of the gospel. Evil and unrepentant evildoers will not ultimately or eternally flourish. So Paul can speak about "that day when, *according to my gospel*, God judges the secrets of men by Jesus Christ" (Romans 2:16, italics added). For Paul too, as for Jesus, preaching the gospel included explaining and proclaiming the kingdom of God, as both judgment and salvation. He finished his life doing exactly that (Acts 28:23, 31).

The response to the gospel of the kingdom of God that was called for by Christ himself, by the apostles and by all faithful evangelists ever since, is the twin response of repentance and faith. They are the demands that come along with the promise—both demand and promise being intrinsic to the nature of the reign of God. If God is king then salvation is promised. But if God is king then change is required. Or as Stott succinctly puts it, "This reign or rule of God is exercised from the throne by Jesus, *who bestows salvation and requires obedience.* These are the blessing and the demand of the kingdom" (italics added).

But repentance is much more than the "change of mind" that popular preaching often explains as the meaning of *metanoia*. With its deep roots in the Old Testament, it involved a turning away from the idolatries and evils of life lived in rebellion against God, and a turning back to God in radically changed life and behavior (see, for example, the strong definition of what repentance means in Jeremiah 7:3-7). Jesus cannot have meant anything less in his call for repentance than what John the Baptist had already outlined in explanation of what some typical "fruits that befit repentance" might look like (Luke 3:8).

Rightly, then, and with full biblical authenticity, Stott quotes René Padilla with approval, that "without ethics there is no real repentance." And since biblical ethics includes more than our personal piety but also our social engagement in the world we live in, he makes this remarkable, powerful and challenging assertion, "Thus *social responsibility becomes an aspect not of Christian mission only, but also of Christian conversion.* It is impossible to be truly converted to God without being thereby converted to our neighbor." Paul would have agreed and added that it is impossible to be truly reconciled to God without being reconciled to your enemy (Ephesians 2:14-18). John too would have agreed, and added that it is impossible to claim to love God without loving your brother and sister (1 John 4:20-21).

The gospel of the kingdom of God then *is* good news for the world, but it also *becomes* good news for people when they respond in faith *and* in repentance that is demonstrated in obedience, that is, in practical, ethical change of life.

Stott rightly castigates those who drive any kind of wedge between accepting Jesus by faith as Savior and submitting to him in obedience as Lord. He acknowledges that some people do so with the worthy motivation of protecting the doctrine of justification by grace alone through faith alone, but he urges that the separation between faith and obedience (as if you could have one without the other) is unbiblical. I agree. Paul's expression "the obedience of faith," standing as his missionary goal at the beginning and end of

Romans (Romans 1:5; 16:26), captures precisely the integration of both, in a way that shows he would have agreed entirely with James that justifying faith has to be faith that proves itself in obedience (James 2:14-26). The same controversy is still around today in the arguments of those who insist on a sharp demarcation between justification and sanctification. Again, the motivation is understandable—that we must not import good works into the grounds of our salvation. Nothing could be clearer than Paul's words in Titus 3:5, "He saved us, not because deeds done by us in righteousness, but in virtue of his own mercy." But equally nothing could be clearer than Paul's insistence (repeatedly in Titus) that "those who have believed in God may be careful to apply themselves to good deeds" (Titus 3:8; compare Titus 1:8; 2:7, 14; 3:1, 14). Faith and good works are not the same thing, but they belong integrally together in what it means to be a true disciple of Jesus. That distinction and yet integration is classically captured in Ephesians 2:9-10—"not because of works. . . . created in Christ Jesus for good works"—and commended in the lives of new believers when Paul thankfully observes their "work of faith" (1 Thessalonians 1:3).

Stott concludes his chapter with a quotation from the Lausanne Covenant (paragraph 4 on "The Nature of Evangelism"). So perhaps it is appropriate, in the same tradition, to conclude these reflections with a quotation from the Cape Town Commitment. The biblical texts referenced in brackets are part of the original document.

We Love the Gospel of God

As disciples of Jesus, we are gospel people. The core of our identity is our passion for the biblical good news of the saving work of God through Jesus Christ. We are united by our experience of the grace of God in the gospel and by our motivation to make that gospel of grace known to the ends of the earth by every possible means. . . .[15]

The section continues with three paragraphs headed: "a) We love the good news in a world of bad news; b) We love the story the gospel tells; c) We love the assurance the gospel brings."

It then continues:

d) We love the transformation the gospel produces. The gospel is God's life-transforming power at work in the world. "It is the power of God for the salvation of everyone who believes" [Romans 1:16]. Faith alone is the means by which the blessings and assurance of the gospel are received. Saving faith however never remains alone, but necessarily shows itself in obedience. Christian obedience is "faith expressing itself through love" [Galatians 5:6]. We are not saved *by* good works, but having been saved by grace alone we are "created in Christ Jesus *to do* good works" [Ephesians 2:10]. "Faith by itself, if it is not accompanied by action, is dead" [James 2:17]. Paul saw the ethical transformation that the gospel produces as the work of God's grace—grace which achieved our salvation at Christ's first coming, and grace that teaches us to live ethically in the light of his second coming [Titus 2:11-14]. For Paul, "obeying the gospel" meant both trusting in grace, and then being taught by grace [Romans 15:18-19; 16:19; 2 Corinthians 9:13].[16]

five

DIALOGUE

John Stott

My argument so far has been that mission denotes the self-giving service that God sends his people into the world to render, and includes both evangelism and sociopolitical action; that within this broadly conceived mission a certain urgency attaches to evangelism, and priority must be given to it; and that evangelism means announcing or proclaiming the good news of Jesus. This brings us to the third word, *dialogue*, and to the question: Is there any room for dialogue in the proclamation of the good news? It is well known that during the past decade or two the concept of "dialogue with people of other faiths" has become the ecumenical fashion, and that evangelicals have tended to react rather sharply against it. Is our negative reaction justified? And what are the issues anyway?

EXTREME VIEWS

Extreme positions have been taken on both sides of this debate. Evangelical Christians have always—and in my judgment rightly—emphasized the indispensable necessity of preaching the gospel, for God has appointed his church to be the herald of the good news. An eloquent summons to proclamation was issued by Dr. Martyn

Lloyd-Jones in his book *Preaching and Preachers*.[1] His first chapter is titled "The Primacy of Preaching," and on its first page he writes,

> To me the work of preaching is the highest and the greatest and the most glorious calling to which anyone can ever be called. If you want something in addition to that I would say without any hesitation that the most urgent need in the Christian Church today is true preaching, and as it is the greatest and most urgent need in the Church, it is obviously the greatest need for the world also.

Indeed, because the essential problem of the human race is our rebellion against God and our need of salvation, therefore "preaching is the primary task of the Church."[2]

To his passionate advocacy of preaching Dr. Lloyd-Jones sometimes added his distaste for the concept of dialogue: "God is not to be discussed or debated. . . . Believing what we do about God, we cannot in any circumstances allow Him to become a subject for discussion or debate or investigation . . . as if He were but a philosophical proposition."[3] And the same goes for the gospel: the gospel is suitable for proclamation, not for amiable discussion.

Now if by "discussion" we have in mind the work of clever diplomats at the conference table, whose objective is to satisfy (even appease) everybody, and whose method is to reach consensus by compromise, I find myself in wholehearted agreement with Dr. Lloyd-Jones. The gospel is a nonnegotiable revelation from God. We may certainly discuss its meaning and its interpretation, so long as our purpose is to grasp it more firmly ourselves and commend it more acceptably to others. But we have no liberty to sit in judgment on it, or to tamper with its substance. For it is God's gospel not ours, and its truth is to be received not criticized, declared not discussed. Having said this, however, it is necessary to add that, properly understood, "dialogue" and "discussion" are two different things. Dr. Lloyd-Jones's rejection of both may be seen as somewhat extreme.

At the other extreme there is a growing dislike for preaching, or at least for preaching of an authoritative or dogmatic kind. Proclamation is said to be arrogant; the humble way of communication is the way of dialogue. It would be difficult to find a more articulate exponent of this view than Professor J. G. Davies. In his opinion, "Monologue is entirely lacking in humility: it assumes that we know all and that we merely have to declare it, to pass it on to the ignorant, whereas we need to seek truth together, that our truth may be corrected and deepened as it encounters the truths of those with whom we are in dialogue."[4] Further, "monologue . . . is deficient in openness," whereas "dialogue involves complete openness."[5] Professor Davies goes on:

> To enter into dialogue in this way is not only difficult, it is dangerous. Complete openness means that every time we enter into dialogue our faith is at stake. If I engage in dialogue with a Buddhist and do so with openness I must recognize that the outcome cannot be predetermined either for him or for me. The Buddhist may come to accept Jesus as Lord, but I may come to accept the authority of the Buddha, or even both of us may end up as agnostics. Unless these are *real* possibilities, neither of us is being fully open to the other. . . . To live dialogically is to live dangerously.[6]

For myself I regard this as an intemperate overstatement. It is true that good Christian preaching is always dialogical, in the sense that it engages the minds of the listeners and speaks to them with relevance. But it is not true to say that all monologue is proud. The evangelist who proclaims the gospel is not claiming to "know it all," but only to have been put in trust with the gospel. We should also, as I believe and shall soon argue, be willing to enter into dialogue.

In doing so we shall learn from the other party both about their beliefs and also (by listening to their critical reaction to Christianity) about certain aspects of our own. But we should not cultivate a total "openness" in which we suspend even our convictions concerning the truth of the gospel and our personal commitment to Jesus Christ. To attempt to do this would be to destroy our own integrity as Christians.

DIALOGUE IN THE BIBLE

In this dialogue about dialogue, perhaps the place to begin is with definition. A more simple and straightforward definition I have not found than that framed at the National Evangelical Anglican Congress held at Keele in 1967: "Dialogue is a conversation in which each party is serious in his approach both to the subject and to the other person, and desires to listen and learn as well as to speak and instruct."[7]

After this definition it is important to note that the living God of the biblical revelation himself enters into a dialogue with human beings. He not only speaks but listens. He asks questions and waits for the answers. Ever since his question went echoing among the trees of the Garden of Eden ("where are you?"), God has been seeking his fallen creature, and addressing questions to them. Of course the approach of the Infinite to the finite, of the Creator to the creature, of the Holy to the sinful has always been one of gracious self-disclosure. Nevertheless, the form his revelation has taken has often been dialogical. "Gird up your loins like a man," he said to Job. "I will question you, and you shall declare to me" (Job 38:3; 40:7). And his address to Israel through the prophets was full of questions.

"Come now, let us reason together,"
    says the LORD. (Isaiah 1:18)

"What wrong did your fathers find in me
    that they went far from me?" (Jeremiah 2:5)

"Why do you complain against me?" (Jeremiah 2:29)

Have you not known? Have you not heard?
  Has it not been told you from the beginning?
  Have you not understood from the foundations of the
    earth? (Isaiah 40:21)

How can I give you up, O E'phraim!
  How can I hand you over, O Israel! (Hosea 11:8)

Jesus too, who himself as a boy was found in the temple "sitting among the teachers, listening to them and asking them questions" (Luke 2:46), during his public ministry entered into serious conversations with individuals like Nicodemus, the Samaritan woman and the crowds. He seldom if ever spoke in a declamatory, take-it-or-leave-it style. Instead, whether explicitly or implicitly, he was constantly addressing questions to his hearers' minds and consciences. For example, "When . . . the owner of the vineyard comes, what will he do to those tenants?" (Matthew 21:40). Again, "which of these three, do you think, proved neighbor to the man who fell among the robbers?" (Luke 10:36). Even after the ascension, when he revealed himself to Saul of Tarsus on the Damascus road, and the prostrate and blinded Pharisee appeared at first to have been crushed by the vision, Jesus addressed him a rational question: "Why do you persecute me?" and provoked the counterquestions "Who are you, Lord?" and "What shall I do, Lord?" (Acts 9:4-5; 22:10).

When later Saul began his great missionary journeys as Paul the apostle, it is instructive to notice that some form of dialogue was an integral part of his method. Luke not infrequently uses the verb *dialegomai* to describe an aspect of his evangelism, especially during the second and third expeditions. True, there is some uncertainty about the precise meaning of the verb. In classical Greek it meant to "converse" or "discuss" and was particularly associated with the so-called dialectic as a means of instruction and persuasion developed in different ways by Socrates, Plato and Aristotle. In the Gospels it is once used of the apostles' argumentative discussion with each other over who was the greatest (Mark 9:34). In reference to Paul's ministry, Gottlob Schrenk, in the *Theological Dictionary of the New Testament*, says that it refers to the "delivering of religious lectures or sermons" but has no reference to "disputation."[8] The Arndt-Gingrich lexicon, on the other hand, though conceding that it sometimes means "simply to speak or preach" (for example, Hebrews 12:5), maintains that it is used "of lectures which were likely to end in disputations."[9] The context certainly suggests this too.

Thus in the synagogue at Thessalonica for three weeks "Paul . . . argued with them from the scriptures, explaining and proving that it was necessary for the Christ to suffer and to rise from the dead, and saying, 'This Jesus, whom I proclaim to you, is the Christ.'" Luke then adds: "some of them were persuaded" (Acts 17:1-4). Here five words are brought together—*arguing, explaining, proving, proclaiming* and *persuading*—which suggest that Paul was actually debating with the Jews, hearing and answering their objections to his message. In Athens we are told that he "argued" both "in the synagogue with the Jews and the devout persons, and in the market place every day with those who chanced to be there" (Acts 17:17). That last clause is an important addition because it shows that Paul's reasoning approach was with casual Gentile passersby as well as with Jews in the synagogue. In Corinth he "argued in the synagogue every sabbath, and persuaded Jews and Greeks" (Acts 18:4), while at Ephesus he first "entered the synagogue and for three months spoke boldly, arguing and pleading about the kingdom of God" and then for two years "argued daily in the hall of Tyran'nus" possibly for as long as five hours a day (Acts 19:8-10; compare Acts 18:19).

Paul also used the same method in Christian preaching, for during the famous "breaking of bread" at Troas, during which the young man Eutychus fell asleep with nearly disastrous consequences, *dialegomai* is again used to describe Paul's address (Acts 20:7, 9). The last example is also interesting, because we find Paul having a dialogue with the procurator Felix, arguing with him in private about "justice and self-control and future judgment" until Felix grew alarmed and terminated the conversation (Acts 24:25). In summary, then, we may say that Paul included some degree of dialogue in most if not all his preaching, to Christians and non-Christians, to Jews and Gentiles, to crowds and individuals, on formal and informal occasions. Indeed, to add a final text, Paul seems to have expected all the disciples of Jesus to be involved in continuous dialogue with the world, for he urged the Colossians, "Let your speech always be gracious, seasoned with salt, so that you may know how you ought to answer every one" (Colossians 4:6). Here are Christians in such close contact with "outsiders" (Colossians 4:5) that they are able both to speak to them (with gracious and salty speech) and to answer their questions.

The kind of "dialogue" that was included in Paul's ministry was, however, very different from what is often meant by the word today. For Paul's dialogue was clearly a part of his proclamation and subordinate to his proclamation. Moreover, the subject of his dialogue with the world was one that he always chose himself, namely, Jesus Christ, and its object was always conversion to Jesus Christ. If this was still the position, few who hesitate about dialogue would disagree with it. But often the modern dialogue of Christians with non-Christians seems to savor rather of unbelief, than of faith, of compromise than of proclamation. It is time now to investigate this argument against dialogue. Afterward I will seek to marshal some arguments in favor of true dialogue. Then I shall conclude with some contemporary examples.

THE ARGUMENT AGAINST DIALOGUE

The conservative Christian's argument against dialogue as bordering on treason against Jesus Christ can best be understood historically.

The World Missionary Conference at Edinburgh in 1910 took place in an atmosphere of great confidence. I do not call it "self-confidence," because certainly their confidence was in God. Nevertheless, they confidently predicted the imminent collapse of the non-Christian religions. W. H. Temple Gairdner in his official account of the conference could write, "The spectacle of the advance of the Christian Church along many lines of action to the conquest of the five great religions of the modern world is one of singular interest and grandeur."[10] This mood was rudely shaken by the outbreak of the First World War four years later. And at the second missionary conference at Jerusalem in 1928 the atmosphere was already different. Delegates were aware of the growth of secularism, and even suggested that against this universal enemy a common religious front was necessary.

Ten years later, in 1938, the third ecumenical missionary conference was held at Tambaram near Madras. Its key figure was the Dutchman Hendrik Kraemer, whose book *The Christian Message in a Non-Christian World* had been written and published shortly before the conference assembled.[11] Partly under the influence of Karl Barth's dialectic, in which he opposed religion to revelation as human religiosity over against God's Word, Kraemer stressed that there was a fundamental "discontinuity" between the religions of humanity and the revelation of God. He rejected both aggressive Christian missions on the one hand and on the other the notion that Christ was the fulfillment of non-Christian religions, and in their place he urged the uncompromising announcement of the gospel, although "in a persuasive and winning manner."[12] He called the church to repossess its faith "in all its uniqueness and adequacy and power," and added: "We are bold enough to call men out from these (sc. other religions) to the feet of Christ. We do so because we believe that in him alone is the full salvation which man needs."

As the Tambaram conference closed, the black storm clouds of the Second World War, and of the new paganism it threatened to unleash, were already darkening the horizon, and when the war ended and ecumenical activity began again, "the coming dialogue between east and west" that Kraemer had foretold was already being canvassed by other voices. Both Protestant and Roman Catholic theologians began to formulate very differently from Kraemer the relation between Christianity and other religions. In 1963 H. R. Schlette could write that "anyone who determines his ethical and actual individual way of life on the basis of an authentic desire to live a human life according to an order founded on truth, attains salvation."[13] Similarly, Karl Rahner began to popularize the idea that sincere non-Christians should rather be thought of as "anonymous Christians": "Christianity does not simply confront the member of an extra-Christian religion as a mere non-Christian but as someone who can and must already be regarded in this or that respect as an anonymous Christian."[14] In consequence, "the proclamation of the gospel does not simply turn someone absolutely abandoned by God and Christ into a Christian, but turns an anonymous Christian into someone who also knows about his Christian belief in the depths of his grace-endowed being by objective reflection and by the profession of faith." Similar thinking is expressed by Raimundo Pannikar in *The Unknown Christ of Hinduism*.[15]

One of the fundamental beliefs of scholars who think and write like this today is that Christ is already present everywhere, including other religions. This being so, it is in their view presumptuous of the Christian missionary to talk of "bringing" Christ with them into a situation; what they do is first to "find" Christ already there and then maybe to "unveil" him. Some go further still. They not only deny that missionaries take Christ with them, or can be the media of Christ's self-revelation to the non-Christian; they even suggest that it is the non-Christian who is the bearer of Christ's message to the Christian.

But is Christ present in the non-Christian world? In our increasingly pluralistic society and syncretistic age this is the basic theological question that we cannot dodge. It would be facile to reply with a bare "yes" or "no." We need rather to ask ourselves what Christ's apostles taught on this crucial issue. We will look in turn at statements of Peter, Paul and John.

Peter began his sermon to Cornelius: "Truly I perceive that God shows no partiality, but in every nation any one who fears him and does what is right is acceptable to him" (Acts 10:34-35). Some have argued from this assertion that sincere religious and righteous people are saved, especially because the story begins with an angel's statement to Cornelius that "your prayers and your alms have ascended as a memorial before God" (Acts 10:4). But such a deduction is inadmissible. To declare that a man who fears God and practices righteousness is "acceptable" to him cannot mean that he is "accepted" in the sense of being "justified." The rest of the story makes this plain. This sincere, God-fearing and righteous man still needed to hear the gospel. Indeed, when Peter later recounted to the Jerusalem church what had happened, he specifically recorded the divine promise to Cornelius about Peter, namely, that "he will declare to you a message by which you will be saved" (Acts 11:14). And the Jerusalem church reacted to Peter's account by saying, "then to the Gentiles also God has granted repentance unto life" (Acts 11:18). It is clear then that, although in some sense "acceptable" to God, Cornelius before his conversion had neither "salvation" nor "life."

In his two sermons to heathen audiences, in Lystra and in Athens, the apostle Paul spoke of God's providential activity in the pagan world. Although in the past God had allowed all the nations "to walk in their own ways," he said, yet even then "he did not leave himself without witness, for he did good" to all people, especially by giving them rain, fruitful seasons, food and happiness (Acts 14:16-17).

To the Athenian philosophers Paul added that God the Creator was the sustainer of our life ("since he himself gives to all men life and breath and everything") and the Lord of history ("having de-

termined allotted periods and the boundaries" of all human "habi-
tation") intending that people "should seek God, in the hope that
they might feel after him and find him." For "he is not far from each
one of us" since, as heathen poets had said, "in him we live and
move and have our being" and "we are indeed his offspring." What
these truths and the Athenians' knowledge of them did, however,
was not to enable them to find God but rather to make their idolatry
inexcusable. For, having overlooked it in the past, God "now . . .
commands all men everywhere to repent" (Acts 17:22-31).

This sketch Paul filled out in the early chapters of Romans. He
affirms there very clearly the universal knowledge of God and of
goodness in the heathen world. On the one hand God's "invisible
nature, namely, his eternal power and deity" are "clearly perceived
in the things that have been made," God having "shown it to them"
(Romans 1:19-20). On the other hand, people know something of
God's moral law, for he had not only written it on stone tablets at
Sinai; he had written it also on human hearts, in the moral nature
they have by creation (Romans 2:14-15). So to some degree, Paul
says, all human beings know God (Romans 1:21), know God's law
and "know God's decree" that lawbreakers "deserve to die" (Romans
1:32). This revelation of God to all people, sometimes called "general
revelation" (because made to all people), or "natural revelation"
(because given in nature and in human nature), is not, however,
enough to save them. It is enough only to condemn them as being
"without excuse" (Romans 1:20; compare Romans 2:1; 3:19). For the
whole thrust of the early chapters of Romans is that, although
people know God, they do not honor him as God but by their wickedness suppress the truth they know (Romans 1:18, 21, 25, 28).

We turn now to John, and especially the prologue to the Fourth
Gospel. Here he describes Jesus as "the Logos of God," and "the
light of men" (John 1:1-4). He also affirms that the light is contin-
ually shining in the darkness and that the darkness has not overcome

it (John 1:5). Next he applies these great axioms to the historical process of revelation. He says of the Logos, whom he later identifies as Jesus Christ, "The true light, which enlightens everyone, was coming into the world." Indeed, "he was in the world" all the time (John 1:9, 10 NRSV). Long before he actually "came" into the world (John 1:11) he "was" already in it and was continuously "coming" into it. Moreover, his presence in the world was (and still is) an enlightening presence. He is the real light, of which all other lights are but types and shadows, and as the light he "enlightens everyone." Thus "every human person," Scripture gives us warrant to affirm, possesses some degree of light by his reason and conscience. And we should not hesitate to claim that everything good, beautiful and true, in all history and in all the earth, has come from Jesus Christ, even though people are ignorant of its origin. At the same time we must add that this universal light is not saving light. For one thing it is but a twilight in comparison with the fullness of light granted to those who follow Jesus as "the light of the world" and to whom is given "the light of life" (John 8:12). For another thing, people have always "loved darkness rather than light, because their deeds were evil." Because of our willful rejection of the light we are under condemnation (John 3:18-21).

The witness then of Peter, Paul and John is uniform. All three declare the constant activity of God in the non-Christian world. God has not left himself without witness. God reveals himself in nature. God is not far from any person. God gives light to every human being. But as a whole human race we reject the knowledge we have, prefer darkness to light and do not acknowledge the God we know. That knowledge by itself does not save us; it condemns us for our disobedience. Even our religiosity is a subtle escape from the God we are afraid and ashamed to meet.

We do not therefore deny that there are elements of truth in non-Christian systems, vestiges of the general revelation of God in nature. What we do vehemently deny is that these are sufficient for salvation and (more vehemently still) that Christian faith and non-Christian faiths are alternative and equally valid roads to God. Although there is an important place for "dialogue" with people of other faiths (as I shall shortly argue), there is also a need for "encounter" with them, and sometimes even for "confrontation," in which we seek both to disclose the inadequacies and falsities of non-Christian religion and to demonstrate the adequacy and truth, absoluteness and finality of the Lord Jesus Christ.

Such encounter with people of other faiths, however, should not be abrasive or hostile. Even if we need to expose the falsehood of other religions when compared to the biblical revelation, we do not do so in order to ridicule them or their adherents. Ridicule and mockery can never be consistent with love for our neighbor, or even our enemy, of another faith. We need to see the person of a different faith first and foremost as a human being, made in the image of God, whom we are to love for Christ's sake and with whom we can establish a living, personal friendship. And we need to remember that in any such encounter, even when we have the opportunity to present the biblical faith and explain how and where it differs from, or indeed condemns, all other forms of human religion and idolatry, it is ultimately not us but the Holy Spirit who convinces and convicts people of the truth about God, sin and the Lord Jesus Christ.

So, as we come to consider the true nature of dialogue and what can be said in its favor, we must start from the assumption that it should not and need not compromise our fundamental convictions about Christ and the truth of God's revelation in Scripture. Only when we are assured that a true Christian dialogue with a non-Christian is not a sign of syncretism but is fully consistent with our belief in the finality of Jesus Christ are we ready to consider the arguments by which it may be commended. They are four.

THE ARGUMENT FOR DIALOGUE

First, true dialogue is a mark of *authenticity*. Let me quote from the statement of the World Council of Churches assembly at Uppsala, making a point with which I fully agree:

> A Christian's dialogue with another implies neither a denial of the uniqueness of Christ, nor any loss of his own commitment to Christ, but rather that a genuinely Christian approach to others must be human, personal, relevant and humble. In dialogue we share our common humanity, its dignity and fallenness, and express our common concern for that humanity.[16]

If we do nothing but proclaim the gospel to people from a distance, our personal authenticity is bound to be suspect. Who are we? Those listening to us do not know. For we are playing a role (that of the preacher), and for all they know we may be wearing a mask. Besides, we are so far away from them, they cannot even see us properly. But when we sit down alongside them like Philip in the Ethiopian's chariot, or encounter them face-to-face, a personal relationship is established. Our defenses come down. We begin to be seen and known for what we are. It is recognized that we too are human beings, equally sinful, equally needy, equally dependent on the grace of which we speak. And as the conversation develops, not only do we become known by the other, but we come to know them. They are human beings too, with sins and pains and frustrations and convictions. We come to respect their convictions, to feel with them in their pain. We still want to share the good news with them, for we care about it deeply, but we also care now about the one with whom we want to share it. Dialogue puts evangelism into an authentically human context.

Second, true dialogue is a mark of *humility*. I do not mean by this that proclamation is always arrogant, for true proclamation is a setting forth of Jesus Christ as Savior and Lord, and not in any sense or degree a parading of ourselves. What I mean rather is that as we listen to another person, our respect for that person as a human being made in God's image grows. The distance between us diminishes as we recall that if he or she is fallen and sinful, so are we. Further, we realize that we cannot sweep away all their cherished convictions with a brash, unfeeling dismissal. We have to recognize humbly that some of their misconceptions may be our fault, or at least that their continuing rejection of Christ may be in reality a rejection of the caricature of Christ which they have seen in us or in our fellow Christians. As we listen to that other person, we may have many such uncomfortable lessons to learn. Our attitude changes. There may after all have been some lingering sense of superiority of which we were previously unconscious. But now no longer have we any desire to score points or win a victory. We love the other person too much to boost our ego at their expense. Humility in evangelism is a beautiful grace.

Third, true dialogue is a mark of *integrity*. For in the conversation we listen to our friend's real beliefs and problems, and divest our minds of the false images we may have harbored. And we are determined also ourselves to be real. We should both be committed to only one thing—that the truth should emerge. But as a Christian, I know that Christ is the truth, and so I long for Christ himself to "emerge." But since Christ makes demands on all alike, I may well find that my own understanding and commitment are inadequate. So the dialogue will be challenging to myself as well as to the other person. But it is a matter of personal integrity that I respect the freedom and dignity of my dialogue partner and do not expect of him or her anything I am not willing to ask or hope for myself. Such integrity is essential to true dialogue.

Fourth, true dialogue is a mark of *sensitivity*. Christian evangelism falls into disrepute when it degenerates into stereotypes. It is impossible to evangelize by fixed formulae. To force a conversation along predetermined lines in order to reach a predetermined destination is to show oneself grievously lacking in sensitivity both to the actual needs of our friend and to the guidance of the Holy Spirit. Such insensitivity is therefore a failure in both faith and love. Dialogue is essentially mutual listening in order to understand one another. The Lausanne Covenant contains two references to dialogue. On the one hand it says firmly that we "reject as derogatory to Christ and the gospel every kind of syncretism and dialogue which implies that Christ speaks equally through all religions and ideologies."[17] But on the other hand, it says with equal firmness that "that kind of dialogue whose purpose is to listen sensitively in order to understand" is actually "indispensable to evangelism."[18] The principle was stated centuries ago in the book of Proverbs: "If one gives answer before he hears, it is his folly and shame" (Proverbs 18:13).

In conclusion, having looked at some of the arguments against and for the place of dialogue in evangelism, I would like to give examples of it in three different contexts, the first among Hindus in India, the second among Muslims in the Arab world and the third in the industrial areas of Britain.

DIALOGUE WITH HINDUS

My first example is E. Stanley Jones, an American Methodist missionary in India who flourished between the world wars. He was a prolific writer. His two best-known books, in which he described the principles of his work, are probably *The Christ of the Indian Road* and *Christ at the Round Table*.[19]

It was during one of his missions that a Hindu invited him to a tea party in his home in order that he might meet some of the leading Hindus of the local community. They sat in a circle on the floor and talked. Jones asked them what their reaction would be if Christ were to come to India direct, disassociated from Westernism. The mayor of the city interrupted: "I hear you speak about finding Christ. What do you mean by it?" In reply Jones told the story of his conversion.

"Now tell me," said the mayor, "how *I* could find him."[20] Out of that conversation Jones's famous Round Table Conferences grew. He would invite about fifteen adherents of other faiths—mostly educated people like judges, government officials, doctors, lawyers and religious leaders—and five or six Christians, mostly Indians.

In the dialogue that developed, the emphasis was neither on the rival civilizations of East and West, nor on the rival Scriptures of Hindus and Christians, nor even on the rival personalities of Krishna and Christ, but on what each man's religion meant to him in his own experience. This has been criticized, for example by Hendrik Kraemer, and we cannot help agreeing that human testimony does seem rather to have eclipsed the divine objective testimony to Christ in Scripture. Nevertheless, God honored it. Once a Hindu who had written a savage assault on Christianity, using the latest ammunition supplied by the Rationalistic Association of Britain, of which he was a member, was challenged to speak at a deeper personal level and was immediately disconcerted and silenced. Then a Christian youth with bare feet and wearing simple homespun spoke naturally of what the Lord Jesus meant to him. "There were milleniums of spiritual and social culture between the rest of the group and this youth," wrote Jones, but no one could gainsay the reality, the authenticity with which he spoke.[21]

Two particular aspects of Stanley Jones's "Round Table" method impress me. The first is his insistence on fairness and mutual respect. Much Western writing about Hinduism had been very polemical, and had unjustly concentrated on the caste system and on idolatry, child widows and the abuses of temple Hinduism rather than on the philosophic thought of the Upanishads and the Bhagavad Gita. "I felt I would be unfair," wrote Jones, "if I did not let these representatives speak and interpret their own faith. . . . Each was given the chance to say the best he could about his own faith."[22] At the beginning of each conference Jones would say, "Let everyone be perfectly free, for we are a family circle; we want each one to feel at home, and we will listen with reverence and respect to what each man has to share." As a result, the old "battle of wits" gave place to an atmosphere of "deep seriousness."[23] Jones writes,

> We have tried to understand sympathetically the viewpoint of the other man. . . .
>
> The deepest things of religion need a sympathetic atmosphere. In an atmosphere of debate and controversy the deepest things, and hence the real things of religion, wither and die. . . .
>
> The Crusaders conquered Jerusalem and found in the end that Christ was not there. They had lost him through the very spirit and methods by which they sought to serve him. Many more modern and more refined crusaders end in that same barrenness of victory.[24]

Yet this does not mean that Jones was indifferent to the results of his Round Table Conferences, for he was an evangelist. The second impressive point about his conferences is that in them all the supremacy of Jesus Christ was apparent.

> There was not a single situation that I can remember where before the close of the Round Table Conference Christ was not in moral and spiritual command of the situation.
>
> At the end everything else had been pushed to the edges as irrelevant and Christ controlled the situation. . . .
>
> No-one could sit through these Conferences and not feel that Christ was Master of every situation, not by loud assertion, or through the pleading of clever advocates, but by what he is and does.[25]

At the close of one conference a Hindu said, "Today eight of us have spoken and none of us has found; five of you Christians have spoken and all of you seem to have found. This is very extraordinary." During another conference a Hindu lawyer got up, took the flowers from the table, walked across the room, laid them at the feet of a Christian, touched his feet and said, "You have found God. You are my guru."[26]

DIALOGUE WITH MUSLIMS

My second example concerns not the Hindu but the Muslim world. There has been an honorable succession of scholarly and dedicated Christian missionaries to Muslims. One has only to mention the names of Henry Martyn, Samuel Zwemer and W. H. Temple Gairdner to realize what great men of God have given their minds and their lives to the task of communicating Christ to the followers of Muhammad. In my own generation one of the best-known names in this field is Bishop Kenneth Cragg. Bishop Cragg's full statement appears in his book *The Call of the Minaret*.[27] He interprets the muezzin's call not only as an explicit summons to prayer addressed to Muslims, but also implicitly as a call to Christians to respond to the challenge of the Muslim world. So his book is divided into two main parts, the first titled "Minaret and Muslim," in which he expounds the essentials of Muslim belief, and the second "Minaret and Christian," in which he issues his fivefold call to us—a call to understanding, to service, to retrieval (the attempt to retrieve the situation in which Muslims are so deeply suspicious of Christians), to interpretation and to patience.

In reading the book, two particular emphases have struck me. The first is Cragg's stress on what he calls "the ambition for understanding."[28] If we want to be understood, we must first ourselves struggle to understand. And the kind of understanding he envisages is not merely the academic knowledge that may be gained by a study of Islam but the far more intimate awareness that comes from the fullest meeting with Muslims. It is from people, not just from books, that we shall come to understand. The Christian "must strive to enter into the daily existence of the Muslims, as believers, adherents and men."[29]

To begin with, the Christian must understand what Islam means to the Muslim. We must "seek to know it, as far as may be, from within. We wish to hear at the minaret what it is which greets every rising sun and salutes every declining day for millions of contemporary men, and thus to enter with them across the threshold of the mosque into their world of meaning."[30] But next the Christian must also understand how Christianity looks to the Muslim. The Christian must feel the shame of the Crusades and of the bitter medieval polemic against Islam, and grasp the Muslim's abhorrence of Western imperialism and secularism, and his or her utter incomprehension of the West's unjust espousal of Israel at the Arabs' expense. The Christian must also strive to understand what Cragg calls the Muslim's "massive misunderstandings" of Christian theology—of the Christian doctrines of God and the Trinity, of Christ and the cross, and of salvation.[31]

But the minaret's call to the Christian is not to understanding only. It is also, secondly, to action, and that both negatively and positively. Cragg uses the word *retrieval* to indicate the work of restitution that we Christians have to perform. "Among the factors contributing to the rise of Islam," he writes, "was the Christian failure of the Church. It was a failure in love, in purity, and in fervor, a failure of the spirit. . . . Islam developed in an environment of imperfect Christianity," even of a "delinquent Christianity."[32] So the Christian

> yearns to undo the alienation and to make amends for the past by as full a restitution as he can achieve of the Christ to Whom Islam is a stranger. The objective is not, as the Crusaders believed, the repossession of what Christendom has lost, but the restoration to Muslims of the Christ Whom they have missed. . . .
>
> Let it be clear that the retrieval is not territorial. . . . The retrieval is spiritual. It aims not to have the map more Christian

but Christ more widely known. . . . The retrieval does not mean taking back cathedrals from mosques, but giving back the Christ. . . . To restore Christ transcends all else.[33]

Already Cragg's concept of "retrieval" has become positive. It leads naturally to his next call, which is for interpretation.

If Christ is what Christ is, He must be uttered. If Islam is what Islam is, that "must" is irresistible. Wherever there is misconception, witness must penetrate: wherever there is obscuring of the beauty of the cross it must be unveiled: wherever men have missed God in Christ He must be brought to them again. . . .

We present Christ for the sole, sufficient reason that He deserves to be presented.[34]

So Cragg gives himself to the work of interpretation, and in so doing traverses five major theological areas—the Scriptures, the person of Jesus, the cross, the doctrine of God and the church. Throughout he pleads for patience, for "patience with monumental misunderstandings which must somehow be removed," indeed for "that travail in patience which is the Christian mission."[35]

Bishop Stephen Neill writes similarly moving words:

Christians must persist in their earnest invitation to true dialogue; they must exercise endless patience and refuse to be discouraged. And the burden of all their invitation must be "Consider Jesus." . . . We have no other message. . . . It is not the case that the Muslim has seen Jesus of Nazareth and has rejected him; he has never seen him, and the veil of misunderstanding and prejudice is still over his face.[36]

DIALOGUE IN INDUSTRIAL BRITAIN

My third example of Christian dialogue brings us to post-Christian Britain, and to the concern of Bishop David Sheppard for the unreached industrial masses of our own country. After serving as a curate in Islington, he then served for eleven years as warden of the Mayflower Family Centre in Canning Town, one of the poorest parts of east London, before becoming bishop of Woolwich in 1969 and then bishop of Liverpool. My quotations are from his book *Built as a City*.[37] His overriding concern is that

> the Church's life in big cities has been marked by its inability to establish a strong, locally rooted Christian presence among the groups that society leaves without voice or power. . . .
>
> Great efforts have been made over the years by many churches in urban and industrial areas. . . . But in spite of it all locally rooted churches with strong local leadership are rarely to be seen.[38]

Consequently urban mission "is not a marginal subject for Christians" but rather "one of the priorities today in God's work." "The gap between Church and world, and especially the world of industry and manual work, is historically wide and contemporaneously massive."[39] What, if anything, could be done?

Being a modest man, David Sheppard told no dramatic success story. But he did lay down certain basic indigenous principles: "The Church which will make Jesus Christ and His claims a serious adult proposition will need to have at least four characteristics: a Church of and for the area; a believing and worshipping Church; a common life providing unjudging and thought-provoking fellowship, and local leaders and decision-makers."[40] Then after the principles he gives some illustrations of how an indigenous, working-class church can emerge. He writes first of the need for "bridge-building." Christians have to care enough to give priority in their time "to join together with other people in the community," and together to identify and then to tackle some of the important social issues of their own locality.[41]

From bridge building he moves to friendship. He tells us that in 1960 he and his wife, Grace, made a decision: "we set aside every Thursday evening as a couple to meet couples who did not come to church but with whom we had good links." On alternate Thursdays they visited couples in their homes and entertained couples in their own home.

> We said in the invitation that there was a discussion at the end of the evening. In our flat there was always background music, for a visit to a vicar's home is a nerve-racking adventure for non-church people, and sitting on the edge of chairs in silence is to be avoided. A cup of tea, gossip, sometimes a noisy game called Pit, another cup of tea and some sandwiches and half an hour's discussion. On evenings like these after some had gone home, and in visits to homes, a high proportion of the best conversations started at 10.30 p.m.[42]

From bridge building through friendship expressed in informal evenings of relaxed discussion they moved to a more serious "searching-group." "Five couples came. They already had the self-confidence that they would not be thought foolish whatever ideas they expressed. I learned then just how powerful a learning weapon has been created when a 'talking-group' has come into being, whose members sense that the others feel the same way about life."[43] After two and half years, David Sheppard could write, "a number of local couples were convinced Christians." Canon David Edwards, reviewing the book, commented, "His book is pre-eminently a call to patience in real life and real love. He summons us to keep on keeping on."[44]

I hope and believe that these three examples, although from very different contexts—Hindu, Muslim and the post-Christian West— all illustrate the same marks of a true Christian dialogue, which I have called authenticity, humility, integrity and sensitivity. Dialogue is a token of genuine Christian love, because it indicates our steadfast resolve to rid our minds of the prejudices and caricatures that we may entertain about other people, to struggle to listen through their ears and look through their eyes so as to grasp what prevents them from hearing the gospel and seeing Christ, to sympathize with them in all their doubts, fears and "hang-ups." For such sympathy will involve listening, and listening means dialogue. It is once more the challenge of the incarnation, to renounce evangelism by inflexible slogans, and instead to involve ourselves sensitively in the real dilemmas that people face.

six

REFLECTIONS ON DIALOGUE

Chris Wright

John Stott's lifelong commitment to the "uniqueness and finality" of the Lord Jesus Christ as Savior, Lord and God, along with his submission to the truth and authority of the Bible, compelled him to contend against any theology or ideology that appeared to threaten either. Religious pluralism came squarely into that category. He was, however, careful to distinguish between the social facts of religious *plurality*, and the ideology of relativistic religious *pluralism*.[1] On the one hand, it is an obvious fact that people of many different faiths live together in the world, and in many contexts do so in close proximity. Given that reality, Stott affirmed that people need, at the very least, to talk to one another and seek to understand one another, simply as an act of human respect and dignity. In that sense, he saw no problem with interfaith dialogue and indeed welcomed and encouraged it (as this chapter explains). But on the other hand, the theology or ideology of religious *pluralism* claims that all religions have their own independent validity as "ways of salvation" (however that may be defined), but that *no* religion has an absolute understanding of ultimate truth, or provides the only, exclusively unique way to "God" (again, however that may be defined). Dialogue within that framework of assumptions then becomes either a syncretistic attempt to find as much common ground as we can all affirm together (while abandoning our clashing distinctives), or an openness to be corrected in one's religious understanding by the persuasiveness of the other party's convictions. Such relativistic dialogue Stott condemned as resting on assumptions that biblical faithfulness to the uniqueness of Christ could not accept.

My own very modest and limited engagement with this topic is another area where our paths crossed. I first met John Stott personally in 1978, in the immediate post-Lausanne years, as one of many younger evangelicals in whom he took a mentoring interest. So he was supportive and encouraging when I went with my family to India in 1982 to teach the Old Testament at the Union Biblical Seminary, Pune. While I was there, I was invited by David Wenham, then editor of *Themelios*, a journal for theological students, to contribute an article on a Christian approach to other religions. Although I was living in the multireligious land of India, I was not engaged in either evangelism among, or dialogue with, people of other faiths in that country (though I was teaching and interacting daily with students whose ministry was certainly in that context), so I stuck to what I knew—the Scriptures. So the article was published as "The Christian and Other Religions: The Biblical Evidence."[2] Having read this article, John Stott invited me, during our home leave in the United Kingdom, to deliver a lecture in April 1986 at his recently founded London Institute for Contemporary Christianity on "The Uniqueness of Christ in the Context of Religious Pluralism." The article and lecture were then combined and expanded in a small booklet published by All Nations Christian College in 1990, *What's So Unique About Jesus?*[3] Finally, this too was revised and expanded to full book length and published in 1997 as *The Uniqueness of Jesus*.[4] John Stott was kind enough to write a foreword, showing his own assessment of the matter in his opening words, "The greatest challenge to Christianity today is without doubt religious pluralism, with its denial of the uniqueness and finality of Jesus Christ."

I do not know whether Stott would have continued to consider it the "greatest challenge" in the following years. He certainly addressed a whole range of other issues that challenge the Christian faith in *Issues Facing Christians Today*, and in later years he was convinced that climate change was a major threat to the earth itself, and therefore needed to be taken far more seriously by Christians. Whatever may have been his personal taxonomy of "challenges," it is interesting that he did not take on the issue of religious pluralism himself in any major single book on the topic. However, he did address it tangentially in at least two chapters of other composite works, in four successive editions of *Issues Facing Christians Today* between 1984 and 2006, and in *The Contemporary Christian* (1992).[5]

CLARIFYING INCLUSIVISM

When Stott wrote the present book in 1975, the familiar classification (in academic circles at least) of Christian approaches to other religions as "exclusivist," "inclusivist" and "pluralist" had not yet been forged. It seems to have originated with Alan Race in 1984, and Stott refers to that source in a very brief summary of the three positions in *The Contemporary Christian* (1992).[6] However, even without that name, Stott is contending in this chapter not only with relativistic pluralism, but also with views that have since come to be labeled inclusivism.

That term has become rather slippery, however, and indeed many Christian theologians engaged in reflection, dialogue and mission among people of other faiths would now say that the issues "on the ground" are far too complex to be captured in such a simple triple classification. Nevertheless, in order to clarify and comment on Stott's argument here, it might be helpful to offer a concise definition of each position, as provided by Harold Netland.

> *Exclusivism* maintains that the central claims of Christianity are true, and that where the claims of Christianity conflict with those of other religions, the latter are to be rejected as false. Christian exclusivists also characteristically hold that God has revealed himself definitively in the Bible and that Jesus Christ is the unique incarnation of God, the only Lord and Savior. Salvation is not to be found in the structures of other religious traditions.
>
> *Inclusivism*, like exclusivism, maintains that the central claims of the Christian faith are true, but it adopts a much more positive view of other religions than does exclusivism. Although inclusivists hold that God has revealed himself definitively in Jesus Christ and that Jesus is somehow central to God's provision of salvation for humankind, they are willing to allow that God's salvation is available through non-Christian religions. Jesus is still held to be, in some sense, unique, normative, and definitive; but God is said to be revealing himself and providing salvation through other religious traditions as well. . . .
>
> *Pluralism* parts company with both exclusivism and inclusivism by rejecting the premise that God has revealed himself in any unique or definitive sense in Jesus Christ. To the contrary, God is said to be actively revealing himself in all religious traditions. Nor is there anything unique or normative about the person of Jesus. . . . Christian faith is merely one of many equally legitimate human responses to the same divine reality.[7]

Now it is clear, from Stott's chapter on dialogue, that he stands firmly in the first camp, and that he rejects the third position as incompatible with biblical Christianity. However, within the second, position, inclusivist, there are some elements he accepts and some he rejects. The question he asks, "Is Christ present in the non-Christian world?" cannot be answered (he wisely point out) with a simple "yes" or "no." In fact, the answer has to be both, in different senses. For Christ is both the revelation of God's truth as well as the mediator of God's salvation.

So to the extent that we find any *truth* embedded in other religious systems, we must attribute that to the general revelation of God. So, yes, Christ is there in the truth known through general revelation. But knowledge of some truth does not constitute salvation, and since other religions do not tell the story of what God has done to save the world through Jesus Christ, then, no, they cannot therefore be means of salvation. So, the answer to the question above, "Is Christ present in the non-Christian world?" (meaning the world of other religions), would be: in general revelation, yes; but in salvation, no.

Mainline Protestant theologians, like Stott himself, positively affirm this nuanced answer. They agree that "all truth is God's truth" and therefore "truth in Christ"—who is Truth. Such truth remains true even if it is known and believed within the context of religious systems that contain much else that is false. In that sense, Christ remains central to the inclusivist position as to the exclusivist. But they reject the greater, *salvific* inclusivism found in the documents of the Roman Catholic Second Vatican Council and the influential theology of Karl Rahner, who was an official adviser at it. This is the form of "inclusivism" that is generally rejected by evangelicals: the view that other religions can function (by God's providential permission) as means of salvation for those who never hear of Christ—but the salvation they mediate is in some way still salvation *through Christ and accomplished by Christ.*

Stott refers very briefly to Rahner's "anonymous Christianity" theology, but it may be helpful to expand it a little.[8] The following is excerpted from my own book.

To summarise Rahner's view, God's universal saving grace is so powerfully seeking people that those who have as yet had no contact with the Christian gospel are "allowed" to find in their own religion "a positive means of gaining a right relationship to God and thus for attaining salvation, a means which is therefore positively included in God's plan of salvation." He regards sincere non-Christians as "anonymous Christians," in virtue of the grace of Christ which they have received and unwittingly responded to in their own faiths. Thus, people can be saved by God's grace and by Christ, without actually belonging to the visible Christian church. The sincere Hindu, for example, will be saved by Christ, but it is through the "sacraments" of Hinduism that Christ saves him. He is in fact an "anonymous Christian."

Rahner's "anonymous Christianity'" has been the target of much debate and plenty of criticism. Many critics say that it is patronising towards people of other religions to think we are doing them a favour by regarding them as anonymous Christians. . . . It is easy to imagine what Christian reaction would be if we were to be told by ardent representatives of Islam, that we are in fact "anonymous Muslims."[9]

Stott responds to this form of salvific inclusivism with a survey of apostolic examples and teaching, drawn from Peter, Paul and John. He then concludes,

We do not therefore deny that there are elements of truth in non-Christian systems, vestiges of the general revelation of God in nature. What we do vehemently deny is that these are sufficient for salvation and (more vehemently still) that Christian faith and non-Christian faiths are alternative and equally valid roads to God.

I agree with that assessment. However, I would differ somewhat from the way Stott presents the specific case of Cornelius. Inclusivists argue that Cornelius was in some sense "saved" by being acceptable to God even before Peter arrived to tell him the good news about Jesus, and therefore, they argue, others who in some way "fear God and do what is right" may be saved without hearing about Jesus. Stott denies such a simplistic conclusion. But I think we need to be more nuanced than the simple question "Was Cornelius already saved or not?" Here is how I have discussed Cornelius elsewhere:

> To ask the question that way is somewhat off-beam. First of all, it is clear from the whole context that Peter's statement [Acts 10:34-35, in which Peter says, "Truly I perceive that God shows no partiality, but in every nation any one who fears him and does what is right is acceptable to him"] is not merely a general affirmation that everybody everywhere is saved. It is Peter's recognition . . . that the gospel of Jesus had now broken down the distinction between Jew and Gentile. . . . Peter's point, then, was not that God saves everybody, but that God welcomes anybody. . . .
>
> Secondly, one has to have regard to the unique historical context of the event. In a sense, Cornelius, before his hearing about Jesus, was in the same position as those Gentiles in the Old Testament who came to believe in the living God and act accordingly. . . .
>
> However, unlike the Old Testament believers, Cornelius lived in the generation in which the Messiah had actually come. . . .
>
> Cornelius thus becomes a key turning point in the book of Acts in the story of how the gospel went to the Gentiles. . . . The whole point of the story seems to be: now that Jesus the

Messiah has come, salvation must be preached in his name.
... It is misusing the story to suggest that the favourable comments on Cornelius' "Old Testament behaviour" before he
was evangelised imply that evangelism in general is somehow
unnecessary.[10]

To conclude these reflections on "inclusivism": it seems best to me
that, if we continue to use the three terms "exclusivist," "inclusivist"
and "pluralist" at all (and as I said, many if not most Christian theologians who tackle the question of other faiths would say that the
classification is too simplistic for the exceedingly complex reality),
then we should reserve the middle word for the position described
earlier as "salvific inclusivism." That is, the view that Christ not only
includes within himself whatever truths of general revelation may
be found in the teachings of other religions, but also that the salvation Christ accomplished can somehow be mediated through the
"sacraments" of other faiths. People can be saved *by* Christ but
through their sincere practice of their own religion. That kind of
inclusivism therefore attributes some saving capacity, function or
validity to other religions. That is a form of inclusivism that both
John Stott and I reject.

That is very different from the view adopted by some evangelicals, who hold firmly to all the elements defined above within the
"exclusivist" paradigm (especially that salvation is to be found only
and exclusively in the cross and resurrection of Christ), but who
leave open the question as to whether God may save some people
(by grace and through Christ) who never hear of him in their earthly
lifetime but may turn to God in some form of repentance and faith.

That issue will be discussed in the next chapter, but for the
moment, I would prefer not to call such a position "inclusivist"
(though the label has been applied to me). It is rather "exclusivist"
(salvation is exclusively through Christ), but without being *restric-*

tivist (meaning that salvation is restricted to, that is, actually possible only for, those who hear about Jesus Christ—that is, the evangelized). And it is certainly *not* "inclusivist" in the sense of affirming that people can be saved *through the mediation of* their own religion. The very idea that salvation comes through religion (any religion) at all is roundly and regularly denied by the Bible itself. More on this, however, in the next chapter.

JOHN STOTT IN DIALOGUE

The four words that Stott uses to describe the quality of true dialogue that sacrifices nothing of the uniqueness and truth of the Christian faith while remaining open and respectful to other people—*authenticity, humility, integrity* and *sensitivity*—could without question be applied to the man himself, though he would have strongly disapproved of me saying so! I do not know whether Stott ever had the opportunity to engage in sustained personal dialogue with persons of other major world religions, but within the wider Christian world he often found himself in disagreement (sometimes radical disagreement) with nonevangelical perspectives (and even with some evangelicals!). His customary practice, whenever it was possible, was to invite those who had criticized him, or with whom he had disagreed in public or on paper, to come and visit him and talk together—often over breakfast, or afternoon tea. He believed it was important to *listen*, to seek to understand as well as to be understood, to clarify where there were real and significant differences, and where there could be agreement. He would read widely in the writings of those with whom he disagreed in careful, annotated, detail—something he once told me he sometimes found to be a distressing but necessary exercise. Unfortunately, it has to be said, many of those who have been quick to dismiss Stott himself (usually on the hearsay of some other Christian leader or commentator) have not taken the trouble to do the same.

Two examples of his principles in action may be mentioned. Ironically, in spite of Stott's own appeals for the legitimacy of respectful dialogue, both examples caused him trouble and loss of respect in some quarters.

A liberal-evangelical dialogue. That is the subtitle of the book that is the record of a sustained dialogue through correspondence between David Edwards and John Stott in 1988.[11] David Edwards, a prominent English Anglican church leader, church historian and writer within the liberal Catholic tradition was also a critical admirer of John Stott. For a while they both served in different churches in London as Anglican clergymen, with Edwards about eight years Stott's junior. Aware of the rising evangelical movement in the United Kingdom that owed much to Stott's leadership in the 1960s and '70s, and having read all Stott's books (including this one) and his wider contributions such as the Lausanne Covenant, Edwards set out, with a historian's interest, to explore and critique the evangelical theology that Stott represented. He invited Stott to respond to each chapter of his book, which begins, in fact, with a remarkably detailed and warm appreciation of all that Stott was doing at All Souls Church and in the wider evangelical world.

The book's chapter titles indicate the breadth of the subject matter—and how well Edwards had identified the core elements in evangelical faith and practice.

1. The Power of the Gospel

2. The Authority of the Scriptures

3. The Cross of Christ

4. The Miraculous Christ

5. The Bible and Behaviour

6. The Gospel for the World

In each chapter Edwards affirms his own classic liberal understanding of those topics (within his personal faith as a Christian) and then radically questions the way evangelicals such as Stott present them. Each chapter is then followed by a full-length response by Stott, arguing point by point, and with detailed exegesis of biblical texts (Stott's responses alone contribute some thirty-five thousand words to the book).

What is remarkable about the book is the spirit of the interchanges. Both men combine a willingness for robust challenge of each other's positions with a gracious tone and a respectful appreciation of the force of each other's counterarguments. Stott is happy to accept criticism of evangelicals when it is deserved, for example where some traditional views go way beyond what is clear from Scripture. He is also very ready to state with all humility when he has not come to a clear decision on certain points, or has not yet resolved his own mind over some testing points of doctrine over which learned theologians have debated for centuries. Both men respect the integrity of the other one's personal faith and commitment to Christ, but both seriously challenge the way the other articulates, teaches and justifies their respective theological understandings.

For Stott, clearly a lot is at stake. After all, the subjects of all the chapters are at the very core of evangelical commitment: the saving power of the gospel, the Bible, the cross, the historicity of the Gospels, the authority of the Bible in Christian social engagement, and the urgency of world mission. So he does not hesitate to defend the evangelical position on all of these topics with vigor and sustained argumentation. He exposes the inadequacies and contradictions of theological liberalism and the way it distorts or deviates from traditional biblical understanding of our faith. However, each response is framed as a letter beginning "My dear David," and ending "Yours ever, John," and he addresses Edwards throughout as "you." The tone is gracious and friendly, even if the disagreement is fundamental. And inasmuch as the kind of liberalism represented by Edwards is still around (though tending to be much less friendly or respectful in its rejection of evangelical convictions), the book is still well worth reading as a model of intelligent, thorough, biblical and cogent response to many of the accusations that are still made against orthodox Christian doctrines. In other words, this is dialogue exactly as Stott claimed in 1975 that it should be: marked by authenticity, humility, integrity and sensitivity, but without surrendering the truth of the gospel.

"A Common Word." We live now in a post-9/11 world. And over a decade later we live also in an ISIS-threatened world. It is increasingly difficult to envisage respectful interfaith dialogue between Christians and Muslims, marked by authenticity, humility, integrity and sensitivity—though of course it still does take place.

In 2007 a remarkable document emerged from the Muslim community. It was in the form of an open letter signed by 138 internationally prominent Muslim leaders (academics, politicians, writers and clerics) and addressed to the leaders of major Christian communities, including the Roman Catholic pope; various patriarchs of the Russian, Greek, Syrian, Coptic and other Orthodox churches; and a range of Protestant denominations—Lutheran, Anglican, Reformed, Methodist and Baptist, and the World Council of Churches. Under the title, "A Common Word Between Us and You," the letter urged Christians and Muslims worldwide to seek to live in peace and justice, on the foundation that at the core of both faiths lies the twin imperatives to love God and love our neighbor. The document quotes from the Old Testament and the Gospels in making this point, along with of course the Qur'an.[12]

Christian response varied between warm and enthusiastic welcome, leading to efforts to make it the foundation for wider dialogue and combined efforts for peace building, and cautious suspicion that it was little more than a rather cynical form of Islamic *dawa*, or "mission," to soften up Christians and call them to accept

Islam as essentially no different from their own faith. Somewhere in between uncritical welcome and outright rejection, the World Evangelical Alliance published a well-crafted response that, while welcoming the tone of "A Common Word" and agreeing on the common longing for peace and justice, made quite clear the Christian commitment to the uniqueness and deity of Jesus Christ, and called on Muslims to recognize the rights of Christians in Islamic countries.[13]

One particular response was organized by a group of theologians at Yale Divinity School. They wrote a lengthy reply titled "'A Common Word' Christian Response."[14] In it they welcome the Muslim leaders' overture, recognize that there is indeed "common ground" in the teaching of love for God and neighbor, and receive the document as a kind of mutual handshake. "We receive the open letter as a Muslim hand of conviviality and cooperation extended to Christians worldwide. In this response we extend our own Christian hand in return, so that together with all other human beings we may live in peace and justice as we seek to love God and our neighbors."

Before publishing their response, however, the Yale group wrote to a very large number of Christian leaders around the world inviting them to sign their letter. Included among those so invited were John Stott and me. Before agreeing to sign it, however, the two of us very deliberately did three things together.

First, we read the Yale response carefully to see whether it could be construed as compromising any essential Christian truth, such as the deity of Jesus Christ, or the distinctiveness and finality of God's revelation in the Bible, or the legitimacy of Christian witness to Muslims. We concluded that it did not. We accepted that the Yale response was not an exercise in apologetics, or an attempt to define the whole of the Christian faith in response to Islamic doctrine, but simply an openhanded gesture of friendship, and a desire to build a better commitment to peace and justice on whatever common ground could be established—without denying that there were many crucial areas where there would be no common ground at all.

Second, we wrote to those we knew personally as evangelical friends among the Yale theologians and asked them very directly whether the Yale response intended or implied in any way that evangelism among Muslim people should be deemed out of order— theologically or practically. We were concerned that the document not be understood or used in a way that would undermine the calling of those who seek to share the good news of Jesus, with loving sensitivity, gentleness and respect, among people in majority Islamic communities—sometimes at considerable cost, and many of them our friends. We received several replies from those who had produced the Yale response, assuring us that this was not at all the intent, but rather, on the contrary, the irenic spirit of the response could open doors for such sensitive witness. Two of those replies are quoted later in this chapter.

Third, we wrote to a number of our personal friends who live and work in majority Islamic contexts—many of them Arab Christians and Langham scholars. We asked them the same basic questions and sought their advice as to whether we should or should not add our signatures to the Yale response. We did not want to take any action that would embarrass or betray those for whom this is not a matter of polite interfaith dialogue but often a matter of daily existential stress and potential danger. With only two exceptions (in the correspondence we had), they all affirmed that we should sign, and indeed several of them signed it themselves and are included in the list at the end of the document.

Reassured in these various ways, John Stott and I added our names to the list of signatories. When the document was subsequently published, we were encouraged (and not a little surprised) to see how many others among those we knew as convinced evangelicals and "thought leaders" in the world of evangelical theology and mission had also signed it. We felt ourselves to be in good company!

Not surprisingly, however, the criticisms trickled in. I say "trickled" because actually they were not very many. But they were often quite fierce, and usually along the lines that John Stott had (unbelievably!) signed a document that equated "the Christian God" with "Allah," that did not affirm the deity of Jesus, that did not preach the necessity of the atoning work of the cross, that did not primarily seek to convert Muslims, and so on. I answered many of them individually, on John's behalf, but eventually we crafted the following agreed response to send to any further critics:

A Common Word and the Yale Response

John Stott and Chris Wright, when invited to sign the Yale Response to A Common Word, studied both documents very carefully. We did this not only because of their intrinsic significance, but also because those inviting us to do so (and many of those who have signed the Yale Response) are close personal friends with unquestionable, strong and life-long evangelical commitment, some of whom either are citizens of Islamic countries and bear courageous witness to the gospel in such contexts, or are leaders of movements and organizations that are deeply committed to sharing the good news of Jesus Christ with Muslims.

We wrote to those who had framed the Yale Response seeking clarification and to ensure that neither the message nor the intention behind it, was in any way to be understood as denying the necessity of sensitive witness to Muslims about the non-negotiable claims of Jesus Christ as only Lord and Saviour, and our duty to bear witness to the truth of God that we see revealed in him.

The following quotes are extracts from what we received in reply from those involved in drafting the Yale Response and the invitation to Christian leaders to sign it:

Let me assure you that I in no way want to exclude the possibility of sensitive witness to Christ to Muslims. I am fully in support of such witness, and would myself not sign the document if it implied prohibition of sensitive evangelism. I consider the widening of possibility for free witness as one primary reason for engaging the Muslim letter and the Muslim community as a whole; indeed, I consider our whole response as one form of witnessing—not the only one, but certainly an essential one—to the incredible love of God for the ungodly.

The passion which motivates me to engage in this kind of discussion is my desire to make it possible for 1.3 billion Muslims to consider meaningfully the claims of Jesus Christ—not just as a prophet whose words have been changed, abrogated or superseded, but as supremely attractive Savior and Lord. I also want to remove the obstacles which cause Muslims to associate the Gospel of Christ with militaristic forms of "Christianity" which they find repugnant.

I agree totally with the position that the Lausanne Covenant takes on the question of dialogue and evangelism: "Our Christian presence in the world is indispensable to evangelism, and so is that kind of dialogue whose purpose is to listen sensitively in order to understand. But evangelism itself is the proclamation of the historical, biblical Christ as Saviour and Lord, with a view to persuading people to come to him personally and so be reconciled to God." I also agree with John Stott's official commentary on the Covenant, in which he writes: "Dialogue with non-Christians is not only right but is also (like presence) indispensable. Dialogue is a much-misused word. Some people are using it to describe a situation of compromise in which the Christian renounces his own Christian commitment and regards the Gospel as open to debate! That kind of dialogue we have already rejected (in paragraph 3) as 'derogatory to Christ and the Gospel.' But, properly defined, a dialogue is a conversation in which both parties are serious, and each is prepared to listen to the other. Its purpose is to listen sensitively in order to understand. Such listening is an essential prelude to evangelism, for how can we share the good news relevantly if we do not understand the other person's position and problems?"

In our response letter to the Muslims we have not presented the entirety of the Gospel, but we have tried to bear sensitive witness to Jesus Christ and even mention the forgiveness of sins through what Jesus did "at the end of his life." Muslim readers have told me that they of course understand that we are referring to the atoning death of Christ on the cross. I know personally—and have met privately—with quite a number of the prominent Muslim leaders who signed "A Common Word," and I can assure you that I have shared with each of them the message of forgiveness of sins and eternal life through the atoning death and resurrection of Christ who is the eternal Word of God—God himself—manifest in human flesh.

I believe that the dialogue process which "A Common Word" is opening up will give us opportunity to raise with Muslim leaders the important issue of religious freedom in their countries, including freedom to evangelize.

We recognize that the Yale Response does not "preach the gospel," in all its detail. It was never intended as a creedal statement of all that Christians believe, but merely as an act of responding to A Common Word. It is a letter, not a tract. It extends a hand of friendship in the spirit of the command of Jesus to "love your neighbor," and indeed, to "love your enemies,"—which is a pre-requisite to meaningful evangelistic communication.

There are some who urge us to be suspicious of anything said or done by Muslims, and who see ulterior motives in A Common Word. They may be right or wrong. We are not naïve or unaware of many distressing facts and strong arguments put forward by those who did not sign the Yale Response or who criticize those of us who did. However, our conviction is that, whatever the motives or intentions of Muslims (which are varied and complex), *we* as Christians are called to respond and behave out of the heart of the Christian gospel, which commands us to love our neighbour and our enemy, as obedient disciples of our crucified and risen Lord. Part of such love includes willingness to engage in respectful conversation with fellow human beings from whom we radically differ, without in any way compromising our total commitment to the uniqueness of Jesus Christ, the finality of God's revelation in him, the centrality and necessity of the cross for our salvation, and the mandate of evangelism. All these things, along with the rest of our evangelical faith, we gladly and heartily continue to affirm.

John Stott and Chris Wright

I think the spirit and content of that short document illustrates and encapsulates what Stott considered to be the essence of a true, respectful but uncompromised, dialogue.

Finally, since the Cape Town Commitment was read to him

slowly over several days, I know that he endorsed what it has to say on this issue. Section IIC, on "Living the Love of Christ Among People of Other Faiths," opens with the following paragraphs:

"Love your neighbour as yourself" includes persons of other faiths.

. . . We respond to our high calling as disciples of Jesus Christ to see people of other faiths as our neighbours in the biblical sense. They are human beings created in God's image, whom God loves and for whose salvation Christ died. We strive not only to see them as neighbours, but also to obey Christ's teaching by being neighbours to them. We are called to be gentle, but not naïve; to be discerning and not gullible; to be alert to whatever threats we may face, but not to be ruled by fear.

We are called to share good news, but not to engage in unworthy proselytizing. *Evangelism*, which includes convincing rational argument following the example of the Apostle Paul, is "to make an honest and open statement of the gospel which leaves the hearers entirely free to make up their own minds about it. We wish to be sensitive to those of other faiths, and we reject any approach that seeks to force conversion on them."[15] *Proselytizing*, by contrast, is the attempt to compel others to become "one of us," to "accept our religion," or indeed to "join our denomination."

We commit ourselves to be scrupulously ethical in all our evangelism. Our witness is to be marked by "gentleness and respect, keeping a clear conscience" [1 Peter 3:15-16; compare Acts 19:37] . . . .

We affirm the proper place for dialogue with people of other faiths, just as Paul engaged in debate with Jews and Gentiles in the synagogue and public arenas. As a legitimate part of our Christian mission, such dialogue combines confidence in the uniqueness of Christ and the truth of the gospel with respectful listening to others.[16]

seven

SALVATION

John Stott

Mission denotes what God sends his people into the world to do, and of primary importance within this mission of sacrificial service is evangelism, the sharing with others of God's good news about Jesus. Dialogue, a serious conversation in which we listen as well as speak, is an activity closely related to evangelism. On the one hand it is an activity in its own right, whose goal is mutual understanding. On the other, since the Christian is under the constraint of love to bear witness to Christ, dialogue is also a necessary preliminary to evangelism. Indeed it is the truly human and Christian context within which evangelistic witness should be given. To confess this frankly does not destroy the integrity of the dialogue on the ground that it now has an ulterior motive, and has degenerated into an exercise in public relations whose real objective is the conversion of the other person. This candor rather preserves the integrity of the dialogue by preserving the integrity of the Christian who participates in the dialogue. For the Christian would be true neither to him- or herself, nor to their partner in the dialogue, if they concealed either their belief in the universal lordship of Jesus or their longing that their partner will join them in submission to Jesus as Lord. Such submission in penitence and faith is the way of salvation, which is the fourth word we are to consider. What does salvation mean?

THE CENTRALITY OF SALVATION

The word *salvation* itself may be problematic. Some people find salvation language embarrassing, while others assert that it is a meaningless inheritance from the traditional religious vocabulary of the past. Certainly, then, if Christians are to continue to use the word, it needs to be translated into a more modern idiom. This is fine, even essential, on condition that we remain loyal to the biblical revelation. For a translation is one thing (the old message in new words); a fresh composition or reconstruction is something quite different. And my concern is that some contemporary interpretations of the word are radical reconstructions that are far from loyal to the Bible's portrayal of the salvation that God offers humanity through Christ.

It may be good at once to recognize how vital this question is. For it is no exaggeration to say that Christianity is a religion of salvation. The God of the Bible is a God who has kept coming to the rescue of his people, who has taken the initiative to save. Six times in the Pastorals he is called "God our Savior": "'God' and 'Saviour' are synonymous throughout the whole of the Old Testament," writes Michael Green.[1] The same could be said about the New Testament, for the mission of Jesus was a rescue mission. He "came into the world to save sinners" (1 Timothy 1:15). "The Father has sent his Son as the Savior of the world" (1 John 4:14). His very name embodies his mission, for "Jesus" means "God the Savior" or "God is salvation" (Matthew 1:21), and his full title is "our Lord and Savior Jesus Christ" (see, for example, 2 Peter 3:18).

So the whole Bible is a *Heilsgeschichte*, a history of God's mighty saving acts. Indeed, it is more than a chronicle of the past; it is a contemporary handbook of salvation, "able to instruct you for salvation through faith in Christ Jesus" (2 Timothy 3:15). And of course the gospel is called "the gospel of your salvation" (Ephesians 1:13), even "the power of God for salvation to every one who has faith" (Romans 1:16), because it is through the *kerygma* that God chooses to "save those who believe" (1 Corinthians 1:21). This prominence of the salvation theme in biblical Christianity obliges us to ask what it is that God works, that Christ achieves, that Scripture unfolds and that the gospel offers. I have to begin with two negatives.

SALVATION AND PHYSICAL HEALTH

First, salvation does not mean psycho-physical health. There have been those who seek to equate salvation with health, and especially with "wholeness" understood as a kind of composite health embracing body, mind and spirit.[2] Physical and mental healing, we are told, is of the very essence of the gospel of God's grace. Salvation is for the whole person, including the restoration of body, mind and soul to wholeness. At the psychological level, salvation becomes a kind of personal integration, the wholeness of a balanced personality.

Let me be very clear on the precise point at which I am disagreeing with such a view. I am not denying that according to Scripture, disease is an alien intrusion into God's good world, nor that it is often ascribed to the malevolent activity of Satan, nor that God heals both through natural means and sometimes supernaturally (for all healing is divine healing), nor that Jesus' miraculous healings were signs of his kingdom, nor that he showed both indignation toward sickness and compassion toward the sick, nor that illness, pain and death will find no place in the new bodies and the new universe that God is going one day to create. For I believe all those truths, and hope that they are common ground. I would go further and say that a greater measure of health often follows an experience of salvation. Now that psychosomatic medicine attributes many conditions to stress, while social medicine attributes others to environmental causes, it is to be expected that salvation, because it often leads to the relief of stress and to an improved environment, will also sometimes bring healing of mind and body. Moreover, all Christians should be able to affirm joyfully with Paul that the life of Jesus can be manifested in our mortal flesh (2 Corinthians 4:10-11) and that the power of Jesus is made perfect in our human weakness (2 Corinthians 12:9-10; compare 2 Corinthians 4:7). For our new life in Christ can often bring a new sense of physical and emotional well-being.

What I do deny is that this healing, or indeed any kind of healing—natural or supernatural—either is, or is included in, what the Bible means by the salvation that is now offered to humanity by Christ through the gospel. Of course at the consummation, God will redeem the total creation including our human bodies, and this may rightly be termed full and final salvation, but to assert that healing is as readily and as instantly available today as salvation, or that such healing is part of the salvation that God offers us in Christ by faith now, or that believing Christians have no business ever to be ill, is an attempt to anticipate the resurrection and redemption of our bodies. Not till then will disease and death be no more.

One result of the confusion of salvation and health is that the roles of the doctor and the pastor also become confused. Either the doctor replaces the pastor, or the pastor transforms himself into an amateur physician or psychiatrist. In his perceptive booklet *Will Hospital Replace the Church?* Dr. Martyn Lloyd-Jones, who himself gave up being a consultant physician in order to become a pastor, agrees that the hospital has quite rightly taken over the healing of the sick. Then he adds, "The Hospital does not, cannot, and never will be able to take over the functions of the Church! It is quite impossible for it to do so. . . . The authentic task of the Church is not primarily to make people healthy . . . her essential task is to restore men to right relationship with God. . . . Man's real problem is not simply that he is sick, but that he is a rebel."[3]

At this stage in my argument some may wish to reply that salvation *is* used in the New Testament, particularly in the Gospels, to denote a physical deliverance. They are quite right—at least verbally—and we need to examine their point. *Sōzō* is used of deliverance from blindness (in the case of blind Bartimaeus, Mark 10:52), from leprosy (Luke 17:19) and from an issue of blood (Mark 5:34). In each case Jesus said to the sufferer "your faith has saved you," which each time the Authorized Version renders "thy faith hath made thee whole." The same was said of a crowd of people who were sick with unspecified diseases. As many as touched Christ's garment, we are told, "were made well," which in the Greek is *esōzonto*, "were saved," and in the Authorized Version "were made whole" (Mark 6:56, compare Acts 14:9; James 5:15). But *sōzō* is also used of deliverance from drowning ("Save, Lord; we are perishing," Matthew 8:25; compare Matthew 14:30 and Acts 27:20, 31, 34, 43–28:4) and even from death ("Save yourself, and come down from the cross! . . . He saved others; he cannot save himself" (Mark 15:30-31; compare John 12:27; Hebrews 5:7).

All this is true. But what does it prove? Are we to argue from these uses of the verb "to save" that wherever the New Testament promises salvation to believers it is offering them not only deliverance from sin but also a kind of comprehensive insurance against physical ills of every kind, including disease, drowning and even death? No. It would be impossible to reconstruct the biblical doctrine of salvation in these terms. Salvation by faith in Christ crucified and risen is moral not material, a rescue from sin not from harm, and the reason why Jesus said "your faith has saved you" to both categories is that his works of physical rescue (from disease, drowning and death) were intentional signs of his salvation, and were thus understood by the early church.

We need to remember that the miracles of Jesus were constantly called *sēmeion*, signs of his kingdom, signs of his salvation. Further, the apostles recognized them to be such, and no doubt used these miracle stories in their preaching and teaching. Jesus' well-known words "your faith has saved you" were spoken to the fallen woman who anointed his feet and whom he forgave (Luke 7:48-50). They were also spoken to the blind man, the leprosy sufferer and the woman with the issue of blood not because their cure was their salvation, but because it was a dramatized parable of it.

The form-critical interpretation of the Gospels strongly suggests such an evangelistic use of these well-known incidents. For example, sin is a chronic inward moral disease, which no human being can cure, and if we turn to human remedies we shall not improve but rather get worse. So let the sinner put out the hand of faith and let her but touch the hem of Christ's garment, and she will be made whole, that is, saved. Again, do the storms of sinful passion and even of the wrath of God threaten to engulf us? Then let us cry to Jesus Christ, "Save, Lord; we are perishing," and immediately he will still the storm, and we shall not perish but be saved, and go on to enjoy the peace and calm of his salvation. This is how the early church used these stories of physical deliverance. They believed Jesus had intended them to be illustrations of salvation, not promises of safety or health.

Similarly, the apostle Peter after healing the congenital cripple outside the temple gate could move straight from the means by which "this man has been saved" (*sesōtai,* RSV "has been healed") to the affirmation that "there is salvation [*sōtēria*] in no one else, for there is no other name under heaven given among men by which we must be saved [*sōthēnai*]" (Acts 4:9, 12). The man's healing was "a notable sign" (Acts 4:16) of his salvation.

SALVATION AND POLITICAL LIBERATION

Second, salvation is not sociopolitical liberation. There are theologians whose doctrine of salvation locates our chief human predicament not in our physical and mental sicknesses, but in our social and political structures. They therefore reinterpret salvation as the liberation of deprived and disadvantaged people from hunger, poverty and war; from colonial domination, political tyranny, racial discrimination and economic exploitation; from the ghettos, the political prisons and the soulless technology of the modern world. Not disease but oppression is the problem; so salvation is justice, not health. This reconstruction of salvation dominated the World Council of Churches in the 1960s and '70s.

The emphasis in this interpretation of salvation is on key words like *humanization, development, wholeness, liberation* and *justice.* Let me say at once, not only that these things, and the liberation of people from every form of oppression, are a desirable goal, pleasing to God the Creator, but also that Christians should be actively involved in pursuing that goal alongside other men and women of compassion and goodwill. For God created all people and cares for all people. He means human beings to live together in peace, freedom, dignity and justice. These things in every society are the concern of God, for the God of the Bible is the God of justice as well as of justification, and he hates injustice and tyranny. Further, we evangelicals have often been guilty of opting out of our social and political responsibilities. We are to blame for this neglect. We should repent of it and not be afraid to challenge ourselves and each other that God may be calling many more Christians than hear his call to immerse themselves in the secular world of politics, economics, sociology, race relations, community health, development and a host of other such spheres for Christ.

THE THEOLOGY OF LIBERATION

The strongest advocates of this view of salvation are those who espouse the "theology of liberation." And the earliest exponent of such theology, at least in the awareness of readers in the Western world, is Gustavo Gutiérrez. The original Spanish version of Gutiérrez's book *A Theology of Liberation* was published in Peru in 1971, and then in English several years later.[4] Subtitled *History, Politics and Salvation,* this is the fullest and most thorough attempt that has yet been made to interpret biblical salvation in terms of the liberation of the oppressed.[5] The background to the book is threefold: Latin America the "oppressed continent," the Roman Catholic Church and its *aggiornamento,* and Marxist economic theory. I admire the deep compassion of Gutiérrez for the exploited, his insistence on solidarity with the poor, his emphasis on social "praxis" instead of unpractical theorizing, and his call to the church for "a more evangelical, more authentic, more concrete and more efficacious commitment to liberation."[6] Several times he quotes with approval Marx's famous dictum that "the philosophers have only *interpreted* the world . . . ; the point, however, is to *change* it."

We should have no quarrel with the goal he defines, namely, "liberation from all that limits or keeps man from self-fulfilment, liberation from all impediments to the exercise of his freedom." This is fully biblical. God made humanity in his own image; we should oppose all that dehumanizes it. Again, "the goal is not only better living conditions, a radical change of structures, a social revolution; it is much more: the continuous creation, never ending, of a new way to be a man, a *permanent cultural revolution.*"[7]

What are the means to this end? One of the recurrent themes of the book is that history is the process in which humankind grows in self-consciousness, "gradually takes hold of the reins of his [*sic*] own destiny," wins its freedom and thus creates a new society.[8] In sociological and technological terms, humans have indeed "come of age." They now possess in full measure that "dominion" that God told them to exercise at the beginning of creation (Genesis 1:26-28).

All this—the need for people to free and to fulfill themselves, and to take responsibility for the restructuring of their society—is biblical and right. Both the end and the means are well defined. It is when the author begins to theologize, to try to present social liberation as if this were what Scripture means by salvation, and so to dispense with evangelism in favor of political action, that—reluctantly but decidedly—I part company with him.

Gutiérrez himself asks the basic question, "What relation is there between salvation and the historical process of the liberation of man?" It is, he adds, "the classic question of the relation between . . . faith and political action, or in other words between the Kingdom of God and the building up of the world."[9] He hangs back from identifying the two. But he comes very close to it, and in order to do so indulges in some extremely dubious exegesis.

He all but obliterates the distinction between church and world, Christian and non-Christian, in order that he may apply to all human beings the biblical teaching about God's saving work. Whether they are conscious of it or not, he writes, "all men are in Christ efficaciously called to communion with God." Indeed this, he dares to add, is "the Pauline theme of the universal lordship of Christ, in whom all things exist and have been saved."[10] It also "gives religious value in a completely new way to the action of man in history, Christian and non-Christian alike. The building of a just society has worth in terms of the Kingdom, or in more current phraseology, to participate in the process of liberation is already in a certain sense a salvific work."[11]

In the chapter titled "Encountering God in History" he again universalizes the work and the presence of God. Beginning with the "temple" imagery of Scripture, he goes on to make the statement, entirely unwarranted even on his own premises, that "the Spirit sent by the Father and the Son to carry the work of salvation to its fulfilment dwells in every man." Again, "since God became man, humanity, every man, history is the living temple of God." And Christ's "liberation creates a new chosen people, which this time includes all humanity."[12] There is absolutely no biblical justification for such statements. On the contrary, the New Testament authors constantly contradict this notion by insisting on the distinction between those who are in Christ and those who are not, those who have the Spirit and those who do not (for example, Romans 8:9; 1 John 5:12).

Is there no place, then, in Gutiérrez's scheme for conversion? Yes, but it is fundamentally "conversion to the neighbour."[13] He has already affirmed that "man is saved if he opens himself to God and to others, even if he is not clearly aware that he is doing so." The struggle to be unselfish and "to create an authentic brotherhood among men" is itself a response to God's grace, whether the people concerned explicitly confess Christ as Lord or not.[14] Indeed, the only way to love God is to love my neighbor, the only way to know God is to do justice.[15] Now certainly a true love and knowledge of God must issue in love and justice to our neighbor, but to put this the other way around and make the knowledge of God the consequence of doing justice, and even to equate the two, is uncommonly like a doctrine of salvation by good works.

The author keeps urging that beyond and through "the struggle against misery, injustice and exploitation the goal is the *creation of a new man*."[16] He knows that this is both a Marxist and also a biblical expression. But he betrays no embarrassment that although the words are the same, the sense in which they are used may be different. The "one new man" or "single new humanity" of which Paul writes is God's creation by Christ's death and God's gift to those who are personally in Christ (Ephesians 2:15-16; 2 Corinthians 5:17). It is hard to believe that Gutiérrez seriously thinks this is the same as the "creation" through Marxism of a new social order and lifestyle for all people whether Christian or not.

Although liberation from oppression and the creation of a new and better society are definitely God's good will for humanity, it is necessary to add that these things do not constitute the "salvation" that God is offering the world in and through Jesus Christ. They could be included in "the mission of God," as we have seen, insofar as Christians are giving themselves to serve in these fields. But to call sociopolitical liberation "salvation" and to call social activism "evangelism"—this is to be guilty of a gross theological confusion. It is to mix what Scripture keeps distinct—God the Creator and God the Redeemer, the God of the cosmos and the God of the covenant, the world and the church, common grace and saving grace, justice and justification, the reformation of society and the regeneration of humanity. For the salvation offered in the gospel of Christ concerns persons rather than structures. It is deliverance from another kind of yoke than political and economic oppression.

THE HERMENEUTICAL QUESTION

My deep uneasiness about the form of liberation theology espoused within the ecumenical movement is basically hermeneutical. It concerns the treatment of Scripture, both Old Testament and New Testament, with which its proponents attempt to buttress it. Other critics than myself have alluded to the misuse of Scripture at ecumenical assemblies. It is sometimes arbitrarily selective (omitting what is inconvenient), and at other times extremely cavalier (twisting what seems convenient in order to support a preconceived theory). One Roman Catholic observer at the Salvation Today Bangkok conference in 1973, for example, lamented that although the conference had talked a lot about "salvation," it had not listened to how the apostle Paul spoke of it. Nobody had mentioned justification by faith or everlasting life.

The main biblical evidence adduced for the sociopolitical interpretation of salvation is drawn from the Old Testament, namely the liberation of Israel from its Egyptian oppressors. Gustavo Gutiérrez leans heavily on this interpretation of the exodus. The people of Israel were slaves, suffering economic exploitation and a brutal form of population control. In their bondage they "groaned" and cried to God, and God told Moses he knew their oppression and had "come down to deliver [or liberate] them" (Exodus 3:7-10). Years later at the Red Sea they were told to "stand firm, and see the salvation of the LORD." When the rescue was complete, it was written "thus the LORD saved Israel," and Israel became known as "the people whom thou hast redeemed" (Exodus 14:13, 30; 15:13).

We must ask, however, whether this biblical narrative can be applied to any or every group of oppressed people, and whether it can be regarded as the kind of liberation that God intends or promises for all the oppressed. Surely the answer must be "no."

Certainly oppression in every form is hateful to God. Certainly too God is active in the history of every nation. So much so that his word through Amos drew an analogy between Israel on the one hand and the Philistines and Syrians on the other: "Did I not bring up Israel from the land of Egypt, and the Philistines from Caphtor and the Syrians from Kir?" (Amos 9:7). But this was to assert that Israel could not monopolize Yahweh as if he were a tribal deity; it did not deny the special relationship that God had established between himself and his people Israel. On the contrary, it was again through Amos that God asserted the uniqueness—and therefore the moral implication—of this relationship:

> You only have I known
>   of all the families of the earth;
> therefore I will punish you
>   for all your iniquities. (Amos 3:2; compare Psalm 147:20)

It was this same special relationship that lay behind the exodus. God rescued his people from Egypt in fulfillment of his covenant with Abraham, Isaac and Jacob and in anticipation of its renewal at Mount Sinai (Exodus 2:24; 19:4-6). He made no covenant with the Syrians or the Philistines, and neither did his providential activity in their national life make them his covenant people. In Scripture, "salvation" and "covenant" always belong together. Hence in the

New Testament the exodus becomes a picture of our redemption from sin by Christ, not a promise of liberation for all politically oppressed minorities.

We can have no objection to the use of the word *salvation* in a political sense, provided it is clear that we are not talking theologically about God's salvation in and through Christ. When the New Testament handles Old Testament promises of salvation, it interprets them in moral rather than material terms. Perhaps the most striking example is the song of Zechariah, in which the "horn of salvation" that God had raised up, according to his promise through the prophets "that we should be saved from our enemies," is understood in terms of serving God "in holiness and righteousness," while John the Baptist will "go before the Lord to prepare his ways, to give knowledge of salvation to his people in the forgiveness of their sins" (Luke 1:67-79).

Another popular biblical passage used by those who affirm that salvation can be defined in sociopolitical terms is our Lord's quotation from Isaiah in the Nazareth synagogue:

The Spirit of the Lord is upon me,
 because he has anointed me to preach good news to the poor.
He has sent me to proclaim release to the captives
and recovering of sight to the blind,
 to set at liberty those who are oppressed. (Luke 4:18)

Here three main categories of people are mentioned—the poor, the captives and the blind—and liberation theologies assume that literal, physical conditions are envisaged. But can we take this so easily for granted? It is true that during his ministry Jesus opened the eyes of the blind, and certainly the blind should arouse our Christian compassion today. But Christ's miraculous restoration of sight was a sign that he was the light of the world; it can hardly be taken as an instruction to us to perform similar miraculous cures today. Jesus also ministered to the poor and had some disconcerting things to say to the rich. Yet it is well known that "the poor" in the Old Testament were not just the needy but the pious whose hope and trust were in God. The first Beatitude cannot possibly be understood as making material poverty a condition of receiving God's kingdom, unless we are prepared to turn the gospel upside down. What then of captives and the oppressed? There is no evidence that Jesus literally emptied the prisons of Palestine. On the contrary, the main prisoner we hear about (John the Baptist) was left in prison and was executed. What Jesus did do, however, was to deliver people from the spiritual bondage of sin and Satan, and to promise that the truth would set his disciples free.

Please do not misunderstand me. Material poverty, physical blindness and unjust imprisonment are all conditions that in different degrees dehumanize human beings. They should provoke our Christian concern and stimulate us to action for the relief of those who suffer in these ways. My point, however, is that deliverance from these things is not the salvation that Christ died and rose to secure for us.

I have one further exegetical point to make regarding the attempt to interpret salvation in terms of social liberation. It concerns the instructions that the apostles give to slaves in the New Testament. Although they do not directly attack the institution of slavery, yet Paul insists that slaves are to be treated "justly and fairly" (Colossians 4:1). This was a revolutionary assertion, for the concept of "justice" for slaves was never contemplated in the Roman Empire. Indeed, it is this demand for justice that undermined the institution and in the end destroyed it. Further, although Paul does not incite slaves to rebellion, civil disobedience or self-liberation, he does encourage them, if they can gain their freedom, to avail themselves of the opportunity. He thus recognizes that slavery is an offense to human dignity. "Do not become slaves of men," he writes. But then he adds these significant words: "he who was called in the Lord as a slave is a freedman of the Lord. . . . So, brethren, in whatever state each was called, there let him remain with God" (1 Corinthians 7:20-24). The importance of this teaching should be clear. Slaves who can gain their social freedom should do so, for this is God's will for them. But if they cannot, let them remember that in Christ, whatever their social condition, they are still free people! Their slavery cannot inhibit their deepest liberty as human beings who have been set free by Jesus Christ, and neither can it destroy their dignity as those whom God has accepted. They can stay even in their slavery "with God." No doubt I am laying myself open to the old charge of religious drug peddling, of yet more "opium for the people" (recalling Marx's aphorism that "religion is the opium of the people"). But such an accusation would not be fair. It would never be legitimate to use those two words "with God" to condone oppression or to justify an uncritical acquiescence in the status quo. Rather, they can transform every situation. For they tell us that Jesus Christ gives an inward freedom of the spirit that even the most oppressive tyrant cannot destroy. Think of Paul in prison: was he not free?

So far I have been largely negative. I have tried to argue from Scripture that the "salvation" that Christ once died to win and now offers to the world is neither psycho-physical healing nor socio-political liberation. In rejecting these attempted reconstructions I have also tried to guard myself against misunderstanding. It is necessary to balance my negatives with three positive assertions. First, God *is* greatly concerned for both these areas, namely, our bodies and our society. Second, one day both body and society *will* be redeemed. We shall be given new bodies and shall live in a new society. Third, love compels us meanwhile to labor in both spheres, seeking to promote physical health (by therapeutic and preventive means) and seeking to create a radically different social order that will bring people freedom, dignity, justice and peace. Nevertheless, having emphasized the importance of these things to God and therefore to us, we still have to affirm that they are not the salvation that God is offering human beings in Christ now.

The Lausanne Covenant expresses the tension clearly:

> We affirm that God is both the Creator and the Judge of all men. We therefore should share his concern for justice and reconciliation throughout human society and for the liberation of men from every kind of oppression. Because mankind is made in the image of God, every person, regardless of race, religion, color, culture, class, sex or age, has an intrinsic dignity because of which he should be respected and served, not exploited. . . . Although reconciliation with man is not reconciliation with God, nor is social action evangelism, nor is political liberation salvation, nevertheless we affirm that evangelism and sociopolitical involvement are both part of our Christian duty. For both are necessary expressions of our doctrines of God and man, our love for our neighbor and our obedience to Jesus Christ. The message of salvation implies also a message of judgment upon every form of alienation, oppression and discrimination, and we should not be afraid to denounce evil and injustice wherever they exist.[17]

SALVATION AND PERSONAL FREEDOM

What is salvation, then? It is personal freedom. True, it sometimes results in increased physical and mental health, as we have seen. True also, it has far-reaching social consequences for, as the Lausanne Covenant puts it, "the salvation we claim should be transforming us in the totality of our personal and social responsibilities."[18] Nevertheless, salvation itself, the salvation Christ gives to his people, is freedom from sin in all its ugly manifestations and liberation into a new life of service, until finally we attain "the glo-

rious liberty of the children of God." Georg Fohrer, in Gerhard Kittel's *Theological Dictionary of the New Testament*, makes it clear
that salvation words are primarily negative and emphasize what we
are saved from. Thus in the Greek world salvation was first and
foremost "an acutely dynamic act in which gods or men snatch
others by force from serious peril," whether perils of battle or of the
sea, of judicial condemnation or illness.[19] Hence in Greek literature,
doctors, philosophers, judges, generals, rulers and especially the
emperor are numbered among human "saviors."

The commonest salvation verb in the Old Testament has the
basic idea of broadness or roominess as opposed to the narrowness
of some oppression. It thus indicated deliverance out of some imprisonment into spaciousness "through the saving intervention of
a third party in favour of the oppressed and in opposition to the
oppressor." "The thought," Fohrer continues, "is neither that of self-
help nor of co-operation with the oppressed. The help is such that
the oppressed would be lost without it."[20] It may be a city that is
rescued from a besieging army, a nation from a foreign regime, the
poor from injustice, or individuals from some personal calamity.

All this is an important background for our understanding of the
salvation of *God*. He is the living God, the Savior; idols are dead and
cannot save. And when God saves his people, he not only rescues
them from the oppressor but he saves them for himself. "You have
seen what I did to the Egyptians," he said, "and how I bore you on
eagles' wings and brought you to myself" (Exodus 19:4). This is the
theme already mentioned that "salvation" and "covenant" belong
together. Similarly the "new song" of praise to Christ in heaven
declares, "thou wast slain and by thy blood didst ransom men for
God" (Revelation 5:9).

Now *freedom* is a popular word today. But unfortunately most
contemporary talk about freedom is negative. Dictionaries define
it negatively. One says it is "the absence of hindrance, restraint, con-

finement, repression." Another says that to be free is to be "not enslaved, not imprisoned, unrestricted, unrestrained, unhampered." And the dictionaries are only reflecting common usage. But we must never define freedom in purely negative terms. Indeed the insistence on a positive understanding of freedom is a distinctively Christian contribution to current debate. Michael Ramsey has written, "We know what we want to free men *from*. Do we know what we want to free men *for*?" He goes on to insist that our striving for those freedoms "which most palpably stir our feelings" (that is, freedom from persecution, arbitrary imprisonment, racial discrimination, crippling hunger and poverty) should always be "in the context of the more radical and revolutionary issue of the freeing of man from self and for the glory of God." Such freedom, he continues, is seen perfectly in Jesus alone: "He is free from someone and free for someone. He is free from self, and free for God."[21]

So we shall now examine the New Testament doctrine of salvation, in the three phases or tenses in which the Bible speaks of it (past, present and future). In each case we shall observe how the negative and positive aspects complement each other. "Liberation" is a good rendering of salvation, not least because it hints at the liberty into which the liberated are brought.

FREEDOM FROM JUDGMENT FOR SONSHIP

First of all, in its past phase, "salvation" is liberation from the just judgment of God on sin. It is not just that we had guilt feelings and a guilty conscience, and found relief from these in Jesus Christ. It is that we were actually and objectively guilty before God and have now received a free remission of our guilt, which caused the bad feelings and bad conscience. The reason why the gospel is "the power of God for salvation" is that in it "the righteousness of God is revealed" (namely, his righteous way of declaring the unrighteous righteous), and the reason for this revelation of the righteousness of

God in the gospel is the revelation of "the wrath of God . . . from heaven against all ungodliness and wickedness of men who by their wickedness suppress the truth." This logical sequence of thought in Romans 1:16-18 links the power of God, the righteousness of God and the wrath of God. It is because his wrath is revealed against sin that his righteousness is revealed in the gospel and his power through the gospel to believers.

In this past phase, salvation is the equivalent of justification, which itself is the opposite of condemnation. All those who are "in Christ" are *sesōsmenoi* (Ephesians 2:8), that is, they are those who have been saved. Likewise, they are *dikaiōthentes* (Romans 5:1), those who have been justified. Both words are participles in the past tense, indicating something that has already taken place through faith in Christ. Indeed, Romans 10:10 specifically equates the two, for "man believes with his heart and so is *justified*, and he confesses with his lips and so is *saved*." This justification has been made possible only because of the propitiatory sacrifice of Christ (Romans 3:24-26). There is "no condemnation for those who are in Christ Jesus" only because God sent his own Son "in the likeness of sinful flesh and as a sin offering" and "condemned sin in the flesh," that is, in the flesh in which Jesus came (Romans 8:1-3). Of course the wrath of God is not like human wrath, nor is the propitiation of Christ like heathen propitiations. But once all unworthy elements have been eliminated (namely, the concept of the arbitrary wrath of a vengeful deity being placated by the paltry offerings of humans), we are left with the biblical propitiation in which God's own love sent his own dear Son to appease his own holy wrath against sin (1 John 2:2; 4:10).

In their unfolding of the first phase of salvation, however, the apostles go further than the propitiation of God's wrath, and further even than God's justification of the sinner, which is his acceptance of them as righteous in God's sight. Paul emphasizes that we are saved *from* wrath and *for* sonship. God sent his Son not just to redeem us but also to adopt us into his family. Our judge becomes our father, and the Holy Spirit himself enables us to cry to him "Abba, Father," thus bearing witness with our own spirit that we are indeed his children. So then we are no longer slaves, but children (Romans 8:14-17; Galatians 4:4-7). Now we are free to live as free men and women.

FREEDOM FROM SELF FOR SERVICE

Second, we turn now to the present phase of salvation. For salvation in the New Testament is as much a present process as a gift received in the past. If you ask me if I am saved, and if I think biblically before I answer, I could just as truly reply "no" as "yes." Yes, I have indeed been saved by the sheer grace of God from his wrath and from my guilt and condemnation. But no, I am not yet saved, for sin still dwells within me, and my body is not yet redeemed. It is the common tension in the New Testament between the "now" and the "not yet."

It is well known that the verb *sōzō* is sometimes used in the New Testament in the present tense, as well as in the aorist and the perfect. Christians are *hoi sōzomenoi* ("those who are being saved"). This is partly because it is recognized that our salvation has not yet been brought to completion. *Hoi sōzomenoi* ("those who are being saved") are contrasted with *hoi apollymenoi* ("those who are perishing"), for *they* have not yet perished, and *we* have not yet reached the new creation (compare 1 Corinthians 1:18; 2 Corinthians 2:15; Acts 2:47). Another reason for the present tense is that during the interim between our justification and our glorification comes that process called sanctification, the gradual transformation of the believer by the Spirit of Christ into the image of Christ "from one degree of glory to another" (2 Corinthians 3:18) until in the end we shall be fully conformed to the image of God's Son (Romans 8:29; compare 1 John 3:2).

Moreover, since Jesus Christ into whose image we are being changed is "the second man" or "second Adam" (Romans 5 and 1 Corinthians 15), the pioneer of the new humanity, we ourselves who are in Christ are sharers in this new humanity. To become Christian is in a real sense to become human, because nothing dehumanizes more than rebellion against God, and nothing humanizes more than reconciliation to God and fellowship with God. But to assert joyfully that salvation includes humanization is not at all the same thing as saying that humanization (rescuing people from the dehumanizing process of modern society) equals salvation.

The ecumenical argument seems to run like this: Salvation according to the New Testament makes people human; therefore whatever makes people human is salvation. But this kind of reasoning is as deficient in logic as in theology. One might just as well say: "Aspirin relieves pain; therefore whatever relieves pain is aspirin."

Salvation as a present process is expressed in two surprising apostolic commands. "Work out your own salvation," Paul writes, calling on the Philippians to exhibit in practical, everyday living the salvation that God is working within them (Philippians 2:12-13), while the apostle Peter stresses the need of his readers to "grow up to salvation" (1 Peter 2:2). Since in the previous verse he has told them to put away all malice, deceit, insincerity, envy and slander, it is evident that he regards these things as babyish and that the "salvation" he wants them to grow up into is again Christlikeness of behavior.

In this present salvation too we should emphasize the positive. We are being delivered from the bondage of self-centeredness into the liberty of service. Jesus spoke of our being the slaves of sin, and there is no slavery worse than imprisonment in oneself. Luther described fallen humanity as *homo incurvatus in se*, "man curved or bent inwards upon himself." From this prison Jesus Christ liberates us. He warns us that if we insist on "saving" ourselves, holding on to our own life in selfishness, we shall lose ourselves. By contrast, only if we are prepared to lose ourselves by giving ourselves away in service to him and to others, shall we ever truly find ourselves (Mark 8:35). It is only when we die that we live, only when we serve that we are free.

This present salvation, this liberation from the shackles of our own self-centeredness into the freedom of service, brings more thoroughgoing demands than we are often prepared to recognize. To quote from the Lausanne Covenant again, "the results of evangelism include obedience to Christ, incorporation into his church and responsible service in the world."[22] Unless we are truly delivered from a slavish conformity to tradition, convention and the bourgeois materialism of secular culture, unless our discipleship is radical enough to make us critical of establishment attitudes and indignant over all forms of oppression, and unless we are now freely and selflessly devoted to Christ, church and society, we can hardly claim to be saved, or even to be in the process of being saved. Salvation and the kingdom of God are synonymous (compare Mark 10:23-27), and in the kingdom the authority of Jesus is absolute.

It is impossible to grasp the fullness of this present phase of salvation, as depicted in the New Testament, without feeling ashamed of our contemporary Christian failures. We tend so to glory in our past salvation as a free gift already received that we neglect the call to "grow up to salvation" and to give ourselves wholeheartedly with our fellow believers to the service of God and humanity. If we reflect on the challenge of his present sense of "being saved," we should recognize that the church itself needs liberation—liberation from all that is false to the demands of discipleship to the Lord Jesus Christ, and contrary to the transforming and renewing power of the gospel.

FREEDOM FROM DECAY FOR GLORY

Third, moving to the future aspect, God's salvation, which is both a gift and a continuing process, is also the object of our Christian hope. We were saved in hope of being saved, and the "hope of sal-

vation" is the helmet that the Christian soldier wears (1 Thessalonians
5:8; compare Romans 8:24).

Each day brings this salvation closer, for "salvation is nearer to us
now than when we first believed" (Romans 13:11; compare 1 Peter 1:5,
9). We do not, however, cherish the kind of utopian vision that
Gustavo Gutiérrez describes in his chapter "Eschatology and Politics." On the contrary, "we reject as a proud self-confident dream
the notion that man can ever build a utopia on earth. Our Christian
confidence is that God will perfect his Kingdom and we look forward
with eager anticipation to that day and to the new heaven and earth
in which righteousness will dwell and God will reign for ever."[23]

What will it be, this final salvation? To begin with, it will be a
deliverance from the wrath to come (Romans 5:9; 1 Thessalonians
1:10; 5:9). More than that, it will include "the redemption of our
bodies." For our bodies share with the whole creation a "bondage
to decay" that makes the creation groan as if in labor and makes us
groan inwardly as well. We long for our new bodies (which will be
liberated from physical frailty, a fallen nature and mortality) and for
the new universe (in which there will be no oppression but only
righteousness). This prospect the New Testament also depicts in
positive rather than merely negative terms. For our inward groaning
is a longing for our "adoption as sons," when our sonship will be
revealed in its fullness. Similarly, the whole creation will not just
"be set free from its bondage to decay" but will "obtain the glorious
liberty of the children of God" (see Romans 8:18-25; 2 Peter 3:13).

I have tried to show that in each phase of personal salvation
Scripture lays its emphasis not so much on our *rescue* (from wrath,
from self, from decay and death) as on the *freedom* that this rescue
will bring—freedom to live with God as our Father, freedom to give
ourselves to the service of others, and finally the "freedom of glory"
when, rid of all the limitations of our present fallen existence, we are
free to devote ourselves without reserve to God and to each other.

Are we saved? Yes, and "we rejoice" (Romans 5:2-3, 11). Are we saved? No, and in this body with the whole creation, "we groan inwardly" as we wait for the consummation. We rejoice and we groan: this is the paradoxical experience of Christians who have been saved and are being saved, and at the same time are not yet finally saved.

So the gospel is the good news of salvation, and like Paul we must be able to declare that we are not ashamed of it. For as Michael Green rightly says at the end of his thorough study *The Meaning of Salvation*, "there is still a hunger for salvation" in today's world.[24] And God's good news is still his power unto salvation to those who believe. He still saves believers through the *kerygma*, the announcement of Jesus Christ.

Finally, we must exhibit what we proclaim. Dr. Rhadakrishnan, Hindu philosopher and former president of India, is said to have commented to some Christians, "You claim that Jesus Christ is your Saviour, but you do not appear to be more 'saved' than anyone else." Our message of salvation is bound to fall on deaf ears if we give no evidence of salvation in a changed life and lifestyle. This applies to nobody more directly than to the preacher of the gospel. "The most effective preaching," writes John Poulton, "comes from those who embody the things they are saying. They *are* their message. . . . Christians . . . need to look like what they are talking about. It is *people* who communicate primarily, not words or ideas. . . . Authenticity gets across from deep down inside people. . . . What communicates now is basically personal authenticity."[25] And personal Christian authenticity is an authentic experience of salvation.

eight

REFLECTIONS ON SALVATION

Chris Wright

I t is no exaggeration to say that Christianity is a religion of salvation," John Stott affirms. He could have said "the religion," rather than "a religion," for, as he goes on to say, the God of the Bible is the God of salvation. No other word so frequently and comprehensively defines God in biblical revelation than that he is the God who saves, when all other alleged gods fail to do so. "Salvation belongs to our God," sings the polyphonic choir of redeemed humanity (Revelation 7:10)—and to no other. This is something so distinctive of the biblical faith that it can be stressed even more strongly than Stott had space to do in this book. I devoted a whole chapter to it in my book *Salvation Belongs to Our God* (written, as it happens, at Stott's request, when he was editorial adviser to the series Global Christian Library). I shall expand here on the resounding claims that Stott makes near the beginning of his chapter.[1]

Salvation not only defines the particularity and uniqueness of the biblical God, but even, according to the Bible, defines the very *identity* of God. Sometimes Old Testament writers simply say, "Yahweh *is* salvation" (see, for example, Exodus 15:2; Deuteronomy 32:15). In the Psalms we see that Yahweh is above all else the God who saves. The Hebrew root *yasha* ("to save") occurs 136 times in the Psalms (adding up to 40 percent of all the uses of this word in the whole Old Testament). Yahweh is

- the God of my salvation, or God my Savior (Psalms 18:46; 25:5; 51:14, etc.)

- the horn of my salvation (Psalm 18:2)

- the Rock of my salvation (Psalms 89:26; 95:1)

- my salvation and my honor (Psalm 62:6-7)

- my Savior and my God (Psalm 42:5)

Turning to the New Testament, we find an angel instructing Joseph to call Mary's son Jehoshua (Joshua, Jeshua—or in its Greek form, Jesus), for "he will save his people from their sins" (Matthew 1:21). Jesus' name means, *"Yahweh is salvation."* As believers bow at the name of Jesus, they declare God to be the saving God of the Bible. Paul contributes to this theme particularly in the tiny letter to Titus, which displays a most astonishing concentration of salvation language—in the space of three short chapters, Paul piles up the phrases either "God our Savior" or "Christ our Savior" seven times.

The God revealed as Yahweh in the Old Testament, and as Jesus of Nazareth in the New Testament, is above all else the God who saves. That is the distinctive mark of his uniqueness, and the defining mark of his identity.

THE SCOPE OF SALVATION—WHAT DOES IT INCLUDE?

Stott's passion for clarity leads him to make some sharp distinctions and definitions. Reacting against the kind of radical reframing of Christian salvation language, in terms of healing from sickness or (more pervasively) liberation from economic and political oppression, that had strongly influenced the liberal theology of the ecumenical movement in the 1960s and '70s, Stott insists that biblical salvation is neither of those two things. Or, to be more precise, he was well aware that physical healing and justice for the oppressed are both good things in themselves—things that the Bible shows that God desires and Christians should be concerned about— but he did not see them as included in *the* salvation "which God works, which Christ achieves, which Scripture unfolds and which the gospel offers" (to quote his classic phraseology).

The definite article is significant. Again and again Stott insists on his careful, delimiting definition (in each case below, the italics are my own addition):

- "*the* salvation that God offers humanity through Christ"
- "*the* salvation that is now offered to humanity by Christ through the gospel"
- "these things do not constitute *the* 'salvation' that God is offering the world in and through Jesus Christ."
- "deliverance from these things is not *the* salvation that Christ died and rose to secure for us."
- "*the* 'salvation' that Christ once died to win and now offers to the world is neither psycho-physical healing nor sociopolitical liberation."
- "*the* salvation Christ gives to his people"

Nevertheless, Stott insists on two other points, and concedes a third, in order to guard himself against misunderstanding. But these balancing points seem to me, however, to lead to some difficulty and tension in his overall argument.

First of all, in line with all that he has argued in the first chapter about the holistic nature of Christian mission, he insists that Christians *ought* to be involved in works of healing and in sociopolitical engagement on behalf of the poor and oppressed. "Love compels us to labor in both spheres, seeking to promote physical health (by therapeutic and preventive means) and seeking to create a radically different social order that will bring people freedom, dignity, justice and peace." So he argues that working for "liberation from oppression and the creation of a new and better society . . . could be included in the 'mission of God,' insofar as Christians are giving themselves to serve in these fields." But such work is not part of, or connected to, God's salvation, in Stott's mind (at least as far as he expresses it in this chapter). This seems to me to create an odd disjunction between our theology of mission and our theology of salvation, when it would seem that the Bible holds them very closely together. It seems odd to separate off one part of *our* mission (the social aspect, which Stott believed to be fully mandated in the Bible) from the full biblical content of God's *saving* work.

Second, Stott is fully aware, of course, and mentions it several times, that *ultimately* (eschatologically) the saving, redemptive work of God *will* include complete healing of the body (with the ending of all suffering, disease and death), and *will* include the complete establishment of justice and peace (with the ending of all oppression and violence) in the new creation. He does not at all deny that "illness, pain and death will find no place in the new bodies and the new universe that God is going one day to create." On the contrary, he affirms three positives:

First, God *is* greatly concerned for both these areas, namely, our bodies and our society. Second, one day both body and society *will* be redeemed. We shall be given new bodies and shall live in a new society. Third, love compels us meanwhile to labor in both spheres, seeking to promote physical health (by therapeutic and preventive means) and seeking to create a radically different social order that will bring people freedom, dignity, justice and peace.

So again, somewhat oddly, although biblically speaking salvation *will* include these great eschatological blessings, these things are *not* included in "the salvation that is now offered to humanity by Christ through the gospel."

This disjunction (between evangelism that offers salvation, and social engagement that is pleasing and obedient to God but not connected to salvation) is what governed the structure of the relevant paragraph in the Lausanne Covenant:

> We affirm that God is both the Creator and the Judge of all men. We therefore should share his concern for justice and reconciliation throughout human society and for the liberation of men from every kind of oppression. Because mankind is made in the image of God, every person, regardless of race, religion, color, culture, class, sex or age, has an intrinsic dignity because of which he should be respected and served, not exploited. . . . Although reconciliation with man is not reconciliation with God, nor is social action evangelism, nor is political liberation salvation, nevertheless we affirm that evangelism and sociopolitical involvement are both part of our Christian duty. For both are necessary expressions of our doctrines of God and man, our love for our neighbor and our obedience to Jesus Christ. The message of salvation implies also a message of judgment upon every form of alienation, oppression and discrimination, and we should not be afraid to denounce evil and injustice wherever they exist.[2]

It is clear in that paragraph that Christian social engagement is rooted in the doctrine of God as Creator, rather than being connected to God's work in salvation—until, that is, the final curious sentence that applies "the message of salvation" precisely to those areas, presumably because Stott could not forget his biblical awareness that God's salvation will eventually eliminate all "evil and injustice wherever they exist."

Third, the concession that Stott makes is that the Bible actually does use the vocabulary of "saving" and "salvation" in a very broad variety of ways, including healing and political liberation.[3] But he reduces the impact of this, once again by insisting that "the biblical doctrine of salvation" cannot be equated to "a kind of comprehensive insurance against physical ills of every kind, including disease, drowning and even death." Such miracles were "signs of salvation," not the thing itself.

How are we to respond to these things? It is very clear that Stott is anxious, and rightly so, to protect the biblical meaning of salvation on two fronts. On the one hand, he does not want it to be mutated into a purely material, physical, social or political kind of "liberation" that leaves the underlying problem of sin and evil and their ultimate and eternal consequences untouched and so has no time or place for the necessity of evangelism and personal regeneration through Christ. On the other hand, he is resisting an over-realized eschatology that imagines that all the ultimate blessings of salvation that the Bible speaks of in the new creation can be promised and enjoyed in our present life in this world.

However, it seems to me that a better way to obtain the same objectives—that is, to preserve the full biblical conception of salvation while avoiding a merely physical or political interpretation—would be *not* to "divide up" salvation in terms of its "content" (since the Bible in so many places in both Testaments fills the word with such a richness of content—all associated with God's saving work), and then bracket out some parts and say they are not included in "the salvation that God offers through Christ." Rather, it would be better to follow Stott's own secondary instinct, which has to do not so much with the content of salvation as with the *timing* of our experience of its full content. In other words, we need to recognize that within the wholeness of biblical salvation (*all* of which is entirely the work of God and ultimately accomplished through Christ), there is that which we can be *assured* of here and now, and that which we may not necessarily *experience* here and now in this life, but will gloriously celebrate as reality in the new creation. In other words, we can make a distinction between present and eschatological dimensions of salvation, while holding both within the total "package" of what Christ accomplished and the gospel offers.

So what exactly can we promise to those who turn to God in repentance and faith? The Bible consistently affirms that if sinners repent and trust in the saving work of Christ they can know the forgiveness of sins, they can be assured of salvation from God's wrath on the last day, and they can be sure they have received the gift of eternal life. God guarantees that, *in relation to sin and its eternal consequences*, we have been saved, we are being saved, and we will be saved, all based on the cross and resurrection of Jesus Christ. These things we can confidently trust for ourselves and promise to others based on God's own clear promises.

What about many other things the Bible speaks of in saving language—physical healing, liberation, rescue from danger and death, and so on? These all can happen in this life, and Scripture shows that God can and often does do these things for some people in particular times and places. But can we guarantee that he always will do so for everyone who asks or trusts?

Some Christian ministries claim just this—for example, it is *always* God's will to save you from poverty and make you rich, here and now; it is *always* God's will to save you from sickness and make you well, here and now. Have faith, or enough faith, or the right kind of faith, and all the benefits of God's salvation can be yours here and now. Stott does not mention prosperity gospel teaching in his chapter, but doubtless he would have accused it of that kind of distortion.

So does faith guarantee every kind of salvation the Bible uses the vocabulary of salvation for? Not according to Hebrews 11. In this chapter is a catalog of the saving acts of God in relation to the faith of many Old Testament individuals. Faith was common to all. According to Hebrews 11:32-35, many of them experienced material, physical and military dimensions of God's salvation (Gideon, Barak, Samson, Jephthah, David, Samuel and "the prophets" are given as examples).

But *others did not* experience salvation in this immediate way. Instead, they "were tortured, refusing to accept release . . . suffered mocking and scourging . . . chains and imprisonment . . . were stoned . . . were sawn in two . . . were killed with the sword . . . went about in skins of sheep and goats, destitute, afflicted, ill-treated . . . wandering over deserts and mountains, and in dens and caves of the earth" (Hebrews 11:35-38). So then, the writer tells us, salvation in many senses never came for them, in their earthly lifetimes. *But* "these were *all* commended for their faith."

This passage pushes back against all false and exaggerated claims for instant health and wealth as the inevitable product of faith. The difference in the fates of these individuals did not lie in the presence or absence of faith, but in the mysterious ways of God. We can promise what God unquestionably promises (eternal salvation for those who repent and trust him, and deliverance from all sickness, death and oppression *in the new creation*). But we should not promise what God does not promise (deliverance from all problems or suffering in this life). Whatever measure of healing and justice that God brings to people in this life through our missional engagement in works of love, compassion, peacemaking or justice seeking (however partial and provisional such efforts may be) constitutes anticipatory firstfruits of the ultimate salvation that God has accomplished through Christ for his redeemed people in the new creation.

Stott is fully aware of the temporal distinctions within the biblical understanding of salvation—its past, present and future tenses. He applies them very effectively in the major section of this chapter,

"Salvation and Personal Freedom." As that subheading shows, his emphasis is on the blessings and benefits of salvation enjoyed by the individual believer. There is another dimension, however, that is not adequately addressed in this chapter on salvation, namely the corporate and cosmic (or creational) dimension of salvation. Without a doubt, this is not mere oversight, since Stott had plenty to say on both in later works, and we should recall the point I made in the preface that this book was based on five lectures in which it was impossible to say everything. For the wider, mature reflection of John Stott on the vast dimensions of biblical salvation—including its ecclesial and social outworking, and its ultimate consummation in the new creation, one should invest very profitable time in reading *The Cross of Christ* and *The Contemporary Christian*.[4]

More recent evangelical thinking and writing has happily recaptured something of this biblical fullness of salvation—in all its tenses (past, present and future) and in all its dimensions (personal, social and creational). I am confident that Stott himself would have applauded the biblically balanced and richly hope-filled emphases of the books mentioned in the following endnote, for the prime reason that they remain as committed as Stott himself to affirming that salvation is exclusively the work of the God revealed to us in the Bible (Yahweh the Holy One of Israel, embodied in the Messiah, Jesus of Nazareth, God's Son), and that God has accomplished that salvation exclusively through the incarnation, death and resurrection of Jesus Christ—as the central accomplishment of the great biblical narrative of God's saving work that extends from creation to new creation.[5]

THE HERMENEUTICS OF SALVATION—
HOW SHOULD WE USE THE OLD TESTAMENT?

Writing this book in 1975, John Stott was among the earliest British evangelicals to respond to Latin American liberation theology when it burst on the awareness of the English-speaking world through the translation of Gustavo Gutiérrez's seminal book, *A Theology of Liberation*.[6] Stott's response is characteristic. First, he has clearly studied the book with great care and thoroughness. Second, he seeks to applaud all that he can find that is positive and that he feels evangelicals ought to endorse and learn from. But then, third, he brings a sharp biblical critique, exposing those places where he believes Gutiérrez has gone way beyond what is biblically justifiable, or where he has confused categories that need to be kept distinct. In the following years, others took up the challenge of interacting with liberation theology, in its various flavors—some more evangelically congenial than others.[7]

Stott claims in this chapter that his main point of contention with the kind of liberation theology advocated by Gutiérrez and others is hermeneutical—their handling of Scripture. And in particular, Stott disputed their use of Old Testament texts. He mentions especially their strong use of the exodus narrative. While he wholeheartedly recognizes that the Bible as a whole, and that story in particular, shows that "oppression in every form is hateful to God," and that Christians ought to be in the forefront of exposing and resisting it, he objects to liberation theology's use of the exodus on two fronts. Negatively, he asks "whether this biblical narrative can be applied to any or every group of oppressed people, and whether it can be regarded as the kind of liberation which God intends or promises for all the oppressed. Surely the answer must be 'no.'" And positively, he affirms that the New Testament transforms the exodus into "a picture of our redemption from sin by Christ, not a promise of liberation for all politically oppressed minorities."

I find myself in partial agreement and partial disagreement on both points.

On the first point, I agree that we cannot turn the historical fact of what God did for Israel into an expectation or a promise that God will do the same for every oppressed group in the history of the fallen world. Such a claim would amount to the same kind of distorted "realized eschatology" found in the prosperity gospel— the promise that physical healing and/or material abundance is guaranteed here and now. Nevertheless, we need to balance this with other thoughts.

First, it is clear that the Israelites themselves had a strong expectation that the God of the exodus could, and would, "do it again"— both at the personal level (hence the frequent appeals to God for deliverance from oppression in the Psalms), and at national level (witness the strong "new exodus" themes in the prophets). But, furthermore, we should not forget that Israel was called into existence for the sake of God's ultimate purpose of bringing blessing and the extension of covenant relationship *to all nations*. Of course, this is an eschatological hope, not a present guarantee or an immediate geopolitical agenda. Nevertheless, it does mean that the exodus narrative functions not merely or exclusively as something "for Israel only" (though certainly it was one dimension of their unique identity as God's people), but has a *paradigmatic* purpose also. The God who did this for Israel is in fact the God who is characterized by his love for the alien and the oppressed—in the widest generic sense (Deuteronomy 10:17-19).

Liberation theologians were not wrong, in other words, to see in this narrative a demonstration of God's priorities and concerns. There is a biblically grounded hermeneutical route from the biblical narrative to social engagement with and for the poor, an engagement that seeks justice and liberation from oppression. However, Stott and others are right to complain when liberation theologies simply *equate* any human activity that challenges injustice as *salvation* per se, if it does not include also bringing people into relationship with God through Jesus Christ. The exodus is repeatedly described in the Old Testament as the great primal act of God's *redemption*. Speak of God as "Redeemer" and you think "exodus," in Old Testament

Israel. But the purpose of the exodus was not just to get Israel out of Egypt ("freedom" in a purely geographical and political sense), but to get them to Mount Sinai to enter into covenant relationship with their God and then to live out that relationship of redeemed covenant obedience in the land he would give them. For that reason, a merely sociopolitical use of the exodus, though indebted to part of the story, is seriously deficient even in its use of the Bible.

On the second point, it is manifestly true that the New Testament uses the exodus narrative as a way of understanding Christ's achievement in his cross and resurrection. That is characteristic of the narrative nature of salvation itself in the Bible: the great central story of salvation in the Gospels gathers up and "reenacts" all that God had done in the preceding story of Israel (part of what Paul meant in saying that "Christ died for our sins *in accordance with the scriptures*, that he was . . . raised on the third day *in accordance with the scriptures*," 1 Corinthians 15:3-4), and points forward to the new creation climax which, in Revelation 21–22, draws heavily on the Old Testament yet again. But the exodus is not merely "a picture" of a future spiritual redemption. It was itself a reality—God really rescued people from real oppression that was political, economic and social, as well as spiritual. And the Old Testament repeatedly uses the language of redemption for the exodus as a whole.

So we should not, it seems to me, reduce its full biblical significance to a *spiritual* understanding of redemption from sin and overlook those other dimensions of its paradigmatic force—any more than we should reduce it only to the sociopolitical realm and overlook its intrinsic spiritual significance. Either extreme ends up distorting the way the exodus narrative functions in a full biblical understanding of salvation (and mission). I have discussed this much more fully in a whole chapter of my book *The Mission of God*, and conclude with an appeal for an integrated interpretation of the exodus that gives full value to all its dimensions.[8]

THE STORY OF SALVATION—
CAN OTHER STORIES PREPARE THE WAY?

We have stressed above the narrative nature of salvation in the Bible. That is to say, in the Bible, salvation is not a formula, technique or magic mystery. Salvation is always described as what God has achieved within history through the whole chain of promises and events that center and culminate in Jesus Christ. And that leads to a further point, which we may address here, though it would have been relevant also in relation to Stott's chapter on interfaith dialogue.

This narrative nature of biblical salvation is at the heart of of its uniqueness. When the Bible speaks of salvation, it is not speaking of some common thing that all other religions also believe in, only in different ways. In the Bible, as soon as you mention salvation, you have to tell the story—*this* story, not any other. All other notions of salvation start out from the wrong place—that salvation is something we eventually hope to reach by our own efforts, with a little help from the gods or the gurus. In the Bible God is the *subject*, not the *object*, of salvation. God does it. God achieves it. God is the active subject. We do not have to work for salvation, in order to persuade or manipulate God to grant it to us. And, according to Scripture, God's accomplishment of it is through the events recorded in this narrative history.

In the Bible, salvation is rooted in the "having-happened-ness" of the historical events by which God has acted to save humanity and creation. It is what God has done already in the *past*, and as a result, certain outcomes are assured in the *future*; because of this, we live changed lives in the *present*. Other religions do not save *because they do not tell this story*. They therefore cannot "connect" people to that story and to the Savior, who is the great Subject of the story. They have no gospel, for they do not know the story that alone constitutes the good news.

THE EXTENT OF SALVATION—WHO WILL BE INCLUDED?

One issue that Stott did not tackle in his chapter on salvation in this book, but that he did address later on, is the question of the extent of salvation, or perhaps more accurately, its limits. He has spoken in this chapter often about the salvation that God offers to people through the gospel of Christ. But what about those who never hear about the offer? What about those who never learn about the good news of Jesus Christ? In other words, what is the destiny of the unevangelized?

In *The Contemporary Christian* Stott has a chapter titled "The Uniqueness of Jesus Christ," in which he expounds with his customary clarity what it means to say that Jesus alone is Lord and Savior. At the end, however, he anticipates that his reader might ask exactly the questions above. In seeking to answer, he says, "we need to combine confidence and agnosticism, what we know (because Scripture plainly teaches it) and what we do not know (because Scripture is either unclear or even silent about it)."

He then states "what we know from Scripture," namely: that there is no possibility of self-salvation; that Jesus Christ is the only Savior; "and that salvation is by God's grace alone, on the ground of Christ's cross alone, by faith alone." He then continues:

> What we do not know, however, is exactly how much knowledge and understanding of the gospel people need before they can cry to God for mercy and be saved. In the Old Testament, people were certainly "justified by grace through faith," even though they had little knowledge or expectation of Christ. Perhaps there are others today in a somewhat similar position. They know they are sinful and guilty before God, and that they cannot do anything to win his favour, so in self-despair they call upon the God they dimly perceive to save them. If God does save such, as many evangelical Christians tentatively believe, their salvation is still only by grace, only through Christ, only by faith.[9]

It seems reasonable, in view of this, to include Stott among those who could be called "nonrestrictivist exclusivists" (if it were not for it being such an ugly combination of words!). That is, he was very clear that salvation was exclusively in and through Jesus Christ and nowhere else, and that salvation was exclusively a matter of God's grace, received through repentance and faith. But he was not willing to be dogmatic about whether salvation would ultimately be restricted only to those who, in their earthly lifetime, heard an intelligible explanation of the gospel and put their faith in Jesus Christ. Rather, he would align with those who reverently leave the destiny of all people, evangelized or not, in the hands of the all-just and all-merciful God. It is noticeable how careful Stott is in expressing this possibility, with the words, "Perhaps . . . If . . . tentatively."

This debate on the extent of salvation and the destiny of the unevangelized continues among evangelical theologians and missiologists. The following endnote is the merest sample of some key works on both sides.[10]

My own view in this matter was expressed in my books *The Uniqueness of Jesus* and *Salvation Belongs to Our God*—both of which were read and commended by John Stott, so I have confidence he agreed with the thrust of the arguments outlined below. However, both he and I would want to express this position without extreme dogmatism, and in respectful though disagreeing fellowship with those who hold that salvation is possible *only and exclusively* for those who hear the gospel and exercise conscious faith in the known Jesus of that proclamation.

Several arguments are put forward in support of the view that God will save *through Christ* some who, even though they never hear about Christ in their earthly lifetimes, nevertheless turn to God in some kind of repentance and faith. One relates to Old Testament believers. There were believers in the Old Testament whom we would unquestionably regard as "saved," yet they never knew about the historical Jesus of Nazareth. They were indeed saved *by* Christ (whose death is effective for all human history), but not through *knowing* Christ (in the sense of knowing the story of the life, death and resurrection of Jesus of Nazareth—the New Testament gospel).

Even if we come to the conclusion that Old Testament believers in the covenant nation stood in a special position, the Old Testament also describes how God responded graciously to others who did *not* stand within the covenant nation, such as "converts" like Rahab (Joshua 2), Ruth (Ruth 1:16-17), the widow of Zarephath (1 Kings 17:24) and Naaman (2 Kings 5:15-18), and repentant sinners such as the Ninevites (Jonah). They all joined the community of the saved by coming to exercise faith in the God they encountered through Israelites' witness, so in a sense they could be called "evangelized," even if it was nothing like the New Testament gospel that they heard.

There were also those who were saved who lived long before the redemptive revelation embodied in the history of Israel had even begun—that is, before Abraham—such as Enoch. Enoch's faith is held up also in the New Testament as a model. So the question can be asked: Have there been and are there still other people in similar circumstances as Enoch—that is, who believe God exists and earnestly seek him? And if so, does not God save them in the same way, for the same reason (their faith), and on the same basis—the death of Christ? If, then, the Bible tells us that it was possible for people in those ages before Christ to be saved by Christ without actually knowing Christ, because it was *historically* impossible for them to do so, is it not similarly possible for people today to be saved by Christ even if they do not know him because of *geographical* and other obstacles?

Revelation says that the song of salvation will be sung by "a great multitude which no man could number, from *every* nation, from all tribes and peoples and tongues" (Revelation 7:9, italics added). Such language could be taken in a general or approximate sense. But if we take it in a more intentional sense, then it is affirming that

God will have saved people from *every* ethnic, cultural and linguistic group in the human race throughout history. If that is what Revelation 7:9 intends to say, then the final number of the redeemed will certainly include more than those who have been explicitly evangelized by Christian missionaries in the centuries after Pentecost since many tribes and languages disappeared from the face of the earth long before the New Testament era.

We have to be very careful about what is being said and what is *not*. First, this is not universalism, that everybody will be saved no matter what they believe or how they live. That is clearly contradicted by the Bible. Rather, this view is saying that we are saved by God's grace only, received through the channels of repentance and trust in God's mercy.

Second, this view is not saying that people in any faith are saved by their goodness and sincerity. It is the precise opposite of that. All who will be saved in the end will be saved by the grace of God. The heart of the gospel is that God saves sinners who know they are sinners and turn away from sin and self toward God.

Third, this view is not saying that people in other faiths can be saved through their own religious systems, or that other religions are provisional ways of salvation. The New Testament does not talk of salvation at all except in and through Christ.

Speaking for myself, it seems presumptuous to limit the sovereignty of God's saving grace to the evangelistic obedience of the church. That is to say, while I strongly affirm that people can be saved only and exclusively by Christ, and that the normal way that God brings salvation is through those who know Christ witnessing to those who do not yet, and leading them to repentance and faith, I cannot take the further step of saying that God is somehow unable or not willing to save anybody at any time in human history, unless and until a Christian reaches them with an intelligible explanation of the story of the gospel.

Such a view, if pressed to its theological limits, would mean that in the end, the elect of God will be a subset of those evangelized by us. It would be saying: only those who have been evangelized can be saved, but not all who are evangelized actually are saved; so the total number saved (by God) will be smaller than the total number evangelized (by us). And that seems to restrict the operation of God's grace to the limits of the operation of our human evangelistic efforts.

It seems to me that the Bible gives us grounds to believe that the reverse will be true. That is, those who will have responded to explicit Christian evangelism will be a subset of the finally elect and redeemed. God operates in his sovereign grace to reach out to and touch people to the ends of the earth and at all times of history. The history of Christian mission has many examples of encounters with people who had had an experience of, or some revelation of, the saving grace of God even before Christian missionaries arrived, and who therefore welcomed the news about Jesus with open arms. What the Old Testament prepares us to expect is replicated in the history of crosscultural mission.

The possibility that God may in his sovereign grace save some whom the church may never reach with the gospel (or who died before the church could ever have reached them) does not lessen the church's obligation in mission and evangelism. If God, in the sovereignty of his grace but independently of human evangelistic activity, initiates in the heart of any human a response of repentance and faith that leads to their final salvation through Christ, this will be a matter of rejoicing when we do meet them, here or in the new creation. But it gives us no more valid reason to disobey the Great Commission than does the biblical doctrine of election, though that has also been accused of disincentivizing evangelism. The only way we can be sure, from our perspective, that people are being saved is to be faithful in our witness and see people responding in repentance and faith to Christ.

nine

CONVERSION

John Stott

Mission is the loving service that God sends his people into the world to render. It includes both evangelism and social action, for each is in itself an authentic expression of love, and neither needs the other to justify it. Yet because of the appalling lostness of humanity there is an insistent urgency about our evangelistic task. The nature of evangelism is a faithful proclamation of the good news. Dialogue is its necessary preliminary inasmuch as listening must precede proclaiming, and the salvation that is its goal is personal freedom through Christ, though with unavoidable social implications in anticipation of the eschatological "freedom of glory" when God makes all things new. Our fifth word is *conversion*. It denotes the response that the good news demands and without which salvation cannot be received.

THE CONTEMPORARY DISTASTE FOR "CONVERSION"

Yet *conversion* is another unpopular word today. One reason for this unpopularity is the impression of arrogant imperialism that some evangelists have sometimes given. If ever our evangelism descends to the level of "empire building," "scalp hunting" or boasting about numbers, then of course we bring the word *conversion* into disrepute.

To such perverted forms of evangelism, however, it would be better to apply the term *proselytism*, for evangelism and proselytism are emphatically not identical activities. True, it is difficult to find a satisfactory definition of each, so that Bishop Lesslie Newbigin has written, "One is inclined to conclude that the only workable distinction is that evangelism is what we do and proselytism is what others do."[1]

A helpful distinction has been made by the WCC, when they speak of proselytism as follows:

> Proselytism . . . is the corruption of witness. Witness is corrupted when cajolery, bribery, undue pressure or intimidation is used—subtly or openly—to bring about seeming conversion; when we put the success of our church before the honour of Christ; . . . when personal or corporate self-seeking replaces love for every individual soul for whom we are concerned. Such corruption of the Christian witness indicates lack of confidence in the power of the Holy Spirit, lack of respect for the nature of man and lack of recognition of the true character of the Gospel.[2]

The Lausanne Covenant includes a rather similar statement. It confesses that we are guilty of "worldliness" whenever, "desirous to ensure a response to the gospel, we have compromised our message, manipulated our hearers through pressure techniques and become unduly preoccupied with statistics or even dishonest in our use of them."[3]

Over against the use of coercion and the unseemly spirit of triumphalism one can welcome J. C. Hoekendijk's insistence on the opposite qualities: "To evangelise is to sow and wait in respectful humility and in expectant hope: in humility because the seed we sow has to die, in hope because we expect that God will quicken this seed and give it its proper body."[4]

If such misguided forms of evangelism cause a revulsion against conversion, another reason is the popularity of religious relativism and universalism. For relativism declares that no religion has finality, while universalism declares that no human being is lost. According to some forms of universalist theology, universal salvation has already been accomplished by Jesus Christ. The whole human race has already been reconciled to God by Christ. If that were true, then the only function left to evangelism would be to acquaint the ignorant of this good news, and conversion would cease to indicate a change of any kind except in a person's awareness of their true status and identity.

Scripture does not support this view, however. It is true that God is described as having done something objective and decisive through the cross. Thus, "God . . . through Christ reconciled us to himself" and "in Christ God was reconciling the world to himself" (2 Corinthians 5:18-19). But this does not mean that all human beings have actually been reconciled to God. For now he commits to us the ministry and the message of reconciliation. And this ministry and message are not to inform people that they are already reconciled, but rather to beg people on behalf of Christ: "Be reconciled to God." What validity would such an appeal have if those who hear it are already reconciled to God but simply do not know it? We must never expound God's reconciling work in and through Christ in such a way that it eliminates the contemporary need for people to be reconciled to God. As James Denney expressed it, "It is in virtue of something already consummated on His cross that Christ is able to make the appeal to us which He does, and to win the response in which we receive the reconciliation."[5]

So if we are to be truly biblical in our understanding, we must hold together two truths, first that God was "in Christ" reconciling the world to himself, and secondly that we ourselves must be "in Christ" if we are to receive the reconciliation (2 Corinthians 5:18-21; compare 2 Corinthians 5:17; Romans 5:11).

Further, it is our solemn duty to affirm that those to whom we announce the gospel and address our appeal are "perishing." We proclaim to them the good news of Jesus not because they are saved already but in order that they may be saved from perishing. Our responsibility is to "preach peace" in the sense of promising peace with God through Jesus Christ to those who repent and believe. To preach peace in the sense of announcing smooth words to those still in rebellion against God, of saying "peace, peace when there is no peace"—this is the word of a false prophet, not of a true evangelist of Jesus Christ. The gospel brings warning as well as promise, of the retention of sins as well as the remission of sins (John 20:23). "Beware, therefore," warned the apostle Paul, "lest there come upon you what is said in the prophets: 'Behold, you scoffers, and wonder, and perish'" (Acts 13:40-41). *Perish* is a terrible word. So is *hell*. We should, I think, preserve a certain reverent and humble agnosticism about the precise *nature* of hell, as about the precise nature of heaven. Both are beyond our understanding. But we must be absolutely clear and definite about the awful, eternal *reality* of hell. It is not dogmatism that is inappropriate in speaking about the fact of hell; it is glibness and frivolity. How can we think about hell without tears?

CONVERSION AND REGENERATION

If, then, a response to the gospel is necessary, this response is called conversion. What does it mean? In the New Testament the verb *epistrephō* is usually in the middle or passive voice, and for this reason is six times translated to "be converted" (for example, Acts 3:19 AV). But at the same time it has an active sense and means to "turn." When used in ordinary, secular contexts its first meaning is to "turn around," as for example when Jesus turned around in the crowd to see who had touched him (Mark 5:30). Its other meaning is to "return," as when an unwanted greeting returns to its giver (Matthew 10:13), or the demon determines to return to the house he has vacated (Matthew 12:44), although the more usual verb for re-turning is *hypostrephō,* as when the Bethlehem shepherds returned to their sheep and the holy family to Nazareth (Luke 2:20, 39).

When the same verb is used theologically, it is evident that it has not changed its basic meaning. It still signifies to turn from one direction to another, or to return from one place to another. Thus, Christians can be described as having "turned to God from idols" (1 Thessalonians 1:9; compare Acts 14:15) and also, after "straying like sheep," as having "now returned to the Shepherd and Guardian of your souls" (1 Peter 2:25). Since the turn from idols and sin is usually called "repentance," and the turn to God and Christ "faith," we reach the interesting biblical equation that "repentance + faith = conversion."

What, next, is the relation between conversion and regeneration or the new birth? Certainly each belongs to the other as obverse and reverse of the same coin. We can assert without any fear of contradiction that all the converted are regenerate and all the re-generate are converted. It is impossible to envisage or experience either without the other. Nevertheless, they must be distinguished from each other theologically. Three differences may be mentioned.

First, regeneration is God's act, whereas conversion is a human act. Regeneration is a new birth, a birth "from above" (*anōthen*), a birth "of the Spirit." It is the peculiar work of the Holy Spirit who himself infuses life into the dead. Conversion, on the other hand, is what we do when we repent and believe. True, both repentance and faith are God's gifts, and we could neither repent nor believe without his grace (for example, Acts 11:18; 18:27). Nevertheless, what God's grace does is so to set us free from darkness and bondage as to enable us to do the repenting and the believing. I doubt if we need lose sleep over the question of which comes first. Scripture seems to accord the priority now to the one, now to the other. The really important truth is that they are inseparable.

Second, regeneration is unconscious, whereas conversion is normally conscious. The latter is not always so as a *remembered* conscious act, for many people brought up in a Christian home have loved God and believed in Jesus from their earliest years and cannot recall a period in which they did not believe or a moment when they first did. To such people we must say that convertedness as a condition of life is much more important than conversion as a remembered experience. For adults, however, the turn from idols to the living God, and from sin to Christ, is a conscious act of penitence and faith. But regeneration is unconscious. Its results may well be consciously enjoyed, in terms of assurance, release, communion with God, love, joy and peace. Yet the actual passage from death to life is not a felt experience. Indeed, this is what our Lord seems to have meant when he said to Nicodemus, "The wind blows where it wills, and you hear the sound of it, but you do not know whence it comes or whither it goes; so it is with every one who is born of the Spirit" (John 3:8). The new birth itself is a mysterious work. Its consequences, however, are plain. An analogy with physical birth may be helpful. We were not conscious of the process of being born; our self-consciousness has developed subsequently. However, the fact that we are self-consciously alive is itself proof that we were, at some point in the past, actually born! Similarly the reason we may know we are born again is not because we were consciously aware at the time of what was happening, but because we know that our present spiritual life, perceived in our Christian self-consciousness, or rather God-consciousness, must have originated in a spiritual birth.

The third difference between regeneration and conversion is that the former is an instantaneous and complete work of God, whereas the turn of repentance and faith that we call "conversion" is more a process than an event. There can be no doubt of the suddenness of the new birth. The very imagery of birth makes this clear. For though months of gestation precede it and years of growth follow it, birth itself is a crisis event. We are either born or unborn, just as we are either alive or dead. Further, birth is a complete experience. Once born we can never be more born than at the first moment of emergence from the womb. So with the new birth. Regeneration is not a matter of degrees, as if one person could be more regenerate than another. We may indeed be more or less holy, more or less obedient, more or less like Christ and our Heavenly Father—both in comparison with others and in our own changing journey of discipleship. But we cannot be more or less regenerate, any more than we can be more, or less, born.

There is an evident gradualness about many conversions, however. People begin to become troubled in their conscience and to see the need for repentance. The Holy Spirit begins to open their eyes and they begin to see in Jesus Christ the Savior they need. They may then enter a period of struggle, half resisting, half yielding. They may become like Agrippa "almost persuaded," or like the epileptic boy's father simultaneously believing and unbelieving. Even Saul of Tarsus, who is supposed to have been history's most conspicuous example of sudden conversion, was really nothing of the kind. We are not to imagine that he had his first contact with Jesus Christ on the Damascus road, for he had apparently been "kicking against the goads" of Jesus for some time.

No doubt in the experience of many people there is a point at which the turn called conversion becomes complete, and dawning faith becomes saving faith. Moreover, sometimes people are conscious of this moment. Yet the Holy Spirit is a gentle Spirit; he often takes time to turn people around from self-absorption to Christ. And even then, after we may justly be described as "converted Christians," his work is far from done. For although regeneration cannot grow, the repentance and faith that make up conversion may grow, and indeed must. We need a deeper penitence and a stronger faith. Conversion is only a beginning. Before us lies a lifetime of growth into maturity in Christ, of transformation into the image of Christ.

After this attempt to define conversion, both in itself and in its relation to regeneration, we must now explore certain implications of this radical change.

CONVERSION AND REPENTANCE

First, let us consider conversion and the lordship of Christ. We saw in the chapter on evangelism that repentance and faith are the twin demands of the gospel, and we have already noted in this chapter that the two together constitute conversion. It is the element of repentance that is regrettably absent from much modern evangelistic preaching, although it was prominent in the message of our Lord (for example, Mark 1:15; Luke 13:3, 5) and of his apostles (for example, Acts 2:38; 3:19; 17:30).

What is needed in preaching repentance today is both integrity and realism. In all our evangelism there must be integrity. Our anxiety to win converts sometimes induces us to mute the call to repentance. But deliberately to conceal this aspect of our message is as dishonest as it is shortsighted. Jesus himself never glossed over the cost of discipleship, but rather summoned would-be disciples to "sit down first and count the cost," for he was requiring them if they were to follow him to deny themselves, take up their cross and die. Any kind of slick "decisionism" that sacrifices honesty on the altar of statistics is bound to cause other casualties as well, the victims of our own folly. We are under obligation to teach that a new life in Christ will inevitably bring in its wake new attitudes, new ambitions and new standards. For in Christian conversion not only do old things pass away but in their place new things come (2 Corinthians 5:17).

In addition to integrity, our preaching of repentance and of Christ's lordship requires realism. It is not enough to call people to repentance in vague terms, as if conversion could take place in a kind of mystical vacuum out of which all real life has been sucked. When John the Baptist preached his baptism of repentance, he insisted that people responding must "bear fruits that befit repentance." Neither did he leave it there. He went on to specific issues. The affluent must share their surplus wealth with the deprived. Tax collectors must replace extortion by honesty. And soldiers must never use their power to rob people, but rather be content with their wages (Luke 3:8, 10-14). Jesus evidently did the same, for Zacchaeus was quite clear that for him discipleship would involve refunding his illicit gains. Then he went on to give half his capital to the poor, presumably because most of the folk he had robbed he would never be able to trace. We too need to spell out in realistic and concrete terms the contemporary implications of repentance, conversion and the lordship of Jesus Christ.

CONVERSION AND CHURCH

The second implication of conversion is church membership. Some influential voices have been raised, however, to the effect that converts should not necessarily be required to join the church. Indian Christian theologian Dr. M. M. Thomas, for example, argued for what he called "a Christ-centred secular fellowship outside the church" and—in the context of India—"a Christ-centred fellowship of faith and ethics in the Hindu religious community." He elaborated his position by adding that "conversion to Christ" should not necessarily imply "conversion to the Christian community." Instead converts should seek to build up "a Christ-centred fellowship of faith within the society, culture and religion in which they live, transforming their structures and values from within." In his view this might even include a rejection of baptism as having become "a sign not primarily of incorporation into Christ but of proselytism into a socio-political-religious community." A convert from Hinduism should not be obliged to separate himself "from the Hindu community in the social, legal and religious sense."[6]

Revolutionary as Dr. Thomas's proposals sound, I think we need to respond to them sympathetically. The background to his argument is the disastrous development in India and elsewhere of what is usually called "communalism." It is the rise of a Christian community that, instead of being scattered throughout the non-Christian community as salt and light, becomes isolated from it as a distinct cultural entity on its own. I shall have more to say about this cultural question later.

A second reason why one can understand Dr. Thomas's position concerns the state of the church that converts are expected to join. There is so much about churches, not only in India but everywhere, that is unattractive. There is disunity, lack of integrity, power seeking, even corruption and immorality. We may become very disillusioned with the church and wonder why we would want to bring anyone from "outside" into it. Yet surely, in the light of this, our Christian duty is to seek the renewal of the church, not to avoid or abandon it. For it still remains God's church, unless of course it has totally apostatized from the revealed truth of God. Even the Corinthian church with its bitter factions, tolerated immorality, disorders of public worship and doctrinal uncertainties was nevertheless addressed by Paul as "the church of God which is at Corinth" (1 Corinthians 1:2).

From this contemporary debate we need to turn back to the Bible and to its consistent witness that through the historical process God has been and still is calling out a people for himself, a people who are to be distinct from the world in their convictions and standards, while remaining immersed in it. According to the letter to the Ephesians this redeemed community is central both to the gospel and to history. Further, from the day of Pentecost on, when God's people became the Spirit-filled body of Christ, the apostles expected converts to join it. Peter's summons to the people that very day was not only to repent and believe—as if their conversion could remain an individualistic transaction—but also to be baptized and thus to "save themselves" from that "crooked generation" and be "added" to the new community of the Spirit (Acts 2:40-47). Some kind of transfer from one community to another (I shall later qualify what is meant by transfer) was thus envisaged from the beginning. Baptism, in the New Testament, clearly incorporated converts into the worshiping, teaching, serving community of the church.

Indeed, although a certain "human community" doubtless exists outside Christ, and millions of people are searching for it today in the West's depersonalized technocracy, yet we must maintain that "Christian fellowship" is something different in kind. It has a supernatural origin and quality, for it involves fellowship with God as well as with his people. A Christian congregation that calls people to conversion and so to church membership must exhibit visibly "the grace of our Lord Jesus Christ, the love of God and the fellowship of the Holy Spirit."

CONVERSION AND SOCIETY

Third, we must examine the relation between conversion and social responsibility. Personal conversion leads to social action—or should. That is because a convert to Jesus Christ lives in the world as well as in the church, and has responsibilities to the world as well as to the church. I think it is the tendency of churches to "ecclesiasticize" their members that has made so many modern Christians understandably wary of conversion and church membership. Conversion must not take the convert *out of* the world but rather send him or her *back into* it, the same person in the same world, and yet a new person with new convictions and new standards. If Jesus' first command was "come!" his second was "go!"—that is, we are to go back into the world out of which we have come, and go back as Christ's ambassadors.

Paradoxically, conversion combines a turning away from the world (in the sense of its sin and rebellion against God) with a turning toward the world, in the light of our biblical hope and awareness of God's ultimate redemptive purpose for the world.

With his customary simplicity Archbishop Michael Ramsey summed up the alternatives in one of his addresses to those about to be ordained to the pastoral ministry. He said,

> I suggest that there are three broadly contrasted procedures. It is possible to preach the gospel of conversion without any sight of its social context. It is possible to preach a social gospel which omits the reality of conversion to Christ. Be it your wisdom to preach the gospel of conversion, making it clear that it is the whole man with all his relationships who is converted to Jesus as the Lord of all he is and does.[7]

Commitment to Christ involves commitment to the world into which and for which he came.

In October 1973 during the course of a mission in the University of Dar es Salaam, I was given the privilege of a brief audience of President Julius Nyerere. We talked about the degree of Christians' involvement in Tanzania's national development. President Nyerere then said with great emphasis, "I myself am involved. Every Christian should be involved. I sometimes ask people who call themselves 'committed Christians' what they are committed to. Christ was committed to people. We should be also."

CONVERSION AND CULTURE

Fourth, I come to the question of conversion and human culture. We have already touched on it when discussing church membership. Let me now introduce the subject in this way. Some people think and talk about conversion as if it involved no great upheaval, and little if any change in the convert's lifestyle. Others seem to expect such a complete change as virtually to fumigate the convert from all the supposed contamination of his or her former culture. But conversion is not the automatic renunciation of all our inherited culture. True, conversion involves repentance, and repentance is renunciation. Yet this does not require the convert to step right out of their former culture into a Christian subculture that is totally distinctive. Sometimes we seem to expect them to withdraw from the real world altogether!

In both West and East it is vital for us to learn to distinguish between Scripture and culture, and between those things in culture that are inherently evil and must therefore be renounced for Christ's sake and those things that are good or indifferent and may therefore be retained, even transformed and enriched. In the West, conversion may sometimes seem like a step into an out-of-date past.

> Our congregations demand from every new member not only a conversion but also a change in culture. He has to abandon some of his contemporary behaviour and to accept the older patterns prevalent among the majority of the congregation. The new Christian has to learn the old hymns and to appreciate them. He has to learn the language of the pulpit. He has to share in some conservative political opinions. He has to dress a bit oldfashioned. . . . In brief, he has to step back two generations and undergo what one may call a painful cultural circumcision.[8]

In the Majority World too, and wherever a non-Christian religion dominates a country's culture, Christians need great wisdom to discern between what may be retained and what must be renounced. In many cases new converts adopt too negative an attitude to their former culture. This may have several serious consequences. Christians who break loose entirely from the society in which they were nurtured may find themselves rootless and insecure, and may even—with conventional restraints removed—lapse into moral license. They may even develop a Christian "communalism" that gives them a new security in which to live but cuts them off from their former friends and relatives. Also they may arouse opposition. When Christians are seen as undermining the fabric of traditional society, they are regarded as dangerous fanatics and provoke fierce, irrational hostility.

There have been examples of this from the earliest days of the church, as when the Jews accused Stephen of teaching "that this Jesus of Nazareth will . . . change the customs which Moses delivered to us" and when some merchants of Philippi accused Paul and Silas of "disturbing our city" because "they advocate customs which it is not lawful for us Romans to accept or practice" (Acts 6:14; 16:20-21). In both cases, although one context was Jewish and the other Roman, the issue concerned "customs," either the abandonment of old customs or the introduction of new ones. Culture consists of customs, and people feel threatened when their customs are disturbed. Of course, in one sense Jesus Christ is always a disturber of the peace, because he challenges all inherited custom, convention and tradition, and insists that the whole of life must come under his scrutiny and judgment. Yet it is not a necessary part of our Christian allegiance to be iconoclasts, and to destroy the culture of the past for no better reason than that it is old or that it was part of our pre-conversion life. Culture is ambivalent because human beings themselves are ambivalent. As the Lausanne Covenant expressed it, "Because man is God's creature, some of his culture is rich in beauty and goodness. Because he has fallen, all of it is tainted with sin and some of it is demonic."[9] So "culture must always be tested and judged by Scripture," and we need discernment to evaluate it.

Writing against a Muslim background, Bishop Kenneth Cragg sums up well the relation between conversion and culture:

> Baptism, bringing persons within the church, means their incorporation by faith into the supranational fellowship of Christ. It does not, properly understood, deculturalise the new believer; it enchurches him. That "enchurchment," as its impact widens, bears creatively upon all areas of its context. The new

Christian becomes responsible to Christ for his old setting and to his old setting in the new truth. But he is not thereby "going foreign." All that is not incompatible with Christ goes with him into baptism. Conversion is not "migration"; it is the personal discovery of the meaning of the universal Christ within the old framework of race, language and tradition.[10]

CONVERSION AND THE HOLY SPIRIT

The fifth and last aspect of conversion to be developed is its relation to the work of the Holy Spirit. This is the note on which I believe it is right to conclude, for much of what I have written thus far may have seemed too human-centered and human-confident. Mission, I have urged, is what *we* are sent into the world to do. In evangelism *we* do the proclaiming and in dialogue *we* do the listening. Salvation is what *we* long that our friends will receive. And conversion describes (even in the New Testament) what *we* do, both when we ourselves turn to Christ and when we turn others to Christ. Thus people are said in the Acts to "turn to the Lord" (for example, Acts 9:35; 11:21), and Jesus himself spoke of our need to "turn" and humble ourselves like children if we are ever to enter God's kingdom (Matthew 18:3-4). Also John the Baptist was to "turn many of the sons of Israel to the Lord their God" (Luke 1:16), while the apostle Paul was to "turn" many Gentiles "from darkness to light and from the power of Satan to God" (Acts 26:17-18; compare Acts 26:20 and James 5:19-20). But all this language of human activity is seriously misleading if it is taken to mean that in the end mission is a human work and conversion a human achievement.

This is precisely the impression that we often give, however. In this pragmatic age the church easily slips into the outlook of the world and supposes that the key to evangelistic success is business efficiency. So we publish our manuals of instruction on do-it-yourself evangelism and perfect our ecclesiastical methodologies. Mind you, I happen myself to believe in efficiency, and have never found any reason why Christians should be conspicuous for their inefficiency! At the same time, we must never degrade evangelism into being merely or even mainly a technique to be learned or a formula to be recited. Some people seem to look forward with relish to the time when the evangelistic work of the church will be computerized, the whole job will be done by machines instead of people, and the evangelization of the world will be the ultimate triumph of human technology!

In contrast to the proud, self-confident mood of the modern age, the apostles' humble reliance on the power of the Holy Spirit stands out in bold relief. They believed (and we should believe with them) that people are dead in trespasses and sins, blind to spiritual truth, and slaves of sin and Satan. In consequence, they cannot "turn" themselves or save themselves. Neither can any of us "turn" other people or save them. Only the Holy Spirit can open their eyes, enlighten their darkness, liberate them from bondage, turn them to God and bring them out of death into life. Certainly repentance and faith are plainly declared in the New Testament to be a human duty (Acts 2:38; 16:31; 17:30), but, as we have seen, they are also the gift of God (for example, Acts 11:18; Ephesians 2:8; Philippians 1:29). And however perplexing this antinomy may be, it is necessary in our human-centered world to assert it, so that we may humble ourselves before God.

We are all familiar with the development of modern psychological techniques—in advertising (overt and subliminal), in government propaganda, in the deliberate inducement of mass hysteria and in that most wicked assault on the human personality called "brainwashing." But we Christians must make it clear beyond all doubt that evangelism is an entirely different kind of activity. We must refuse to try to bludgeon people into the kingdom of God.

The very attempt is an insult to the dignity of human beings and a sinful usurpation of the prerogatives of the Holy Spirit. It is also unproductive. For one inevitable result of evangelism by unlawful means (what Paul called "disgraceful, underhanded ways," 2 Corinthians 4:2) is the leakage from the church of those whose conversion has thus been "engineered."

Some words of caution now need to be added, lest we draw unwarranted deductions from the necessity of the Holy Spirit's work in evangelism. Let me mention briefly four conclusions that trust in the Holy Spirit cannot justify.

First, trust in the Holy Spirit is no excuse for shoddy preparation. "There is no need for me to prepare before preaching," somebody argues; "I shall rely on the Holy Spirit to give me the words. Jesus himself promised that it would be given us in that hour what we are to say." Such talk sounds plausible, until we remember that misquotation of Scripture is the devil's game. Jesus was referring to the hour of persecution, not of proclamation, and to the prisoner's dock in a law court, not the pulpit in a church. Trust in the Holy Spirit is not intended to save us the bother of preparation. The Holy Spirit can indeed give us utterance if we are suddenly called on to speak and there has been no opportunity to prepare. But he can also clarify and direct our thinking in our study. Indeed, experience suggests that he does a better job there than in the pulpit.

Second, trust in the Holy Spirit cannot justify a general antiintellectualism. The "lofty words and wisdom" that Paul renounced were not doctrinal preaching or the use of his mind, but the popular wisdom of the world and the fancy rhetoric of the Greeks. In contrast to the former he determined to be loyal to the foolish message of the cross, and in contrast to the latter he would rely in his human weakness on the "demonstration of the Spirit and of power" (1 Corinthians 2:4). But Paul was no anti-intellectual. His sermons were full of doctrinal substance and reasoning. He and his fellow apostles were not just heralds announcing good news; they were advocates arguing a case. As Wolfhart Pannenberg has written,

> An otherwise unconvincing message cannot attain the power to convince simply by appealing to the Holy Spirit. . . . The convincingness of the Christian message can stem only from its contents. Where this is not the case, the appeal to the Holy Spirit is no help at all to the preacher. . . . Argumentation and the operation of the Holy Spirit are not in competition with each other. In trusting in the Spirit Paul in no way spared himself thinking or arguing.[11]

Third, trust in the Holy Spirit cannot be used to justify irrelevance. Some say rather piously that the Holy Spirit is himself the complete and satisfactory solution to the problem of communication, and indeed that when he is present and active, then communication ceases to be a problem. What on earth does such a statement mean? Do we now have liberty to be as obscure, confused and irrelevant as we like, and the Holy Spirit will make all things plain? To use the Holy Spirit to rationalize our laziness is nearer blasphemy than piety. Of course *without* the Holy Spirit all our explanations are futile. But this is not to say that *with* the Holy Spirit they are also futile. For the Holy Spirit chooses to work through them. Trust in the Holy Spirit must not be used as a device to save us the labor of biblical and contemporary studies.

Fourth, trust in the Holy Spirit does not justify the suppression of our personality. Some seem to imagine that if the Holy Spirit is to be in full control, they must entirely eliminate themselves. But what doctrine of the Spirit is this? Our understanding of biblical inspiration should have protected us from this mistake. For in the process we call "inspiration," the Spirit did not suppress the personality of the human authors, but first fashioned and then fully used it. Although modern Christian communicators cannot lay claim to a comparable inspiration, they may be sure that the same Spirit has no wish to obliterate their personality either.

What is forbidden us is all rhetorical affection; all deliberate contriving of effect; all artificiality, hypocrisy and playacting; all standing in front of the mirror in order to self-consciously plan our gestures and grimaces; and all self-advertisement and self-reliance. More positively we are to be ourselves, to be natural, to develop and exercise the gifts that God has given us, and at the same time to rest our confidence not in ourselves but in the Holy Spirit who deigns to work through us.

All down its history, the Christian church seems to have oscillated from one extreme to the other. At times it is so worldly that it goes to the extreme of self-confidence, as if evangelism were merely a question of business efficiency and human technique. At other times it becomes so otherworldly that it goes to the opposite extreme of self-depreciation, as if evangelism were entirely the work of the Holy Spirit and we had nothing whatever to contribute. But a truly biblical understanding of the purpose of the Spirit to work through some human beings to lead others to conversion would deliver us from both these extremes of self-reliance and self-despair, of pride and laziness.

What Scripture lays on us instead is the need for a proper combination of humility and humanity—the humility to let God be God, acknowledging that he alone can give sight to the blind and life to the dead, and the humanity to be ourselves as God has made us, not suppressing our personal individuality, but exercising our God-given gifts and offering ourselves to God as instruments of righteousness in his hand. I wonder if anything is more needed for the Christian mission in the modern age than this healthy fusion of humility and humanity in our reliance on the power of the Holy Spirit.

ten

REFLECTIONS ON CONVERSION

Chris Wright

H e being dead yet speaketh" (Hebrews 11:4 KJV), words sometimes found on the gravestones of famous Christian preachers or writers, could well be applied to John Stott.[1] Again and again, as I have read and reread the chapters of this small book, I have been amazed at how often he anticipated, in a short paragraph or even a passing sentence, issues that have engaged the minds of Christian theologians—especially missiologists—in debates that have waged on through the following decades. Three such issues in this chapter stand out.

CONVERSION AND "INSIDER MOVEMENTS"

In the section "Conversion and Church," Stott quotes M. M. Thomas, a renowned Indian scholar only a few years older than him.[2]

> Dr. M. M. Thomas, for example, argued for what he called "a Christ-centered secular fellowship outside the church" and— in the context of India—"a Christ-centered fellowship of faith and ethics in the Hindu religious community." He elaborated

his position by adding that "conversion to Christ" should not necessarily imply "conversion to the Christian community." Instead converts should seek to build up "a Christ-centered fellowship of faith within the society, culture and religion in which they live, transforming their structures and values from within." . . . A convert from Hinduism should not be obliged to separate himself "from the Hindu community in the social, legal and religious sense."

What M. M. Thomas "argued for" has, in fact, been happening on a remarkable scale in recent decades, not only in India among people living within a Hindu culture, but in several majority Muslim countries. The phenomenon has come to be referred to as "insider movements"—that is, movements of people to faith in Jesus as Savior and Lord, while remaining "inside" their former and surrounding faith communities, or at any rate not leaving those communities in a visible way by joining an established Christian church (or creating one in the traditional image). Not surprisingly, this is a development that has aroused considerable controversy among both theologians and practitioners of Christian mission.

It is remarkable that, although there is no doubt that Stott disagreed with M. M. Thomas at many points (and said so in some of his other writings), his initial response on this point is far from hostile. He writes, "Revolutionary as Dr. Thomas's proposals sound, I think we need to respond to them sympathetically." He gives two reasons for his "sympathy": First, the "disastrous" results of extracting converts from their cultural environment into Christian churches and communities that are effectively isolated from the wider society, and have little influence as salt and light. And, second, the "unattractive" nature of the church that converts are expected to join. To these sad realities, others could doubtless be added. In some countries the word *Christian* is associated with all kinds of historical baggage (whether deserved or not is beside the point—the perception is reality for many), including the legacy of the Crusades, colonialism and the feeling that Christianity is an alien, "Western religion" imposed by missionaries and imperialists. Since the word *Christian* itself began as a nickname and occurs only three times in the New Testament, the argument goes, why should those who come to faith in Jesus be *required* to adopt a name that is immediately open to distorted assumptions, prejudice and hostility? We should distinguish, it is urged, between the genuine "offense of the cross"—the cost of discipleship itself—from the historic and offensive accretions of Christianity as a religious, cultural and institutional phenomenon.

The controversy over "insider movements" tends to crystallize around a few core questions. Are those who profess faith in Jesus yet retain some or most of their association with the religion of their surrounding cultural community not engaged in a form of syncretism that effectively denies the uniqueness of Jesus Christ? But if the alternative (clear renunciation of their family's and community's religious practice along with public confession of Christ) leads to rejection, expulsion and even (as if often does) death, is that not worse? Or, on the contrary, are those things not the expected cost of confessing Christ, including martyrdom, according to the New Testament?

In missiological circles, the debate has raged over whether insider movements should simply be recognized (where they are even visible to "outsiders" at all), with a humble acceptance of the sovereignty of God's Spirit to work where and how he wishes, or whether such insider movements should actually be fostered and encouraged as a matter of mission strategy, or actively discouraged as a betrayal of the gospel and a serious threat to people's genuine salvation.[3] And for some of us, another question arises: What gives those of us who live in the West, who live and breathe one of the most syncretized forms of Christian faith the world has seen, the right to dictate what does or does not "count" as "real" allegiance to Christ in very different cultures where God is at work? Why must we, in our habitual urge to manage and strategize, be the ones to provide the labels and taxonomies and criteria?

My point here, however, is not to survey that whole missiological debate, but simply to point out how Stott anticipates it as he reflects on what conversion *should* mean, but also what it *need not* mean. I am sure that for all Stott's "sympathy" with M. M. Thomas's call for a more truly indigenous Indian expression of faith in Jesus, he would have been very alert to the dangers of syncretism, and would have been concerned that new converts to Christ, no matter how "inside" they may be, should grow up in Christ, should learn the distinctive truth and unique redemptive story of the whole Bible, and be assured of their identity as communities of Jesus followers— even if all that has to take place somehow without the trappings of institutional Christianity and traditional church structures, where they are alien to that culture. I never had the opportunity to discuss this missiological issue with Stott, but I can imagine he would have handled it with his characteristic balance and discernment: being greatly encouraged by the manifest work of God's Spirit in the empirical fact that many people from diverse religious backgrounds are becoming followers of Jesus (and thereby members of his church, even where no institutional church may exist, or be allowed to), while at the same time being anxious that such discipleship should be protected from the dangers, so evident in the Bible, of mixing the worship of the living God with idolatrous assumptions drawn from an unchallenged surrounding cultural worldview.

Since I do know that he had the whole of the Cape Town Commitment read to him, and rejoiced to agree with it, I expect he would have endorsed its paragraphs (necessarily brief) on the matter. They come within section IIC, "Living the Love of Christ Among People of Other Faiths," and read as follows:

Love respects diversity of discipleship

So called "insider movements" are to be found within several religions. These are groups of people who are now following Jesus as their God and Saviour. They meet together in small groups for fellowship, teaching, worship and prayer centred around Jesus and the Bible while continuing to live socially and culturally within their birth communities, including some elements of its religious observance. This is a complex phenomenon and there is much disagreement over how to respond to it. Some commend such movements. Others warn of the danger of syncretism. Syncretism, however, is a danger found among Christians everywhere as we express our faith within our own cultures. We should avoid the tendency, when we see God at work in unexpected or unfamiliar ways, either (i) hastily to classify it and promote it as a new mission strategy, or (ii) hastily to condemn it without sensitive contextual listening.

A. In the spirit of Barnabas who, on arrival in Antioch, "saw the evidence of the grace of God" and "was glad and encouraged them all to remain true to the Lord [Acts 11:20-24]," we would appeal to all those who are concerned with this issue to:

i. Take as their primary guiding principle the apostolic decision and practice: "We should not make it difficult for the Gentiles who are turning to God [Acts 15:19]."

ii. Exercise humility, patience and graciousness in recognizing the diversity of viewpoints, and conduct conversations without stridency and mutual condemnation [Romans 14:1-3].[4]

CONVERSION, CHURCH AND GOSPEL

Still in that section "Conversion and Church," Stott turns to the Bible and reminds us that the church is not a building or an institution, but a people—indeed *the* people whom God has been, and still is, calling and creating for himself. Stott does not mention the Old Testament by name, but by referring to the Bible's "consistent witness" and "the historical process" he doubtless intends us to understand that God's people span all the ages of both Testaments through the whole Bible story. Then he adds, in one of those amazingly condensed but "pregnant" sentences, "According to the letter to the Ephesians this redeemed community is central both to the gospel and to history."

And of course, not only was he right, but also he anticipates the growing awareness of two things that have become more sharply focused in recent evangelical theology: that the church, by its existence, is an integral part of what the gospel means; and that the church is in its essence missional (which is why it is central also "to history"). Or in technical language, we should neither divorce our ecclesiology from our soteriology, nor our missiology from our ecclesiology.

But why single out Ephesians? The most immediate reason is that it was very much on his mind at the time. When, in 1979, he published his exposition of Ephesians, *God's New Society*, he tells us in the preface that "during the past five years and more I have been studying the text of Ephesians, absorbing its message, feeling its impact and dreaming its dream."[5] So it is not surprising that his sentence quoted above is reflected in two subheadings of his comments on Ephesians 3. After stating that "the major lesson taught by this first half of Ephesians 3 is the biblical centrality of the church," he outlines how "the church is central to history" and "the church is central to the gospel."

As for *history*, Paul speaks about the eternal purpose of God, a divine plan that belongs to history and eternity, the creation of a multinational community of reconciled Jews and Gentiles, "which has no territorial frontiers, which claims the whole world for Christ," "his own new society, the beginning of his new creation." That is a missional understanding of the church, because it sees the church as integral to the ultimate mission of God to bring the whole creation into unity under Christ (Ephesians 1:10).

As for the *gospel*, Paul has argued that God's goal of cosmic integration in chapter 1 has issued in ethnic reconciliation (Ephesians 2:11–3:11) between Jew and Gentile. And he sees that as the peacemaking accomplishment of Christ through the cross (Ephesians 2:14-18), and the outworking of the "mystery" of the gospel itself (Ephesians 3:3-6). The gospel is the good news of what God has done, and that includes the fact that he has created a reconciled community—reconciled to God and to one another in Christ.

> The good news of the unsearchable riches of Christ which Paul preached is that he died and rose again not only to save sinners like me (though he did), but also to create a single new humanity; not only to redeem us from sin but also to adopt us into God's family; not only to reconcile us to God but also to reconcile us to one another. Thus the church is an integral part of the gospel. The gospel is good news of a new society as well as of a new life.[6]

This perception of the church as central to the gospel and mission can be seen in other parts of Paul's writings. In Colossians 1:15-20, he includes the church, the body of which Christ is the head, within his survey of the supremacy of Christ over "all things in heaven and on earth," by right of creation, redemption and inheritance. Paul regards the Christian community of believers in Corinth, for all their faults, as "a letter from Christ" (2 Corinthians 3:2-3), demonstrating the truth and authenticity of the apostolic gospel. He commends their contribution (as Gentiles) to the collection for the

famine-stricken poor in Jerusalem (Jewish believers) as their "obedience in acknowledging the gospel of Christ" (2 Corinthians 9:13).
And he could assure the Gentile believers in Galatia that their faith
in the Messiah Jesus had incorporated them into the spiritual seed
of Abraham—and that that in itself was the substantive demonstration of God's faithfulness to his promise to Abraham, which
Paul expresses with explicitly gospel language. "Scripture, fore-
seeing that God would justify the Gentiles by faith, preached the
gospel beforehand to Abraham, saying, 'In you shall all the nations
be blessed'" (Galatians 3:8).

For Paul, the gospel (the good news that God promised the world)
began in Genesis and is now made visible in the church—and visible
not only on earth. The church, according to Paul in Ephesians 3
(meaning, in context, the church as the new humanity of reconciled
Jews and Gentiles through the cross), is God's showcase to the whole
cosmos of spiritual powers, proving the truth of "the mystery of
Christ" and the accomplishment of God's great redemptive mission:
"Through the church the manifold wisdom of God might now be
made known to the principalities and powers in the heavenly places.
This was according to the eternal purpose which he has realized in
Christ Jesus our Lord" (Ephesians 3:10-11).

And since the church is central to the gospel, how the church
behaves, in living, loving and worshiping together, is a central part
of its witness and mission in the world—as Paul so regularly goes
on to insist. The church is not just the mail carrier delivering the
message, but in itself is an embodiment of the message (however
imperfectly in this fallen world).

This gospel- and mission-centered nature of the church has been
taken up in recent works. It is strongly evident, for example, in the
work of N. T. Wright (so much so that he has sometimes been accused—quite wrongly in my view—as *substituting* ecclesiology for
soteriology).[7] It is also a major concern of Scot McKnight in various

writings, most recently *Kingdom Conspiracy.*[8] My own book *The Mission of God's People: A Biblical Theology of the Church's Mission* stresses the historical continuity of God's people through the whole Bible from Genesis onward, and how they (we) are called into existence to be a people who embody the good news of the biblical gospel, who bear witness to it in word and deed as the essence of our mission—our reason for existence within history.[9] And, like so many other "recent" favorite missiological themes, this understanding of the centrality of the church to both gospel and mission was already heralded in the work of Lesslie Newbigin, who spoke of "the congregation as hermeneutic of the gospel" with the powerful, missional, words, "How is it possible that the gospel should be credible, that people should come to believe that the power which has the last word in human affairs is represented by a man hanging on a cross? I am suggesting that the only answer, the only hermeneutic of the gospel, is a congregation of men and women who believe it and live by it."[10]

As I said, Stott had this theme very much on his mind in the 1970s, and it is evident also in the 1974 Lausanne Covenant. The following words come from paragraph 6, "The Church and Evangelism": "The church is at the very centre of God's cosmic purpose and is his appointed means of spreading the Gospel. But a church which preaches the Cross must itself be marked by the Cross." This leads to an ethical imperative, reminiscent of the way Paul moves from the indicative of the gospel to the imperative that must characterize those who believe and obey the gospel. "[The church] becomes a stumbling block to evangelism when it betrays the Gospel or lacks a living faith in God, genuine love for people, or scrupulous honesty in all things including promotion and finance."[11]

The same integration of ecclesial, missional and ethical dimensions lives on within the Lausanne Movement, in the Cape Town Commitment. It is interesting that the section on the *church* (part

I.9, "We Love the People of God") moves rapidly to the role of the church in relation to mission, and the ethical demands that generates, while the section on *mission* (part I.10, "We Love the Mission of God") moves rapidly to the identity and role of the church and the quality of its life in the world. Ecclesiology and missiology cannot be pulled apart.

> *The people of God are those from all ages and all nations whom God in Christ has loved, chosen, called, saved and sanctified as a people for his own possession, to share in the glory of Christ as citizens of the new creation. As those, then, whom God has loved from eternity to eternity and throughout all our turbulent and rebellious history, we are commanded to love one another. For "since God so loved us, we also ought to love one another," and thereby "be imitators of God . . . and live a life of love, just as Christ loved us and gave himself up for us." Love for one another in the family of God is not merely a desirable option but an inescapable command. Such love is the first evidence of obedience to the gospel, the necessary expression of our submission to Christ's Lordship, and a potent engine of world mission* [2 Thessalonians 2:13-14; 1 John 4:11; Ephesians 5:2; 1 Thessalonians 1:3; 4:9-10; John 13:35].

A) *Love calls for unity.* Jesus' command that his disciples should love one another is linked to his prayer that they should be one. Both the command and the prayer are missional—"that the world may know you are my disciples," and that "the world may know that you [the Father] sent me" [John 13:34-35; 17:21]. A most powerfully convincing mark of the truth of the gospel is when Christian believers are united in love across the barriers of the world's inveterate divisions— barriers of race, colour, gender, social class, economic privilege or political alignment. However, few things so destroy our testimony as when Christians mirror and amplify the very same divisions among themselves. We urgently seek a new global partnership within the body of Christ across all continents, rooted in profound mutual love, mutual submission, and dramatic economic sharing without paternalism or unhealthy dependency. And we seek this not only as a demonstration of our unity in the gospel, but also for the sake of the name of Christ and the mission of God in all the world.[12]

After summarizing the mission of God, as "central to our understanding of God, the Bible, the Church, human history and the ultimate future," the section on mission continues:

Our participation in God's mission. God calls his people to share his mission. The Church from all nations stands in continuity through the Messiah Jesus with God's people in the Old Testament. With them we have been called through Abraham and commissioned to be a blessing and a light to the nations. With them, we are to be shaped and taught through the law and the prophets to be a community of holiness, compassion and justice in a world of sin and suffering. We have been redeemed through the cross and resurrection of Jesus Christ, and empowered by the Holy Spirit to bear witness to what God has done in Christ. The Church exists to worship and glorify God for all eternity and to participate in the transforming mission of God within history. Our mission is wholly derived from God's mission, addresses the whole of God's creation, and is grounded at its centre in the redeeming victory of the cross. This is the people to whom we belong, whose faith we confess and whose mission we share.[13]

And this is the people, we might add, in relation to the theme of Stott's chapter, into which converts are grafted, when they become repentant, trusting and obedient disciples of Jesus Christ—whatever kind of "church" they may or may not be aligned with in their immediate culture and historical circumstances.

CONVERSION, CULTURE AND CONTEXTUALIZATION

The section "Conversion and Culture" in Stott's chapter raises issues that have deep roots in the history of the church (and by that I mean that they go right back into the Old Testament too), and continue to exercise the heads, hearts and hands of mission theologians, strategists and practitioners.

Given the prominence of the "contextualization" debate (or "enculturation" as it has been called in the Roman Catholic church), in the history of Christian mission (and not just in modern times; the Jesuit mission movements struggled with it in India and China), it is well worth remembering that the relationship between the people of God and the cultures that they necessarily inhabit (there is no human life without culture) is an issue in the Bible itself. The New Testament shows the earliest followers of Jesus working hard to relate the claims and challenges of their faith to the cultures of first-century Judaism and then to Greek and Roman cultures. But also in the Old Testament, Israel faced the challenge of a whole sequence of ambient cultures (ancient Mesopotamian, Egyptian, Canaanite, Babylonian, Persian, Greek)—with an all-too-human mixture of successful distinctiveness and abject capitulating accommodation. So much of the message of the Torah and the Prophets is illuminated by understanding this struggle—which was at heart a missional one: would they *live* as a nation among the nations (a culture in the midst of cultures), as the distinctive ("holy") people God had created and called them to *be*? That is a major thrust of the great "sermon" we know as the book of Deuteronomy.[14]

Whatever conversion means, then, it has to take place *within* culture—in dynamic and inescapable engagement with culture. That is clearly so when we examine the biblical language used in relation to the phenomenon itself—whether in the Old Testament, with its constant appeals to Israel to "turn" (in all its meanings—to turn away from other gods, to turn back to the living God and so on), or in the New Testament, with the imperative of the kingdom of God on the lips of John the Baptist and Jesus to their fellow Jews to "repent and believe the good news," or the appeal of Paul to pagan polytheists to turn "from idols, to serve a living and true God" (1 Thessalonians 1:9).[15]

This interaction of conversion and culture was explored in some depth in an issue of the *International Bulletin of Missionary Research* titled "Christian Conversion and Mission." Andrew Walls explored the crucial difference between what is known of Jewish proselytism in first-century Judaism and the nature of Christian evangelism and conversion practiced by Paul and the other apostles among the Gentiles.[16] I surveyed the theme of conversion in both Testaments, noting that it included the radical displacement of all other gods, ethical transformation and significant missional implications connected to the blessing of the nations.[17]

Stott makes some seminal statements in this section, worth quoting again.

> Conversion is not the automatic renunciation of all our inherited culture. True, conversion involves repentance, and repentance is renunciation. Yet this does not require the convert to step right out of his former culture into a Christian subculture that is totally distinctive. . . .
>
> Christians who break loose entirely from the society in which they were nurtured may find themselves rootless and insecure, and may even—with conventional restraints removed—lapse into moral license. They may even develop a Christian "communalism" that gives them a new security in which to live but cuts them off from their former friends and

relatives. Also they may arouse opposition. When Christians are seen as undermining the fabric of traditional society, they are regarded as dangerous fanatics and provoke fierce, irrational hostility.

As we saw earlier, that speaks straight into the controversy over "insider movements." Stott would not, of course, have regarded such a brief observation to be in any sense the last word on a very complex issue. But it does show he was aware of the kind of problems that "insider movements" seek to overcome—however controversial they may then prove to be for theologically minded and mission-committed observers. He writes,

> It is vital for us to learn to distinguish between Scripture and culture, and between those things in culture that are inherently evil and must therefore be renounced for Christ's sake and those things that are good or indifferent and may therefore be retained, even transformed and enriched. . . .
>
> It is not a necessary part of our Christian allegiance to be iconoclasts, and to destroy the culture of the past for no better reason than that it is old or that it was part of our preconversion life. Culture is ambivalent because human beings themselves are ambivalent. As the Lausanne Covenant expressed it, "Because man is God's creature, some of his culture is rich in beauty and goodness. Because he has fallen, all of it is tainted with sin and some of it is demonic." So "culture must always be tested and judged by Scripture," and we need discernment to evaluate it.

As I just said, that process of discernment is evident within the Bible itself. In one of my own earliest books (in which I am sure I was influenced by having read this 1975 book by Stott), I explored how the Old Testament bears witness to Israel's complex relationship to surrounding culture—in ways that echo Stott's first paragraph above. We can observe that Israel's response (evident particularly in the Torah) ranged from total "rejection and prohibition" through "qualified toleration" (for example, of polygamy, divorce and slavery) to "critical affirmation" (for example, of the importance of kinship and family cohesion and viability).[18]

Very soon after Lausanne 1974 and the publication of this book in 1975, Stott gave his mind, his convening authority, his unmatched skills as a conference chairperson and his drafting abilities to a consultation on this pressing issue of gospel and culture. It took place at Willowbank, Bermuda, in January 1978, and it produced "The Willowbank Report—Gospel and Culture." It is an outstanding thirty-six-page document that still offers some exceptionally clear definitions, distinctions, theological reflections and practical recommendations. It begins as follows:

> The process of communicating the gospel cannot be isolated from the human culture from which it comes, or from that in which it is to be proclaimed. This fact constituted one of the preoccupations of the Lausanne Congress on World Evangelization in July 1974. So the Lausanne Committee's Theology and Education Group convened a consultation on this topic to meet in January 1978. It brought 33 theologians, anthropologists, linguists, missionaries and pastors together from all six continents to study "Gospel and Culture." Cosponsored by the Lausanne Committee's Strategy Working Group, it had four goals:
>
> 1. To develop our understanding of the interrelation of the gospel and culture with special reference to God's revelation, to our interpretation and communication of it, and to the response of the hearers in their conversion, their churches and their life style.

2. To reflect critically on the implications of the communication of the gospel cross-culturally.

3. To identify the tools required for more adequate communication of the gospel.

4. To share the fruits of the consultation with Christian leaders in Church and mission.

Many mission agencies and many Christian churches in countries that had been former "mission fields," and were therefore seeking to work through the issues of a postmissionary engagement with their indigenous cultures, found some very helpful guidelines in this document—one of the earliest of the Lausanne Occasional Papers.[19]

The literature on contextualization and the relationship between gospel, mission and culture has grown steadily since the 1970s, as has the number of conferences and consultations convened to wrestle with the issues involved. The following endnote samples only a small selection of titles, some of which include much more extensive bibliographies.[20]

But we should give John Stott himself the final word. As so often, he returned from contemplating all kinds of human questions, strategies, challenges and intentions to summon us to humility before God. Whatever mission may mean to us, it is God's mission we are called to share. Whatever salvation includes, it is God alone who saves. Whatever conversion entails, it is God who does the turning.

In contrast to the proud, self-confident mood of the modern age, the apostles' humble reliance on the power of the Holy Spirit stands out in bold relief. They believed (and we should believe with them) that people are dead in trespasses and sins, blind to spiritual truth, and slaves of sin and Satan. In consequence, they cannot "turn" themselves or save themselves. Nor can any of us "turn" other people or save them. Only the

Holy Spirit can open their eyes, enlighten their darkness, liberate them from bondage, turn them to God and bring them out of death into life. Certainly repentance and faith are plainly declared in the New Testament to be a human duty (Acts 2:38; 16:31; 17:30), but, as we have seen, they are also the gift of God (for example, Acts 11:18; Ephesians 2:8; Philippians 1:29). And however perplexing this antinomy may be, it is necessary in our human-centered world to assert it, so that we may humble ourselves before God.

NOTES

CHAPTER ONE: MISSION

[1]Lausanne Covenant, paragraph 5.

[2]W. A. Visser 't Hooft, in *The Uppsala 68 Report*, ed. Norman Goodall (Geneva: WCC, 1968), 317-18.

[3]Lausanne Covenant, paragraph 6.

CHAPTER TWO: REFLECTIONS ON MISSION

[1]I have explored this dimension of mission in more detail in "People Who Send and Are Sent," in Christopher J. H. Wright, *The Mission of God's People: A Biblical Theology of the Church's Mission* (Grand Rapids: Zondervan, 2010), 201-21.

[2]Cape Town Commitment, I.10. Bible references original to the text of the statement.

[3]I should recall that when I first used this word *missional* in John Stott's presence, he looked somewhat askance. "Is that really a word?" he inquired with an infinitesimally raised eyebrow. He was an avid consulter of dictionaries. To be honest, it is a relatively recent coinage (in 2008 *Christianity Today* referred to it as scarcely ten years old). I explained (as I do in *The Mission of God: Unlocking the Bible's Grand Narrative* [Downers Grove, IL: InterVarsity Press, 2006], 22-25), that it is a *needed* word, since *missionary* has too much baggage, and *missiological* refers to theological reflection on mission. *Missional* means a quality or a dimension that pertains to, or contributes to, or applies to, or is characterized by mission.

[4]J. Andrew Kirk, *What Is Mission? Theological Explorations* (London:

Darton, Longman & Todd, 1999), 20. The phrase "the Bible as a book about mission" of course begs the question. That is to say, it assumes an answer to the question, "Whose mission?" Only when we start our definition of mission by reference to God is it possible to say that the whole Bible is "about mission," or make sense of the idea that it is "written by missionaries for missionaries." The latter phrase can be true, not in the sense that the Bible authors were sent out by the church like modern missionaries, but only in that they were in some sense commissioned by God for *his* purposes, including his purpose in inspiring the writings that were collated into the canon of Scripture. Kirk's language makes sense only when we see the Bible itself as the product of, and witness to, the mission of God.

[5]David Bosch, *Transforming Mission: Paradigm Shifts in Theology of Mission* (Maryknoll, NY: Orbis, 1991), 494. A richly informative compilation of key theological texts in relation to every chapter of Bosch's book is Norman E. Thomas, ed., *Classic Texts in Mission and World Christianity: A Reader's Companion to David Bosch's Transforming Mission* (Maryknoll, NY: Orbis, 1995).

[6]It might be appropriate to add that *The Mission of God* was written after I had left All Nations in 2001 and taken on the leadership of the Langham Partnership, founded by John Stott. As a result, much of the book was written at Stott's own writing retreat, The Hookses, in Wales, and often when we were there together. He took a great interest in the work and encouraged me constantly in it, often discussing this or that topic or biblical text. I think the book aligns well with the trajectory of Stott's own implicitly missional reading of Scripture (even if he could never quite welcome the neologism *missional!*).

[7]Indeed the shift toward seeing mission as not merely an activity of the church, but fundamentally as the purpose and action of the Trinity—the *missio Dei* as it is classically known—goes back much further in ecumenical circles, to the International Missionary Council that met in Willingen, Germany, in 1952. And even earlier, interest in reading the biblical texts from a missionary perspective attracted even the renowned British Old Testament scholar H. H. Rowley, in *Israel's Mission to the World* (London: SCM Press, 1939) and *The Missionary Message of the Old Testament* (London: Carey, 1944).

[8]Lesslie Newbigin, *Trinitarian Doctrine for Today's Mission* (London: Edin-

burgh House, 1963; repr., Carlisle, UK: Paternoster, 1998); *The Open Secret: An Introduction to the Theology of Mission* (Grand Rapids: Eerdmans, 1978); *Foolishness to the Greeks: Gospel and Western Culture* (Grand Rapids: Eerdmans, 1986); *The Gospel in a Pluralist Society* (Grand Rapids: Eerdmans, 1989); *Truth to Tell: The Gospel as Public Truth* (London: SPCK, 1991).

[9]See the Gospel and Our Culture website at gocn.org. A very helpful survey of the different senses in which the phrase "missional hermeneutic" is being used by various scholars (including myself) is provided on this site in an article by George R. Hunsberger, "Proposals for a Missional Hermeneutic: Mapping the Conversation," January 28, 2009, www.gocn.org /resources/newsletters/2009/01/gospel-and-our-culture. See the website for the Newbigin House of Studies at newbiginhouse.org.

[10]See Michael W. Goheen, *Introducing Christian Mission Today: Scripture, History and Issues* (Downers Grove, IL: InterVarsity Press, 2014). This builds on Goheen's earlier work in Craig G. Bartholomew and Michael W. Goheen, *The Drama of Scripture: Finding our Place in the Biblical Story* (Grand Rapids: Eerdmans, 2004). See Scott W. Sunquist, *Understanding Christian Mission: Participation in Suffering and Glory* (Grand Rapids: Baker, 2013).

[11]Stott refers to the practical, loving, serving work of the church in society as a crucial dimension of how local church evangelism works out in practice (and he made sure that his own church practiced it) in his earlier book on evangelism, *Our Guilty Silence: The Gospel, the Church and the World* (London: Hodder & Stoughton, 1967; repr., Leicester, UK: Inter-Varsity Press, 1997), 77. But he does not directly address in that book the question of how evangelism and social action are to be related— theologically and in mission. He did later tackle it briefly, with much the same concern as in this book to avoid the extremes of evangelical withdrawal from the world and ecumenical equation of evangelism with sociopolitical action, in *Christ the Controversialist: A Study in Some Essentials of Evangelical Religion* (London: Tyndale, 1970), 185-89; rev. ed., *Christ in Conflict* (Downers Grove, IL: InterVarsity Press, 2013), 175-181. The issue surged to major importance at and after the Lausanne Congress of 1974.

[12]The impression that Stott made on them, as one who listened attentively and sought to understand their contexts and commitments, is told by themselves in their contributions to Christopher J. H. Wright, ed., *Portraits of a Radical Disciple* (Downers Grove, IL: InterVarsity Press, 2011), 112-18, 119-21.

[13]Lausanne Covenant, paragraph 5.

[14]Kevin DeYoung and Greg Gilbert, *What Is the Mission of the Church? Making Sense of Social Justice, Shalom and the Great Commission* (Wheaton, IL: Crossway, 2011), 59. I think their criticism of Stott somewhat unfairly misinterprets him, but that is an argument for elsewhere.

[15]In addition, one might add, Stott built up a model of gospel-centered, holistic mission in his own church, All Souls, Langham Place, London, that still characterizes its ministry. Stott not only pioneered various fruitful forms of local church evangelism but also initiated ministries among the poor and the homeless, as well as stressing the importance of equipping Christian laypeople for ministry and mission in and through their daily work. Fascinating details of his systematic structuring of the whole life and work of All Souls around such a comprehensive missional agenda are recorded in *Our Guilty Silence.*

[16]The full report of that event is available as Lausanne Occasional Paper 21, www.lausanne.org/content/lop/lop-21. It can also be read, along with other major Lausanne documents between 1974 and 1989, in John Stott, ed., *Making Christ Known: Historic Mission Documents from the Lausanne Movement 1974–1989* (Grand Rapids: Eerdmans, 1997), 165-213.

[17]The Manila Manifesto, paragraph 4, "The Gospel and Social Responsibility," www.lausanne.org/content/manifesto/the-manila-manifesto.

[18] Michael W. Goheen, *Introducing Christian Mission Today,* (Downers Grove, IL: InterVarsity Press, 2014), 82-83; quoting from Lesslie Newbigin, *One Body, One Gospel, One World: The Christian Mission Today* (London: International Missionary Council, 1958), 43-44. David Bosch also adopted Newbigin's distinction favorably: *Transforming Mission* (Maryknoll: Orbis, 1991), 372-73.

[19]John R. W. Stott, *The Contemporary Christian* (Downers Grove, IL: InterVarsity Press, 1992), 337-55.

[20]As early as 1983 I was striving after such a concept of mission in one of my earliest booklets, *The Use of the Bible in Social Ethics* (Cambridge, UK: Grove Books, 1983). I wrote, "The social and evangelistic tasks of the church have to be seen as inseparable parts of its single mission. On the one hand, evangelism which is faithful to the whole biblical gospel must include the social nature of man's constitution, the effects of sin in the realm of social life and relationships, and a challenge to repentance and conversion which has profound effects on that realm. . . . On the other

hand (and this is the more neglected side of the matter), Christian social ethics cannot evade an evangelistic dimension if it is being true to the total biblical basis, motivation, and goal of its operations. . . . Precisely such a unified and integrated [understanding] characterized the public ministry of Jesus: socially effective evangelism; evangelistically effective social action. How many wasted and fruitless hours of argument in Christian gatherings . . . over the imagined competing claims of evangelism and social action would be saved, if it could be seen not only that a fully biblical understanding of mission includes them both, but that in fact each necessarily involves the other, in biblical thought?" (21-22).

[21]Micah Declaration on Integral Mission, September 27, 2001, www .micahnetwork.org/integral-mission. This statement is quoted, along with the Lausanne Covenant, in the Cape Town Commitment, I.10.b.

[22]Cape Town Commitment, I.10.b.

[23]I have since discovered that this imagery of a wheel as a metaphor for integrated mission was used by Martin Alphonse, thinking of a cart-wheel, with its hub integrated through its spokes with the rim. For him, the "hub" was the person and lordship of Jesus Christ—the opening affirmation of the great commission itself. See Martin Alphonse, "Mission on the Move: A Biblical Exposition of the Great Commission," in C. V. Mathew, ed., *Integral Mission: The Way Forward; Essays in Honour of Dr. Saphir P. Athyal* (Tiruvalla, India: CSS Press, 2006), 143-56. See also the interesting collection of essays in Tetsunao Yamamori and C. René Padilla, eds., *The Local Church, Agent of Transformation: An Ecclesiology of Integral Mission* (Buenos Aires: Ediciones Kairos, 2004).

[24]Cape Town Commitment, IID.1.e (italics added).

[25]In preparation for the Cape Town Congress in 2010, the Lausanne Theology Working Group held three consultations in collaboration with the WEA Theological Commission in the preceding years examining each phrase of the familiar slogan "The whole church taking the whole gospel to the whole world." The reports and papers are published in three special issues of *Evangelical Review of Theology*: vol. 33, no. 1 (2009); vol. 34, no. 1 (2010); and vol. 34, no. 3 (2010). The full statement from all three consultations can also be read online at www.lausanne.org/content/twg -three-wholes.

[26]See for example, "Holistic Ministry: Reflections from the Theological Commission of the World Evangelical Alliance," October 2008, www

.worldevangelicals.org/tc/statements/holistic-ministry.htm.

[27]INFEMIT, originally standing for the International Fellowship of Evangelical Mission Theologians, was officially launched in Kenya in 1987, binding together continental mission movements in what was then known as the Two-Thirds World. See its website at http://infemit.org/. It oversees the work of the Oxford Centre for Mission Studies (OCMS) and publishes through Regnum Books. See, for example, René Padilla, "What Is Integral Mission," http://lareddelcamino.net/en/images/Articles /what%20is%20integral%20mission%20cr%20padilla.pdf. The history and current status of the holistic mission movement within the global evangelical community is surveyed in great depth in Brian Woolnough and Wonsuk Ma, eds., *Holistic Mission: God's Plan for God's People* (Oxford: Regnum, 2010). An earlier symposium brought together a number of predominantly Indian scholars to reflect on the holistic nature of mission: see Mathew, ed., *Integral Mission*, foreword by John Stott.

[28]See Dean Flemming, *Recovering the Full Mission of God: A Biblical Perspective on Being, Doing and Telling* (Downers Grove, IL: InterVarsity Press, 2013); Goheen, *Introducing Christian Mission Today*; Sunquist, *Understanding Christian Mission*; Samuel Escobar, *The New Global Mission: The Gospel from Everywhere to Everyone* (Downers Grove, IL: InterVarsity Press, 2003); René Padilla, *Mission Between the Times: Essays on the Kingdom* (Grand Rapids: Eerdmans, 1985); Rosemary Dowsett, *The Great Commission* (London: Monarch, 2001); John Dickson, *The Best Kept Secret of Christian Mission: Promoting the Gospel with More Than Our Lips* (Grand Rapids: Zondervan, 2010); Vinay Samuel and Chris Sugden, eds., *Mission as Transformation: A Theology of the Whole Gospel* (Oxford: Regnum, 2000).

[29]I recall my bemusement when I was asked, in an email, to declare whether I was a "prioritist" or a "holist," and to specify my location on a certain spectrum. I politely declined to label myself according to somebody else's boxes.

[30]Goheen, *Introducing Christian Mission Today*, 232, in his chapter "Holistic Mission: Witness in Life, Word and Deed."

[31]Sunquist, *Understanding Christian Mission*, 320, in his chapter "Witnessing Community: Evangelism and Christian Mission."

[32]The Manila Manifesto, paragraph 4, "The Gospel and Social Responsibility."

³³See the Au Sable Institute website at http://ausable.org and the A Rocha website at arocha.org.

³⁴"On the Care of Creation," Evangelical Environmental Network, accessed April 24, 2015, www.creationcare.org/blank.php?id=39.

³⁵This is a small sample. The later works include substantial bibliographical resources for further exploration of this field. Loren Wilkinson, ed., *Earthkeeping in the Nineties: Stewardship of Creation*, rev. ed. (Grand Rapids: Zondervan, 1991); Ron Elsdon, *Green House Theology: Biblical Perspectives on Caring for Creation* (London: Monarch, 1992); R. J. Berry, *The Care of Creation: Focusing Concern and Action* (Downers Grove, IL: InterVarsity Press, 2000); Edward R. Brown, *Our Father's World: Mobilizing the Church to Care for Creation* (Downers Grove, IL: InterVarsity Press, 2006); Ian Hore-Lacy, *Responsible Dominion; A Christian Approach to Sustainable Development* (Vancouver: Regent College Publishing, 2006); Dave Bookless, *Planetwise: Dare to Care for God's World* (Leicester, UK: Inter-Varsity Press, 2008); Dave Bookless, *God Doesn't Do Waste: Redeeming the Whole of Life* (Leicester, UK: Inter-Varsity Press, 2010); Noah J. Toly and Daniel I. Block, *Keeping God's Earth: The Global Environment in Biblical Perspective* (Downers Grove, IL: InterVarsity Press, 2010); Lowell Bliss, *Environmental Missions: Planting Churches and Trees* (Pasadena, CA: William Carey, 2013); John Stott, *Issues Facing Christians Today*, 4th ed., rev. and updated by Roy McCloughry (Grand Rapids: Zondervan, 2006), 135-60; Wright, *Mission of God*, 397-420; *Mission of God's People*, 48-62, 267-70.

³⁶John Stott, *The Radical Disciple: Wholehearted Christian Living* (Leicester, UK: Inter-Varsity Press, 2010), 55-65.

³⁷Cape Town Commitment, I.7.a-b. Bible references original to the text. Since Cape Town 2010, the Lausanne Movement now also sponsors the Creation Care Network, which produced the "Jamaica Call to Action" after its international consultation in 2012. See www.lausanne.org/content /statement/creation-care-call-to-action.

³⁸John Stott, *The Contemporary Christian* (Downers Grove, IL: Inter-Varsity Press, 1992), 140-42 (italics original).

³⁹"About LICC," London Institute for Contemporary Christianity, accessed April 24, 2015, www.licc.org.uk/about-licc.

⁴⁰Mark Greene, *Thank God It's Monday: Ministry in the Workplace* (Bletchley, UK: Scripture Union, 2009); *The Great Divide* (London: LICC, 2010); *Fruitfulness on the Frontline: Making a Difference Where You Are*

(Leicester, UK: Inter-Varsity Press, 2014). Many others, of course, have written on a biblical and missional understanding of "ordinary work." Outstanding among these are: Paul Stevens, *The Other Six Days: Vocation, Work and Ministry in Biblical Perspective* (Grand Rapids: Eerdmans, 2000); and Timothy Keller, *Every Good Endeavour: Connecting Your Work to God's Plan for the World* (London: Hodder & Stoughton, 2012).

[41]Cape Town Commitment, IIA.3.

CHAPTER THREE: EVANGELISM

[1]Lausanne Covenant, paragraph 6.

[2]Ibid., paragraph 9.

[3]J. I. Packer, *Evangelism and the Sovereignty of God* (Downers Grove, IL: InterVarsity Press, 2008), 45.

[4]W. A. Visser 't Hooft, "Evangelism in the Neo-pagan Situation," *International Review of Mission* 63, no. 249 (1974): 84.

[5]C. H. Dodd, *The Apostolic Preaching and Its Developments* (London: Hodder & Stoughton, 1936).

[6]Ibid., 31.

[7]Ibid., 16, 30.

[8]René Padilla, in J. D. Douglas, ed., *Let the Earth Hear His Voice* (Minneapolis: Worldwide Publications, 1975), 128-29.

[9]Samuel Escobar, in Douglas, ed., *Let the Earth Hear His Voice*, 308.

[10]Lausanne Covenant, paragraph 4.

CHAPTER FOUR: REFLECTIONS ON EVANGELISM

[1]Stott's personal account of his conversion can be read in *Why I Am a Christian: This Is My Story* (Downers Grove, IL: InterVarsity Press, 2003), 14, 29-32. The more detailed account can be found in Timothy Dudley-Smith, *John Stott: The Making of a Leader* (Downers Grove, IL: InterVarsity Press, 1999), 85-102.

[2]I first used the term *ultimacy of evangelism* in *The Mission of God: Unlocking the Bible's Grand Narrative* (Downers Grove, IL: InterVarsity Press, 2006), chap. 13. In a section relating to the necessity of a holistic response to the terrible scourge of HIV/AIDS, I speak of "The ultimacy of evangelism and the nonultimacy of death."

[3]Scot McKnight argues strongly for the need to recover the narrative nature of the gospel, including its roots in the Old Testament promises

of God and the story and hope of Israel, rather than reducing it only to an individual plan of salvation. See McKnight, *The King Jesus Gospel* (Grand Rapids: Zondervan, 2011) and *Kingdom Conspiracy: Returning to the Radical Mission of the Local Church* (Grand Rapids: Brazos, 2014). See also Tom Wright, *How God Became King: Getting to the Heart of the Gospels* (New York: HarperOne, 2012).

[4]Perceiving this universal, missional thrust within the whole Old Testament canon is the argument of, and explains the subtitle of, my book *The Mission of God: Unlocking the Bible's Grand Narrative.*

[5]And indeed God's promise to Eve that her seed would crush the serpent's head (Genesis 3:15) is often referred to as the *protoevangelium*, the "first announcement of the gospel."

[6]Ben Witherington III, *Paul's Narrative Thought World: The Tapestry of Tragedy and Triumph* (Louisville, KY: Westminster John Knox, 1994), 2.

[7]As on many issues, Lesslie Newbigin had already articulated the crucial importance of recovering Christian confidence in the Bible as a universal story that demands to be heard as public truth, not merely one among many books of religion in the world. See especially "The Bible as Universal History," in *The Gospel in a Pluralist Society* (London: SPCK, 1989), 89-102. Newbigin's influence can be strongly felt in Michael W. Goheen, *A Light to the Nations: The Missional Church and the Biblical Story* (Grand Rapids: Baker, 2011).

[8]Andrew Walker explores the nature of the gospel as story, and the seriousness of the loss of that story within Western cultures, in *Telling the Story: Gospel, Mission and Culture* (London: SPCK, 1996).

[9]To mention just a few: Vaughan Roberts, *God's Big Picture: Tracing the Storyline of the Bible* (Downers Grove, IL: InterVarsity Press, 2002); Philip Greenslade, *A Passion for God's Story: Discovering Your Place in God's Strategic Plan* (Carlisle, UK: Authentic, 2002); Michael W. Goheen and Craig G. Bartholomew, *Living at the Crossroads: An Introduction to Christian Worldview* (Grand Rapids: Baker, 2008); Craig G. Bartholomew and Michael W. Goheen, *The Drama of Scripture: Finding Our Place in the Biblical Story* (Grand Rapids: Baker, 2004; 2nd ed., 2014).

[10]The full statement, along with the other documents of the Lausanne Theology Working Group, can be downloaded from the website. See www .lausanne.org/content/twg-three-wholes. The rest of the papers presented at the Chiang Mai 2008 consultation, including my own, "'Ac-

cording to the Scriptures': The Whole Gospel in Biblical Revelation," are published in *Evangelical Review of Theology* 33, no. 1 (2009) and can also be accessed at www.lausanne.org/wp-content/uploads/2007/06/LOP63 -2008ChiangMai-Thailand.pdf.

[11]Texts where this narrative nature of Paul's gospel come to the fore include Romans 1:1-4; 1 Corinthians 15:1-8; Galatians 1:11-12; 3:6-8; 2 Thessalonians 2:13-15 (which presents the story of the gospel in the same order as the story of Old Testament Israel—loved, chosen, saved, sanctified, glory); 2 Timothy 1:10; 2:8.

[12]The various affirmations about the gospel in the Chiang Mai statement are based partly on an exercise that I did in preparation for my own paper at the consultation. I read carefully through all of Paul's letters and identified all the places where he uses the word *gospel*. Then I classified them according to the various nuances of his usage. My concluding paragraph was as follows:

> If we could ask Paul what content he might give to Lausanne's phrase 'the whole gospel' . . . I think he would at least have urged us to understand that the whole gospel is
> - a Christ-centred story to be told
> - a hope-filled message to be proclaimed
> - a revealed truth to be defended
> - a new status to be received
> - a transformed life to be lived
> - a divine power to be celebrated.
>
> And I believe, that in urging us to understand these dimensions, Paul would have directed us continually back to what he knew simply as 'the Scriptures'—our Old Testament, for it was 'in accordance with the Scriptures,' that Jesus died and rose again for our salvation. Our whole gospel, then, must be drawn from the deep well of the whole Bible.

[13]John Stott, *Christ the Controversialist* (London: Tyndale, 1970), 127; *Christ in Conflict*, rev. ed. (Downers Grove, IL: InterVarsity Press, 2013), 129-136.

[14]Compare Wright, *How God Became King*.

[15]Cape Town Commitment, section I.8, on the nature of the gospel.

[16]Ibid.

CHAPTER FIVE: DIALOGUE

[1]Martyn Lloyd-Jones, *Preaching and Preachers* (London: Hodder & Stoughton, 1971).

[2]Ibid., 9, 25.

[3]Ibid., 46, 47.

[4]J. G. Davies, *Dialogue with the World* (London: SCM Press, 1967), 31.

[5]Ibid., 31, 55.

[6]Ibid., 55.

[7]National Evangelical Anglican Congress at Keele, paragraph 83.

[8]Gottlob Schrenk, "διαλέγομαι, διαλογίζομαι, διαλογισμός," in Gerhard Kittel and Gerhard Friedrich, eds., *Theological Dictionary of the New Testament*, trans. Geoffrey W. Bromiley (Grand Rapids: Eerdmans, 1971), 2:93-97.

[9]William Arndt, et al., *A Greek-English Lexicon of the New Testament and Other Early Christian Literature; A Translation and Adaptation of Walter Bauer's Griechisch-Deutsches Wörterbuch Zu Den Schriften Des Neuen Testaments Und Der Übringen Urchristlichen Literatur, 4th Rev. and Augm. Ed., 1952* (Chicago: University of Chicago Press, 1957).

[10]W. H. Temple Gairdner, *Edinburgh 1910: An Account and Interpretation of the World Missionary Conference*, Kindle ed. (HardPress, 2010), 135.

[11]Hendrik Kraemer, *The Christian Message in a Non-Christian World* (London: Edinburgh House, 1946).

[12]Ibid., 302. The notion that Christ was the fulfillment of non-Christian religions was popularized by R. N. Farquhar, *The Crown of Hinduism* (Oxford: Oxford University Press, 1913).

[13]Quoted by Carl F. Hallencreutz in *New Approaches to Men of Other Faiths* (Geneva: WCC, 1969), 78.

[14]Karl Rahner, *Theological Investigations V* (London: Darton, Longman & Todd, 1966), 131.

[15]Raimundo Pannikar, *The Unknown Christ of Hinduism*, rev. ed. (London: Darton, Longman & Todd, 1981).

[16]World Council of Churches assembly at Uppsala, report 2, paragraph 6.

[17]Lausanne Covenant, paragraph 3.

[18]Ibid., paragraph 4.

[19]E. Stanley Jones, *The Christ of the Indian Road* (New York: Abingdon, 1925); *Christ at the Round Table* (London: Hodder & Stoughton, 1928).

[20]Jones, *Christ at the Round Table*, 19, 20.

[21]Ibid., 52.

[22]Ibid., 8, 9.

[23]Ibid., 22, 23.

[24]Ibid., 48, 15, 11.

[25]Ibid., 50, 56.

[26]Ibid., 55, 56.

[27]Kenneth Cragg, *The Call of the Minaret* (Cambridge: Lutterworth, 1956).

[28]Ibid., viii.

[29]Ibid., 189.

[30]Ibid., 34.

[31]Ibid., 319.

[32]Ibid., 245, 262.

[33]Ibid., 245-46, 256-57.

[34]Ibid., 334-35.

[35]Ibid., 355, 347.

[36]Stephen Neill, *Christian Faith and Other Faiths* (Oxford: Oxford University Press, 1961), 65, 66, 69.

[37]David Sheppard, *Built as a City* (London: Hodder & Stoughton, 1974).

[38]Ibid., 11, 36.

[39]Ibid., 16, 245.

[40]Ibid., 256.

[41]Ibid., 258.

[42]Ibid., 259.

[43]Ibid., 260.

[44]David Edwards, review of *Built as a City*, in *Church Times* (January 25, 1974).

CHAPTER SIX: REFLECTIONS ON DIALOGUE

[1]There is also a third, political sense of the word *pluralism*. It can be used not to affirm that all religions are equally true in some ways (or equally false in others), but rather to assure all religions of equal freedom under the law within the protection of a democratic state. This political pluralism makes no moral or theological judgment about the truth claims of different religions but seeks to protect the rights and freedom of people to pursue their own religion. It is, in theory at least, the meaning of *secular* in the Indian constitution, for example.

[2]Christopher J. H. Wright, "The Christian and Other Religions: The Biblical Evidence," *Themelios* 9, no. 2 (1984): 4-15.

[3]Chris Wright, *What's So Unique About Jesus?* (Eastbourne, UK: Monarch, 1990).

[4]Chris Wright, *The Uniquness of Jesus* (London: Monarch, 1997).

[5]John Stott, "Our Plural World: Is Christian Witness Influential," in *Issues Facing Christians Today*, 4th ed. (Grand Rapids: Zondervan, 2006), 71-94. This book, with its four editions, 1984, 1990, 1999 and 2006, is a remarkable compendium of Stott's extensive research and reflection on a wide range of social, political, economic, ecological, medical and sexual issues—all addressed with his characteristic "double-listening" to the world and to the Word, and his staunch commitment to holistic Christian mission with evangelism at its heart. See also "The Uniqueness of Jesus Christ," in *The Contemporary Christian* (Downers Grove, IL: InterVarsity Press, 1992), 296-320.

[6]Alan Race, *Christians and Religious Pluralism* (Maryknoll, NY: Orbis, 1982). See also the helpful discussion of the terms, followed by an even more helpful widening out of the whole issue in relation to our biblical hermeneutics, by Ida Glaser, *The Bible and Other Faiths: What Does the Lord Require of Us?* (Downers Grove, IL: InterVarsity Press, 2005), 19-33.

[7]Harold A. Netland, *Dissonant Voices: Religious Pluralism and the Question of Truth* (Grand Rapids: Eerdmans, 1991), 9-10. Netland later produced an even larger survey of the issues, in which he recognizes that, while the three categories of exclusivism, inclusivism and pluralism serve a useful academic purpose in structuring a survey of the breadth of scholarship, the empirical and experiential reality is far more complex. See *Encountering Religious Pluralism: The Challenge to Christian Faith and Mission* (Downers Grove, IL: InterVarsity Press, 2001). This book has a very thorough and helpful bibliographical guidance to all shades of opinion on the topic.

[8]Rahner's work spanned many years and produced twenty-three volumes in English of *Theological Investigations* (London: Darton, Longman & Todd). However, he summarized his central views on this matter in a lecture published as "Christianity and the Non-Christian Religions," in John Hick and Brian Hebblethwaite, eds., *Christianity and Other Religions* (Glasgow: Collins Fontana, 1980), 52-79. A helpful summary and discussion of Rahner's position can also be found in Michael Barnes, *Religions in Conversation* (London: SPCK, 1989).

[9]Chris Wright, *The Uniqueness of Jesus* (London: Monarch, 2002), 61-62.

[10]Ibid., 136-39.

[11]David L. Edwards with John Stott, *Evangelical Essentials: A Liberal-Evangelical Dialogue* (Downers Grove, IL: InterVarsity Press, 1989).

[12]Details of the document, its signatories and addressees and its essential content can be found at http://en.wikipedia.org/wiki/A_Common_Word _Between_Us_and_You. The full text is available at www.acommonword .com/the-acw-document/.

[13]The World Evangelical Alliance response can be read at www.worldea.org /images/wimg/files/We_Too_Want_to_Live_in_Love_Peace_Freedom _and_Justice.pdf.

[14]The full text of the Yale response can be read at http://faith.yale.edu /common-word/common-word-christian-response.

[15]The Manila Manifesto, paragraph 12.

[16]Cape Town Commitment, IIC.1.

CHAPTER SEVEN: SALVATION

[1]Michael Green, *The Meaning of Salvation* (London: Hodder & Stoughton, 1965), 16.

[2]See, for example, Phyllis Garlick, *Man's Search for Health* (London: Highway, 1952); Evelyn Frost, *Christian Healing* (London: Mowbray, 1949).

[3]Martyn Lloyd-Jones, *Will Hospital Replace the Church?* (London: Christian Medical Fellowship, 1969).

[4]Gustavo Gutiérrez, *A Theology of Liberation: History, Politics and Salvation* (Maryknoll, NY: Orbis, 1973).

[5]The "theology of liberation" is an authentic product of Latin America. Beginning with historical reality rather than with Scripture or tradition, and drawing on the help of the social sciences, it registers its spirited protest against the theologies of North America and Europe. Its best-known exponents apart from Gustavo Gutiérrez are Ruben Alves (*Theology of Human Hope*) and Hugo Assmann (*Oppression—Liberation: A Challenge to Christians*). Orlando Costas distinguishes them by saying that "if Alves is the prophet of the movement, and Assmann is the apologist, then Gutiérrez is the systematic theologian" (in *The Church and Its Mission: A Shattering Critique from the Third World* [London: Coverdale, 1974], 223).

[6]Gutiérrez, *Theology of Liberation*, 145.

[7]Ibid., 27, 32.

[8]Ibid., for example, 29, 36, 37.

[9]Ibid., 45.

[10]Ibid., 71.

[11]Ibid., 72.

[12]Ibid., 93, 194, 158.

[13]Ibid., 194.

[14]Ibid., 151.

[15]Ibid., 194-96.

[16]Ibid., 146.

[17]Lausanne Covenant, paragraph 5.

[18]Ibid.

[19]Werner Foester and Georg Fohrer, "σώζω, σωτηρία, σωτήρ, σωτήριος," in Gerhard Kittel and Gerhard Friedrich, eds., *Theological Dictionary of the New Testament*, trans. Geoffrey W. Bromiley (Grand Rapids: Eerdmans, 1971), 7:965-1024.

[20]Ibid., 973.

[21]Michael Ramsey, *Freedom, Faith and the Future* (London: SPCK, 1970), 15, 12.

[22]Lausanne Covenant, paragraph 4.

[23]Ibid., paragraph 13.

[24]Green, *Meaning of Salvation*, 240.

[25]John Poulton, *A Today Sort of Evangelism* (Cambridge: Lutterworth, 1972), 60-61.

CHAPTER EIGHT: REFLECTIONS ON SALVATION

[1]Some of the material in this chapter is drawn from Christopher J. H. Wright, *Salvation Belongs to Our God: Celebrating the Bible's Central Story* (Downers, Grove, IL: InterVarsity Press, 2008).

[2]Lausanne Covenant, paragraph 5.

[3]Actually, he surveys the broader senses of salvation language only in the New Testament. In my book *Salvation Belongs to Our God*, I surveyed the vocabulary across the whole range of both Testaments. Salvation in the Old Testament (meaning ways in which *God* is the subject of acts of saving people), can include deliverance from oppressors, victory in battle, rescue from enemies and vindication in court. In the New Testament, salvation language is used (of Jesus or God) to include rescue from drowning, recovering from terminal illness, being healed of disease or disability and being rescued from death or threatening dangers. And

in *both* Testaments (not just the New), salvation includes God *saving people from sin.* See *Salvation Belongs to Our God,* chap. 1.

[4]John Stott, *The Cross of Christ,* 20th anniversary ed. (Downers Grove, IL: InterVarsity Press, 2006); *The Contemporary Christian* (Downers Grove, IL: InterVarsity Press, 1992).

[5]Among recent books with a strong emphasis on the eschatological (new creation) fullness of the biblical salvation hope, and its consequent impact on how those who are saved should live here and now in the world, see, for example, John Colwell, ed., *Called to One Hope: Perspectives on the Life to Come* (Carlisle, UK: Paternoster, 2000); Michael Wittmer, *Heaven Is a Place on Earth: Why Everything You Do Matters to God* (Grand Rapids: Zondervan, 2004); Darrell Cosden, *The Heavenly Good of Earthly Work* (Peabody, MA: Hendrickson, 2006); Tom Wright, *Surprised by Hope* (New York: HarperOne, 2007); Stephen Holmes and Russell Rook, eds., *What Are We Waiting For? Christian Hope and Contemporary Culture* (Carlisle, UK: Paternoster, 2008).

[6]Gustavo Gutiérrez, *A Theology of Liberation: History, Politics and Salvation* (Maryknoll, NY: Orbis, 1973).

[7]See, for example, for survey, critique and wider bibliography, J. Andrew Kirk, *Liberation Theology: An Evangelical View from the Third World* (London: Marshall, Morgan & Scott, 1979); Kirk, *Theology Encounters Revolution* (Leicester, UK: Inter-Varsity Press, 1980); David J. Bosch, *Transforming Mission* (Maryknoll, NY: Orbis, 1991), 432-47; Orlando E. Costas, *The Church and Its Mission: A Shattering Critique from the Third World* (London: Coverdale, 1974); José Míguez Bonino, *Doing Theology in a Revolutionary Situation* (Philadelphia: Fortress, 1975); M. Daniel Carroll R., "Liberation Theologies," in A. Scott Moreau, ed., *Evangelical Dictionary of World Missions* (Grand Rapids: Baker, 2000), 574-76; Samuel Escobar, "Latin American Theology," in John Corrie, ed., *Dictionary of Mission Theology* (Downers Grove, IL: InterVarsity Press, 2007), 203-7; John Corrie, "Evangelicals and Liberation Theology," in John Corrie and Cathy Ross, *Mission in Context: Explorations Inspired by J. Andrew Kirk* (Aldershot, UK: Ashgate, 2012), 61-76.

[8]Christopher J. H. Wright, *The Mission of God: Unlocking the Bible's Grand Narrative* (Downers Grove, IL: InterVarsity Press, 2006), chap. 8, "God's Model of Redemption: The Exodus," 265-88.

[9]Stott, *Contemporary Christian,* 319.

[10]The case for the possibility that (or rather more strongly, the affirmation that) some among those who never hear the gospel will nevertheless be saved by God on the basis of the atoning work of Christ (not by their own religions) is made from an explicitly Arminian point of view by Clark Pinnock, *A Wideness in God's Mercy: The Finality of Jesus Christ in a World of Religions* (Grand Rapids: Zondervan, 1992). An even more thorough exploration of the issue, historically, theologically and biblically, is by John Sanders, *No Other Name: An Investigation into the Destiny of the Unevangelized* (Grand Rapids: Eerdmans, 1992). Arguing this case from a strongly Reformed perspective comes the major work by Terrance L. Tiessen, *Who Can Be Saved: Reassessing Salvation in Christ and World Religions* (Downers Grove, IL: InterVarsity Press, 2004). A symposium that canvasses a variety of views but comes down most clearly in its critique of the "possibility of salvation for the unevangelized" position is William V. Crockett and James G. Sigountos, *Through No Fault of Their Own? The Fate of Those Who Have Never Heard* (Grand Rapids: Baker Books, 1991).

CHAPTER NINE: CONVERSION

[1]Lesslie Newbigin, *The Finality of Christ* (London: SCM Press, 1964), 88.

[2]"Christian Witness, Proselytism and Religious Liberty in the Setting of the WCC," WCC *Central Committee Minutes*, 1960, 214, quoted by Philip Potter in his address to the Central Committee in Crete, August 1967.

[3]Lausanne Covenant, paragraph 12.

[4]J. C. Hoekendijk, *The Church Inside Out* (London: SCM Press, 1967), 21.

[5]James Denney, *The Death of Christ* (London: Tyndale, 1951), 86.

[6]M. M. Thomas, *Salvation and Humanization* (Madras: CLS, 1971).

[7]Michael Ramsey, *The Christian Priest Today* (London: SPCK, 1972), 37.

[8]Mark Gibbs and T. R. Morton, *God's Lively People* (London: Fontana, 1970), 206.

[9]Lausanne Covenant, paragraph 10.

[10]Kenneth Cragg, *The Call of the Minaret* (Cambridge: Lutterworth, 1956), 336.

[11]Wolfhart Pannenberg, *Basic Questions in Theology* (London: SCM Press, 1971), 2:34-35.

CHAPTER TEN: REFLECTIONS ON CONVERSION

[1]They are not, of course, on Stott's own gravestone. The words he himself chose to have engraved there are modeled on one of Stott's great heroes,

Charles Simeon of Cambridge (1759–1836), whose epitaph reads, "Whether as the ground of his own hopes, or as the subject of all his ministrations, he 'determined to know nothing but Jesus Christ and him crucified.'" John Stott's gravestone in the Welsh village of Dale, Pembrokeshire, close to The Hookses (the coastal cottage where he wrote most of his books), bears the inscription, "Buried here are the ashes of John Robert Walmsley Stott, 1921–2011, Rector of All Souls Church, Langham Place, London, 1950–1975 and as Rector Emeritus 1975–2011, Who resolved both as the ground of his salvation and as the subject of his ministry to know nothing except Jesus Christ and him crucified. 1 Corinthians 2:2."

[2]This in itself shows something of the breadth of Stott's international reading. M. M. Thomas was a renowned and profound Indian theologian who advocated a more indigenous form of Indian Christianity, had a strong concern for social reform, seeing salvation as humanization, and in his opposition to the oppression of Dalits reflected the liberation theology of Latin America.

[3]A sample of some of the positions taken by different protagonists in the debate can be found on the Lausanne website, for example, Joseph Cummings, "Muslim Followers of Jesus?," accessed April 25, 2015, www .lausanne.org/content/muslim-followers-of-Jesus. The issue also occupied *Christianity Today*, which hosted a series of "Global Conversations" in the year leading up to the Third Lausanne Congress in Cape Town, October 2010. The article and responses can be read in the December 2009 issue, available at www.lausanne.org/global-conversation-articles. A good summary of the whole topic, with further bibliographical links, is also available at http://en.wikipedia.org/wiki/Insider_movement.

[4]Cape Town Commitment, IIC.4.

[5]Later incorporated into the Bible Speaks Today series as *The Message of Ephesians: God's New Society* (Downers Grove, IL: InterVarsity Press, 1979).

[6]Ibid., 126-29.

[7]See especially his groundbreaking *The New Testament and the People of God* (Minneapolis: Fortress, 1992), but also in more recent and popular work, chapters such as "Reshaping the Church for Mission," in *Surprised by Hope* (New York: HarperOne, 2008) and "The Launching of God's Renewed People," in *How God Became King* (New York: HarperOne, 2012).

[8]Scot McKnight, *Kingdom Conspiracy: Returning to the Radical Mission of the Local Church* (Grand Rapids: Brazos, 2014).

[9]Christopher J. H. Wright, *The Mission of God's People: A Biblical Theology of the Church's Mission* (Grand Rapids: Zondervan, 2010).

[10]Lesslie Newbigin, *The Gospel in a Pluralist Society* (Grand Rapids: Eerdmans, 1989), 227.

[11]Lausanne Covenant, paragraph 6.

[12]Cape Town Commitment, I.9a.

[13]Cape Town Commitment, I.10a.

[14]I explore this missional-cultural dimension of Deuteronomy in my commentary: Christopher J. H. Wright, *Deuteronomy*, New International Biblical Commentary (Peabody, MA: Hendrickson, 1996); republished in the Understanding the Bible Commentary (Grand Rapids: Baker, 2012).

[15]It is a sobering fact that the language of *conversion* is directed far more frequently at God's own people than at the foreign nations—though they too can be summoned to "turn . . . and be saved" (Isaiah 45:22). It reminds us that though there may be a moment of specific conversion associated with one's first exercise of repentance and faith, being converted is a lifelong and ever-deepening process of turning, and returning, to love the Lord our God with heart, soul, mind and strength.

[16]Andrew F. Walls, "Converts or Proselytes? The Crisis over Conversion in the Early Church," *International Bulletin of Missionary Research* 28, no. 1 (2004): 2-6.

[17]Christopher J. H. Wright, "Implications of Conversion in the Old Testament and the New," *International Bulletin of Missionary Research* 28, no. 1 (2004): 14-19.

[18]Those are subheadings in the chapter "Culture and Family," in Christopher J. H. Wright, *An Eye for an Eye* (Downers Grove, IL: InterVarsity Press, 1983), now revised and expanded in *Old Testament Ethics for the People of God* (Downers Grove, IL: InterVarsity Press, 2004), 327-62.

[19]"The Willowbank Report—Gospel and Culture" can be accessed at www.lausanne.org/content/lop/lop-2. It is also included in John Stott, ed., *Making Christ Known: Historic Mission Documents from the Lausanne Movement, 1974–1989* (Grand Rapids: Eerdmans, 1997).

[20]The outstanding historian of Christian mission through all its centuries since the New Testament is undoubtedly Andrew F. Walls, and some of his most stimulating articles in this field are collected in *The Missionary Movement in Christian History: Studies in the Transmission of Faith* (Maryknoll, NY: Orbis, 1996). And of course, Lesslie Newbigin had his

customary penetrating insights: for example, "Church Growth, Conversion and Culture," in *The Open Secret: An Introduction to the Theology of Mission* (Grand Rapids: Eerdmans, 1995), 121-59. Other relevant works include Vinay Samuel and Albrecht Hauser, *Proclaiming Christ in Christ's Way: Studies in Integral Evangelism* (Oxford: Regnum, 1989); David J. Hesselgrave and Edward Rommen, *Contextualization: Meanings, Methods and Models* (Grand Rapids: Baker, 1989); David Burnett, *Clash of Worlds* (London: Monarch, 1990); David Smith, *Against the Stream: Christianity and Mission in an Age of Globalization* (Leicester, UK: InterVarsity Press, 2003); Dean Flemming, *Contextualization in the New Testament: Patterns for Theology and Mission* (Downers Grove, IL: InterVarsity Press, 2005); A. Scott Moreau, *Contextualization in World Missions: Mapping and Assessing Evangelical Models* (Grand Rapids: Kregel, 2012); John Corrie and Cathy Ross, eds., *Mission in Context: Explorations Inspired by J. Andrew Kirk* (Aldershot, UK: Ashgate, 2012).

ALSO BY JOHN STOTT

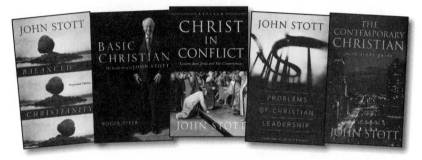

Balanced Christianity
Basic Christianity
Christ in Conflict
Problems of Christian Leadership
The Contemporary Christian

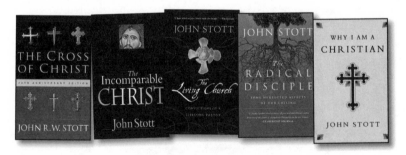

The Cross of Christ
The Incomparable Christ
The Living Church
The Radical Disciple
Why I Am a Christian

ALSO BY
CHRISTOPHER J. H. WRIGHT

Knowing God the Father Through the Old Testament
Knowing Jesus Through the Old Testament (Second Edition)
Knowing the Holy Spirit Through the Old Testament

From the Bible Speaks Today Series:
The Message of Ezekiel
The Message of Jeremiah
The Message of Lamentations

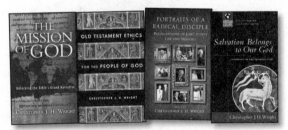

The Mission of God: Unlocking the Bible's Grand Narrative
Old Testament Ethics for the People of God
Portraits of a Radical Disciple: Recollections of
John Stott's Life and Ministry (editor)
Salvation Belongs to Our God: Christian Doctrine in Global Perspective